DATE			

The
Earthworm
Book

The Earthworm Book

How to Raise and Use Earthworms
for Your Farm and Garden

by
Jerry Minnich

 Rodale Press Emmaus, PA

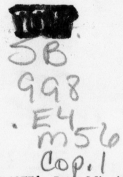

Library of Congress Cataloging in Publication Data
Minnich, Jerry.
    The earthworm book.

    Bibliography: p.
    Includes index.
    1.   Earthworms.   2.   Earthworm culture.   I.   Title.
SB998.E4M56   639'.75'46   77-13405
ISBN 0-87857-193-0

For my father,
Samuel Foelker Minnich

Contents

Introduction

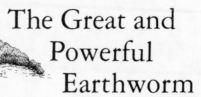

The Great and Powerful Earthworm

"The plough is one of the most ancient and most valuable of man's inventions; but long before he existed the land was in fact regularly ploughed and still continues to be thus ploughed by earthworms. It may be doubted whether there are many other animals which have played so important a part in the history of the world as have these lowly organized creatures."

The year was 1881, and the writer was the great English naturalist Charles Darwin.

The great and powerful earthworm

Darwin, aside from being a genius, had studied the earthworm for more than 40 years. Thus his words were carefully considered as he set them down on paper. But just why did the great Darwin place these "lowly organized creatures" on such a high station among all the tens of thousands of animals of this planet, both past and present? The earthworm, greater than the horse? More powerful than the African elephant? More important to man than the ox or cow?

To all these questions, a resounding *yes*, and therein lie both the earthworm's power and Darwin's genius. The power, the importance of the earthworm lies in its awesome role in the creation of all the agricultural soils of the world. Through history and continuing to the present day, man's great food-growing lands have existed only where earthworms are present to till that soil. Relentlessly, day and night, generation after generation, century after century, through the rise and fall of man's temporal civilizations, the earthworm has done much to create, till, and improve the soil. The earthworm is great and powerful because it has, by its ceaseless churning of the earth, enabled plants to grow and all the terrestrial animals to survive. The earthworm has contributed significantly to man's prosperity, enabling him to grow in numbers and dominate the earth. This is the power of the earthworm—and Darwin's genius lies in the fact that he recognized the earthworm's contribution at a time when virtually everyone else in the world thought about earthworms not at all.

Earthworms are many things to many people. To anglers, they are prime bait—an efficient tool for the catching of fish, because most fish species prefer the common earthworm over any other bait that nature has provided or man has created.

To increasing thousands of Americans, earthworms represent a business, a marketable product that shows greater promise every year. The prime market has always been, and remains, bait fishermen—but farmers and gardeners are constituting an ever-increasing segment of the earthworm-buying population.

For biology teachers, the earthworm has long been valued as a primary laboratory teaching tool, its simple structure easily analyzed by beginning students in both secondary schools and colleges.

Even archaeologists give thought to the earthworm, for by the earthworm's slow and unending work over many centuries many ancient structures have been buried in the earth and thus preserved for future study.

But it is by gardeners and farmers that the earthworm is treasured most highly, for these subterranean denizens play a major role in the creation of compost and humus, improving the soil and enhancing crop production wherever plants can be grown.

As research upon the earthworm continues to increase both in scope and sophistication, we are looking at new ways to make use of this creature's remarkable talents: as an aid in reducing biodegradable solid wastes to humus for farm and garden, as a painless way to reclaim strip mines, as a new source of protein-rich food for both humans and livestock, as a tool in erosion and flood control, and as a multi-indicator of environmental quality. As great as the past of the earthworm has been, its future looks bigger and brighter than ever.

In these pages, I have attempted to bring together all these aspects of the earthworm—its history, characteristics, and behavior, its importance to man in the past and present, and its great promise for the future. For those interested in raising earthworms as a full- or part-time business, I have tried to separate fact from much of the fiction that is being perpetrated today. For the angler, I have presented not techniques on bait fishing, which are readily available elsewhere, but easily applied information that can help the angler maintain a constant supply of worms with little effort. But it is especially for the gardener and farmer that this book has been written, for it is in the production of food for man that the earthworm, as always, finds its most noble role.

Last, in the course of research for this volume, I have been appalled at the tremendous gaps in the scientific literature in this field. It would seem that, after the brilliant start that Darwin gave us nearly a century ago, we have dropped the ball and never quite picked it up. There are scarcely any scientists in the country who are now devoting the bulk of their efforts to earthworm research. Agronomists barely give a tip of the hat to the earthworm, perhaps leaving the job to zoologists. Zoologists tread the earth above the earthworm, studying larger species, insensitive to the earthworm's paramount role in both agronomy and agriculture. We need more activity in nearly every area of earthworm research—in the classification and distribution of species, in the effects of the earthworm upon agriculture, and especially in the earthworm's potential role in helping to feed the world's burgeoning population. We need far more work in discovering the specific effects that various earthworm species have upon various soils and crops. And we need foresighted research that will encourage our using this valuable subterranean ally in solving some of our most pressing environmental problems.

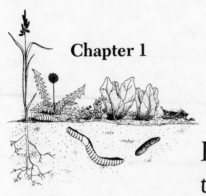

Chapter 1

Introducing
the Earthworm

If you meet an earthworm on some dewy spring night, and wish to address him properly, you may call him *Lumbricus terrestris*, which is likely to be his formal name.

Or, if you are on an informal basis, "night crawler" will do, for the zoologist's *Lumbricus terrestris* is our familiar native night crawler.

Of course, if you live in certain parts of the country, the same worm might be known as a dew worm, nightwalker, rainworm, angleworm, orchard worm, night lion, or any of dozens of other local designations.

One of the difficulties in talking about earthworms is the enormous proliferation of common names that have been given to different worm species—or even the *same* species—in different localities at different times. This confusion has arisen in part because, to the untrained eye, most earthworms look alike. Many gardeners identify five or more completely different species as the "garden worm" simply because they see no difference between the various species that live in garden soil. Some fishermen believe that the night crawler they catch in the evening is the same worm that they find in the top layer of garden soil during a warm spring afternoon. Actually, the night crawler will seldom be found near the soil surface during the warmth of the day.

To compound the problem, scientists have not, until relatively recent times, begun to classify earthworms on a scientific basis. Even Dr. George Sheffield Oliver, who probably knew more about earthworms than anyone in the world during the 1930s, did not mention species names in his

1

well-known book *Our Friend the Earthworm*, but spoke of the "orchard worm, rain worm, angle worm, dew worm, brandling, manure, night crawler, fish worm, night lions, and similarly descriptive names familiar to certain areas of the United States."

It is no wonder that so much misinformation and confusion about earthworms have been spread for so many years. People who have wanted to study earthworms, or more particularly wanted to discover which kinds of earthworms would suit their particular needs, had to guess what each author meant by a "dew worm," or an "orchard worm." For the same reason, we still have very little idea of the population distributions of the various species across the North American continent, since much of the information recorded in past years is untrustworthy because of name confusion.

Science does have a way to bring order out of such chaos, however. Nomenclators are scientists who give names to plants and animals. More particularly, nomenclators give *Latin* names to plants and animals, because only the standard use of this language throughout the Western world (and much of the rest of the world, as well) assures that the earthworm researcher in Brazil will understand just what his counterpart in Belgium is talking about.

On, then, to Latin nomenclature as it applies to our friend, the earthworm:

The earthworm is an animal belonging to the phylum Annelida, the class Chaetopoda, and the order Oligochaeta. In addition, each earthworm belongs to a family (most American species belong to the family Lumbricidae) and also has a genus and species name. A particular kind of earthworm is commonly identified by its genus and species name, which are always given together, in italics, the species name following the genus name (as in *Lumbricus terrestris*). If the same name is mentioned again soon after, the genus name might be abbreviated (*L. terrestris*).

All members of the animal kingdom are divided into nine broad phyla. Earthworms belong to the phylum Annelida (which is Latin for "rings"). All annelids are soft-bodied animals comprised of segments of similar appearance, joined one behind the other. There are more than 6,000 known species of annelids. Most are sea dwellers, the best known of which are the leeches. Among land-dwelling annelids, the earthworm is best known.

Subdividing further, scientists have placed the earthworm into the class Chaetopoda and the order Oligochaeta. All oligochaete have seta (bristles) which are sunk into their body walls and used for locomotion.

There are about 1,800 known species of earthworms in the world (although Henry Hopp, renowned earthworm expert formerly with the United States Department of Agriculture, estimated the total number—known and unknown— to be in excess of 3,000). The most common in Europe and North America belong to the family Lumbricidae, which has approximately 220 known species. There are other families common to other parts of the world—the Glossoscolecidae in Central and South America, the megascolecid group in southern and eastern Asia and Australia, and others. But it seems to be the Lumbricidae, commonly known as the lumbricids, that are most important to world agriculture. First, they are the most active in their soil-building activities, and second they seem to be able to drive out members of other native families (except the Asiatic *Pheretimas*) wherever they are introduced. The European lumbricids have accompanied plants on ship to all parts of the world, where they have quickly replaced native species and, in so doing, often improved soils in these regions.

History

Earthworms and their close relatives have been a part of the earth for so many millions of years that scientists hesitate to guess at their age. Their ancestors were marine worms, existing before there was even soil on this planet and vegetation on its face. As the waters of the earth gradually receded,

3

giving way to dry land, countless creatures underwent the tremendously slow and halting process of adapting themselves to a changing environment. Certain marine worms gradually became adapted to wet and marshy areas, and then to drier and drier land, until they were able to survive in our common forest and prairie soils. Earthworms still retain their ancient roots to the sea, however. Their skin must be moist constantly in order for them to survive, and they are still able to live submerged in water for many months. Their closest annelid relatives are leeches and other marine worms.

Life Span

How long can an earthworm expect to live? Scientists really do not know, which is one indication of the appalling lack of scientific knowledge in this field. In *Biology of Earthworms,* the standard work in its field, authors C. A. Edwards and J. R. Lofty say, "The life span of mature lumbricids in the field is probably quite short, often no more than a few months." This short span, however, is due not to the earthworm's innate inability to live longer, but to the many natural hazards to which the earthworm is subject. It serves as food for birds, moles, shrews, and other animals, and it is easily killed by sudden freezes, changes in soil chemistry, and certain agricultural practices, notably the application of toxic chemicals.

Edwards and Lofty summarize the research of other scientists, indicating that lumbricids have a potential longevity of 4 to 8 years. *Allolobophora longa* has been kept for $10^{1}/_{2}$ years under favorable conditions; *Eisenia foetida* (the brandling worm) for $4^{1}/_{2}$; and *Lumbricus terrestris* (the native night crawler) for 6 years.

Thomas J. Barrett, another noted earthworm researcher, said in his 1947 book *Harnessing the Earthworm,* "In a favorable environment an earthworm will live for many years. One report was given of an observation carried out for a period of fifteen years and the worm under this experiment appeared just as young as ever." Barrett, in considering the earthworm's physical characteristics, surmised that, "barring accidental destruction, he should enjoy comparative immortality in the flesh, remaining eternally youthful through perfect assimilation and elimination."

Nor is Barrett the only researcher to contemplate the potential immortality of the earthworm. Dr. F. J. Trembley, writing in the 3 May 1970 edition of the *Sunday Call-Chronicle* (Allentown, Pa.), muses:

> I have often wondered if *Lumbricus* is inherently immortal. There are many primitive plants and animals in whose life histories there is no place for natural death. They died by an accident but their living stuff does not grow old and die. This state occurs in one-celled organisms and in simple colonial organisms built of a few cells. Earthworms are far advanced over these simple organisms but I have never found a dead one that did not die obviously from some accident or injury. A soft-bodied, dead worm, high in protein, would soon be attacked by scavenger organisms. But, I have caught many thousands of worms for various purposes and I have never found a dead one. Could this organism be one of those which never lost an ancestor by natural death?

Structure of the Earthworm

Pick up an earthworm and examine it carefully.

After only a cursory examination, you can tell that this animal is superbly suited to its environment, equipped with all the physical attributes it needs to do its job with cool efficiency, and shorn of any excess baggage.

You will notice, first, that an earthworm is cool—and slimy. It is cool because it is a cold-blooded animal, like its marine cousins, and it remains cool because it is constantly moist. The evaporation of its moisture helps to keep the earthworm cool, just as perspiration helps to keep us cool on a sultry July day. For us, keeping cool is often no more than a comfort, but for the earthworm it is ever critical, for the earthworm must remain both cool and moist in order to survive. A night crawler, exposed for only a short time to a temperature and humidity that we would find quite comfortable, would quickly become severely impaired or die. For other species, allowable temperatures may be higher, but they are still critical.

The film of mucus on the earthworm's skin helps to hold moisture. It also is essential in the respiratory exchange of atmospheric gases, including oxygen and carbon dioxide. Since earthworms have no lungs, they exchange these vital gases through their body walls.

But the mucus has other important purposes. It serves as a highly effective lubricant, helping to smooth the earthworm's way as it burrows through the roughest of earth, twigs, and stones. And as the earthworm burrows, the mucus is constantly rubbed off, helping to cement the walls of its tunnel, while more mucus is constantly being manufactured. This same lubricant is helpful in the earthworm's escaping its enemies. Many a frustrated robin has lost a fat night crawler because the prey has been able to "worm" its way out of a tight jam.

Last, the mucus serves an important reproductive function. As two earthworms mate, a special mucus is exuded in the sexual region of the worms' bodies, helping to protect the spermatozoa that is being mutually exchanged.

The next thing you might notice about the earthworm is its construction. It is among the most streamlined of all creatures, tapered at both ends, absolutely no protruding appendages or organs showing. What better basic form for burrowing through the earth? The earthworm stalks no prey, and so it needs no fangs. It does its yeoman work in the darkness of earth, and so it needs no eyes. It has no ears to protrude, no awkward arms or legs. Here, you will say, is an animal perfectly constructed to perform efficiently in its environment. And you will be right. The earthworm needs no further evolutionary adaptation. It is perfect, as it has been for millions of years.

Noticeable also in the construction of this earthworm are

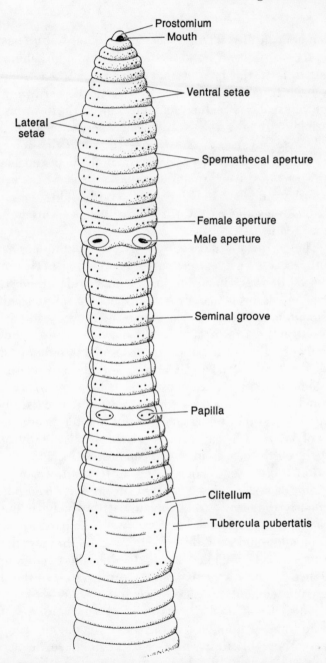

Figure 1 Ventral View of the Anterior Region of *Lumbricus terrestris*

its segments (called *somites*). It is as if Mother Nature pushed together one or two hundred tiny donuts, one behind the other, to form this creature. These somites (a mature worm may have from 115 to 200) help to give the earthworm its tough muscular structure and flexibility. Earthworms are amazingly strong, a relatively high proportion of their body weight given over to muscle tissue. The segmental construction (and the segments run clear through the body) enables an earthworm to drive through hard-packed soil where even a pitchfork would have difficulty, and to push aside stones more than 60 times the earthworm's own weight. This is not a fragile creature.

The earthworm has no head, as such, but it does have a mouth, located at its extreme anterior (the front). The mouth opens on the very first anterior segment (called the *peristomium*) and is protected by an overhanging lobe called the *prostomium*. With the aid of a hand lens, you can observe these structures on a large night crawler. The earthworm literally eats the earth as it burrows through it, either pushing aside the earth or taking it into its mouth, and it uses the prostomium to push aside those objects too large to be eaten. Through the anus, at the extreme posterior (rear) segment, the earth and other mineral and organic matter emerge in the form of *castings* (the earthworm's manure). It is not difficult to view the earthworm as an instant composting machine.

But there is one more feature of the earthworm that is apparent at first glance. Near the anterior end, colored conspicuously differently from the rest of the body, is the *clitellum*. This feature of the earthworm plays a paramount role in copulation and reproduction. In most lumbricids, the clitellum is roughly saddle shaped. It is usually swollen in appearance, especially among adult worms, often to the point where the segments are barely discernible.

Now, if you hold the worm gently and stroke it, from back to front, you might feel tiny bristles along the ring segments. These bristles, called *seta*, might have been completely overlooked by you, but they are vitally important to

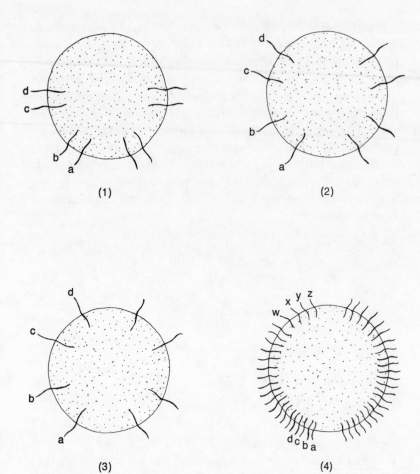

Figure 2 Arrangement of Setae in Earthworms
1, 2, 3, lumbricine arrangement; 4, perichaetine arrangement;
1, closely paired; 2, widely paired; 3, distant-paired

Source: After Edwards, C. A., and J. R. Lofty, *Biology of Earthworms*,
London (1972)

the earthworm, which could not survive without them. The
seta serve first to help the earthworm to move. In its snug
tunnels, or while burrowing through fresh earth, it can

protract all its seta (there are eight on each ring segment, among the lumbricids) while flexing its muscular structure, moving along in a rippling motion, much as a centipede moves with its legs. The seta also help to anchor the posterior end of the night crawler to its tunnel walls while the rest of the worm is searching the surface of the ground for food. The seta, although only about one millimeter long, are amazingly powerful. Both the robin and the angler can testify that many earthworms will break in two rather than be pulled from the ground. Last, the seta aid in copulation by enabling two worms to hold fast to each other, facilitating the exchange of spermatozoa.

Sexual organs.   Earthworms are hermaphrodites—bisexual—each possessing both male and female sexual apparatus. But they are not self-fertilizing. Each worm must copulate with another in order to reproduce, and then each worm will bear a cocoon containing eggs.

The openings of the female sexual glands (called the oviducts, where eggs are formed) are found on the fourteenth anterior segment of all lumbricids. The male pores, from which sperm is omitted, are located on the fifteenth segment (rarely, the thirteenth). Between segments nine and ten, and also ten and eleven, concealed from the naked human eye, are the sperm receptacles.

Internal features.   Let us now take a look at the body wall of the earthworm. Should we take a cross section of this earthworm, we would see first, on the very outer skin, the *cuticle*, a very thin and transparent layer. Underneath the cuticle is the *epidermis*, which consists of a single layer of cells made up primarily of two specific kinds. One of these is the *gland cells* whose job it is to secrete the all-important mucus, and the other consists of the long and slender *epithelial cells* that give body and strength to the earthworm.

In addition, thousands upon thousands of sensory cells are found throughout the epidermis. Working together, they give the earthworm its most important sense—that of touch.

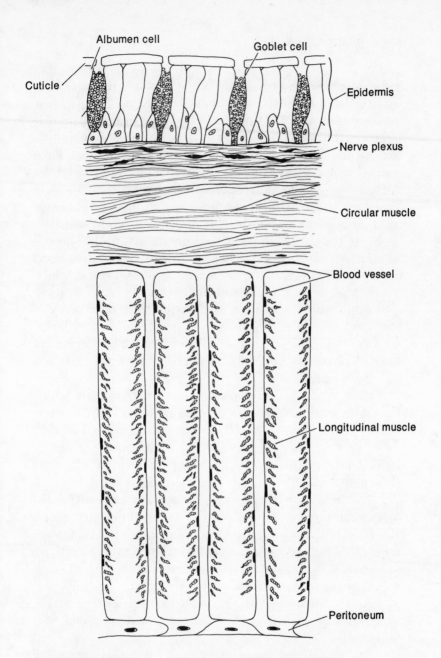

Figure 3 Transverse Section of the Earthworm's Body Wall

Source: After Grove, A. J., and G. E. Newell, *Animal Biology*, London (1962)

Although an earthworm cannot see (at least in our sense of the word) or hear, it is extremely tactile, sensitive to the slightest movement around it. An earthworm can feel the robin as it scratches the ground, and will beat a hasty retreat into its burrow at the bird's approach. Night crawler hunters have learned to tread very, very softly, if they are not to frighten the worms away.

Present also in the epidermis are large numbers of photoreceptor cells, found mostly in the prostomium. These are the "eyes" of the earthworm, and they are located in the "head." Although our earthworm cannot distinguish physical features, it can sense light. Earthworms react negatively to light, which is why they appear on the soil surface only at night, as some species (notably the native night crawler) must do in order to feed and copulate. Earthworms cannot detect red light, however, which is why night crawler hunters place a piece of red cellophane over their flashlights in their stealthy searches for fishing bait.

Contained also in the prostomium are taste cells, which the earthworm uses, in part, to choose his food. Not much is known about these taste cells, although researchers in 1959 found that earthworms can detect sucrose, glucose, and quinine. Undoubtedly, they can detect much more, for they show definite food preferences, as we shall see later.

Just inside the body wall is the *coelom*, a large cavity that extends all the way throughout the length of the earthworm. It is filled with coelomic fluid, and it surrounds the alimentary canal. The coelomic fluid is ejected by the earthworm in times of trouble—when it is too hot, too cold, or when it experiences mechanical or chemical irritation.

At this point, it will be well to stop looking at the earthworm as a cross section, and to take a good look at it lengthwise.

The earthworm's alimentary canal (or gut) is the central feature of its body cavity. And why not? The earthworm is, after all, mainly an eating and composting machine. It eats its own weight in earth, minerals, and organic matter each day, and this job requires an impressive digestive system. The alimentary canal lies in the center of the body cavity. Its wall is comprised of three layers: the interior, which is a mucous layer; the middle, composed of strong muscle fibers and blood vessels; and the outer layer, which is protective.

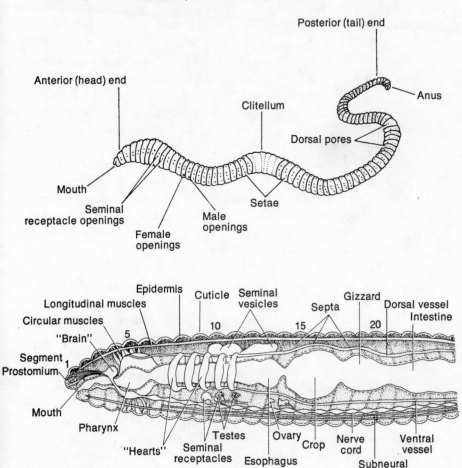

Figure 4 Structure of *Lumbricus terrestris*

Source: After Gaddie, R. E., North American Bait Farms, Inc.

The canal is basically a tube that runs clear through the length of the worm, from the mouth to the anus. Different parts of the canal serve somewhat different purposes, however, and so scientists have given different names to these parts. Just behind the mouth is the *buccal cavity,* the cheek pouch of the earthworm. It is in this region, extending only to the first or second anterior segment, where the taste cells are located. No one knows whether a worm can spit out food it doesn't like, but it certainly can stop eating distasteful food once the food reaches the buccal cavity.

Behind the buccal cavity is the *pharynx,* which connects the mouth to the esophagus. The pharynx extends to about the sixth segment, and is used as a kind of suction pump, drawing in food from the mouth.

The *esophagus* opens from the pharynx and leads to the *crop* and the *gizzard.* The crop feeds food back to the gizzard, which, with the aid of powerful muscular contractions, grinds up the food for further digestion. The sand and other mineral particles that the earthworm consumes act as grinding stones in the gizzard.

Behind the gizzard, which ends at about the twentieth segment in most common species, begins the intestine. It is here, as in our own bodies, that most of the digestion and absorption of the earthworm's food takes place. There are many folds in the inner wall of the intestine, which give the food greatest chance to be fully absorbed.

Between the intestine and the body wall are five pairs of vessels that scientists call, for lack of a better name, "hearts." Although they do not resemble mammalian hearts, their function is much the same. They direct the flow of blood through the earthworm's body. The earthworm has only two major blood vessels, one dorsal (topside) and the other ventral (bottomside). There are many minor vessels and capillaries that carry blood to all parts of the body.

The respiratory system of the earthworm is very rudimentary. There are no lungs or other such apparatus, but oxygen is received through the body wall, where it is taken up by the blood and circulated throughout the earthworm's body.

Nervous system.   In each segment, the nerve cord enlarges into nerve cells to form a ganglion. These ganglia are the centers from which impulses are given off to the other organs of the body from the brain.

The earthworm's "eyes" are single cells scattered on the dorsal epidermis, particularly toward the front end, that detect the color blue most strongly while the color red is hardly noticed. Possibly an internal lenslike cell focuses light rays on a nerve fiber and relays the message to the brain. The earthworm's typical reaction to light is to avoid it by retreating into the ground.

The earthworm's insensitivity to ultraviolet light is perhaps its one evolutionary flaw. When its burrows are flooded by heavy rains, the earthworm will come to the surface. Ultraviolet light rays from the sun can then kill the earthworm in as few as 60 seconds.

The sense of touch is highly developed in the earthworm. It serves the worm well in seeking a sex partner, in detecting predators and avoiding irritants, and in selecting food.

Regeneration.   If you chop a worm in half, will you have two worms, one worm, or no worms? The answer is, in most cases, one worm, perhaps none, and never two. Earthworms have surprising powers of regeneration. For instance, if the worm is severed anywhere along the rear half of its body, it will grow a new tail with fully as many segments as in the original—but never more. The full regeneration process usually takes several months, depending upon the species. (More active species, such as the red worm, regenerate quickly; night crawlers, more slowly.)

If the body is severed within the front half, however, chances for regeneration are reduced. The nearer to the head the body is severed, the less chance there is for regeneration. Researchers have conducted many tests along this line and have found that no earthworm will regenerate if it is severed farther front than the thirteenth anterior segment—and some species need as many as 30 uninjured segments in order to survive. Also, the ease and quickness of regeneration coincide precisely with the number of anterior segments preserved. The nervous system of the earthworm must be preserved for regeneration to occur—and the core of that system lies in the anterior part of the body.

In sum, the gardener need not be unduly disturbed if he should sever a few earthworms while hoeing or spading. There is a better-than-even chance that the injured worms will retreat into their burrows, nurse their wounds, and come back in a few months good as new.

Chemical Makeup

The major chemical constituent of the earthworm is water, comprising from 70 to 95 percent of its body weight. The remaining 5 to 30 percent is mostly protein, forming between 53 and 72 percent of the total dry weight. Fat makes up anywhere from 1 to 17 percent of the dry weight, and mineral matter makes up from 9 to 23 percent, probably depending somewhat on the earthworm's diet. What is important is that the earthworm is largely protein—a reflection of its heavy muscular construction—making it an important food source not only for wildlife but, in some parts of the world, for livestock and even human beings.

Intelligence

No one would claim that an earthworm is one of the more intelligent members of the animal kingdom, at least not in our sense of the word. The earthworm doesn't have much of a brain—it amounts to no more than an insignificant knot of nerve tissue located above the mouth at the third anterior segment—and yet this earthworm does exhibit an ability to learn. The trouble is that it is difficult to separate instinct from intelligence. Combining the two, however, the earthworm has persisted for millions of years with no change necessary in its basic structure or habits. If survival is a product of intelligence, then the earthworm might well be smarter than we humans.

Charles Darwin conducted a great many observations and experiments in attempting to evaluate the earthworm's intelligence. One of the more interesting involved his curiosity about the manner in which earthworms pulled leaves into their burrows. Darwin counted 227 decayed leaves in one group of burrows, and observed that 80 percent were pulled in by the tip, 11 percent by the middle, and 9 percent by the leafstalk. It was apparent that the worms were selecting the manner in which to drag the leaves into their burrows, either by instinct, by trial and error, or by having previously learned the most efficient manner through experience. The last two would indicate intelligence of some kind.

Darwin then conducted an interesting experiment. He brought in some leaves of a rhododendron that was exotic to the area, one with which the worms had no experience. The worms dragged in 73 percent of these leaves by the stalk, 27 percent by the tip, and not one by the middle. Since these percentages were a complete reversal of the former pattern, Darwin concluded that the earthworms were operating on a trial-and-error basis, which does presuppose some intelligence. This behavior pattern is somewhat comparable to the chimpanzee presented with a footstool, a stick, and a high-hanging banana. The chimp might not be able to conceive his course of action abstractly, then carry it out as preconceived, but by trial and error he will eventually stand on the stool and knock down the banana with the stick. So it was with Darwin's earthworms. They could not drag in the leaves by one end, but they did then exhibit the intelligence to try the other end.

In more recent times, earthworms have been run through mazes in thousands of classrooms and laboratories, and have shown themselves capable of being trained—by reward and punishment—to follow a simple course. Surprisingly, researchers have also found that earthworms run a maze with greater efficiency during hours of darkness than in daytime. It is suspected that, since earthworms are nocturnal animals, their nerve tissues might exhibit heightened sensitivity during this active period.

Earthworm Species

The order Oligochaeta comprises 14 families. Some scientists divide these into two groups—red and gray. Families belonging to the red group include Lumbricus, Eisenia, and Dendroboena, and within these families the best-known species are all lumbricids: *Lumbricus terrestris* (the native night crawler), *L. rubellus* (the red worm), and *Eisenia foetida* (the brandling worm). The gray group includes the *Allolobophora* and *Octolasium* genera (both lumbricids), and the best-known species here is *Allolobophora caliginosa* (the field worm).

In general, the red worms live on organic matter—either manure or plant residues—that is in an early state of decomposition. The red worms feed nearer to the surface of the soil than the gray species. Night crawlers leave their castings on top of the soil quite often, while the gray worms leave theirs near the surface but never on it.

In terms of their importance to agriculture and horticulture in North America, night crawlers and field worms are by far the most important, since they are both populous and active in turning the soil. Gray worms, including the field worm, leave a higher percentage of mineral matter in their castings, which is a boon to growing plants. If one had to choose one earthworm species most important to agriculture and horticulture in North America, it would have to be *Allolobophora caliginosa*—the common field worm.

The lumbricids are believed to have been the most recent family on the evolutionary scale, so perfectly designed that they are capable of driving out nearly any other family when they are introduced to foreign regions. Lumbricids are found throughout the temperate and colder regions of the Northern Hemisphere, including Japan and Central Asia, and they are peregrine (introduced) inhabitants of many other areas.

Of the more than 1,800 known species of earthworms, perhaps only eight are of immediate and avid interest to gardeners, farmers, anglers, and commercial breeders in North America. Of these, five are commonly found naturally in fields and gardens, while the other three live naturally only in manure piles, decaying logs, and other very local areas of organic concentration. Two are popular for commercial breeding and sale.

Following are short descriptions of the "Key Eight" earthworms:

Lumbricus terrestris (night crawler; native night crawler; Canadian night crawler; northern native night crawler; dew worm; nightwalker; nightclimber; river walker; beavertail worm; lawn clipper; gumbo worm; rainworm; angleworm; orchard worm; night lion).   This lumbricid is the largest earthworm commonly found in North America. It grows to a length of 4 to 12 inches and is found commonly in lawn, garden, and orchard soils. As its name suggests, the night crawler comes to the surface only at night and in the early dawn hours, to feed, leave castings, and mate. Night crawlers are of great benefit to agriculture, since they burrow deeply into the ground—as far as 15 feet—helping to break up subsoil and interchange organic debris and nutrients for growing plants. No other earthworm species in America penetrates so deeply into the ground.

Night crawlers are prized for fishing bait because of their large size, but they are difficult to raise commercially because of their need for cool temperatures, their slow reproduction rate, and their migratory tendencies. They cannot be kept outdoors in bottomless pits, as red worms can, because night crawlers will soon leave the area.

Allolobophora caliginosa (field worm; common field worm; garden worm; brown worm; gray worm).   Field worms are lumbricids found widely distributed throughout the country, particularly in humid areas and in the South. They are likely to be turned up by the hundreds in gardens during spring and fall digging, and they make good fishing bait. The field worm is smaller than the night crawler, growing from two to eight inches in length, but it is larger than the red worm or other common species. They are not raised widely for bait because their rate of reproduction is slow, they demand cool temperatures, and they can be harvested easily in most backyards during the spring fishing season, making commercial production unnecessary.

Even though the common field worm is not one of the glamour stars of the Oligochaeta, its yeoman service to gardeners and farmers is tremendous. Their populations are generally higher than those of the night crawler, and they turn more soil in total. Field worms do not come to the surface except in times of very heavy rains, and yet they do not burrow deeply into the soil. The fact that their work is done mainly in the area of plant roots endears them further to farmers and gardeners. Last, the field worm will live in soils that may be too infertile for the night crawler, which is an added bonus for gardeners who are attempting to build up soil by encouraging earthworm populations.

Diplocardia verrucosa.   This is a slim worm commonly found in North American agricultural soils, although not in particularly large numbers. Further, their slight construction and relative inactivity make the *Diplocardia* of only marginal help to growing crops. It is a member of the family Acanthodrilidae.

Allolobophora chlorotica (green worm).   This lumbricid is another species that must be mentioned because of its prevalence in North American garden and agricultural soils, even though it is of little help to growing crops. It is the shortest of the species listed here, rarely growing three inches in length, although it is slightly thicker in diameter than the *Diplocardia*. The green worm is perhaps also the most inactive of all these species. Henry Hopp reported finding the green worm "curled up in a semi-dormant condition while the other worms are active." The green worm is, obviously, a slacker.

Pheretima (swamp worm).   This genus of the family Megascolecidae is the only non-European species to have made serious inroads into American agricultural and garden lands. It is a native of India and eastern Asia, and its presence is strong in Australia and other temperate regions where it has been introduced. It is the only genus known to be able to withstand the invasion of the lumbricids.

Pheretimas have been discovered in many parts of the American south, and as far north as Michigan. David Causey, an Arkansas researcher, has said that the *Pheretimas* are "so adaptable that it would appear that they are already the most common earthworm in some parts of the southern half of the state, and are to be found in practically all of the state."

He continues, "As has been pointed out repeatedly by investigators, our native worms seem to be losing out in the competition with foreign species, and are being replaced by European species in the north. In the south the genus *Pheretima* seems to be the successful invader. The conflict between the European forms and the Asiatic *Pheretima* on American soil should prove to be an interesting struggle in the years to come."

(Note: The history of species distributions at various points in geological time is taken up more fully later in this book, in the chapter devoted to earthworm history, chapter 2. It may be said here, however, that most of the common species of North American earthworms have been introduced from other parts of the world. Both the "native" night crawler and the common field worm, for instance, have been introduced from Europe since the time of initial European contact with this continent.)

There are three species of *Pheretimas* so far reported to

be common in North America: *P. californica,* a brownish worm growing to a length of two to five inches; *P. hupeiensis,* a dark cream-colored species of about the same size; and *P. diffringes,* a brownish member which can grow to nearly seven inches. All thrive in garden, agricultural, and stream-bank soils, in general sharing the same conditions as the common field worm. They are surprisingly adaptable, being able to thrive in the Indian subtropics as well as in the northern latitudes of the United States.

Unfortunately, little is known of the *Pheretimas'* contribution to soil fertility. We can surmise that it might be considerable, however, since the *Pheretima* appears to be a very active species. When handled, it will whip back and forth quite vigorously, in snakelike fashion, exhibiting far more energy than either the night crawler or field worm.

The *Pheretima* also has another characteristic that is very interesting and most promising. The Indian researchers S. R. Khambata and J. V. Bhatt, in 1957, reported that the bacillus *E. coli* was usually absent from the intestines of this earthworm species, suggesting that the intestinal secretions of the *Pheretima* might retard the growth of this harmful product of human excreta. The *Pheretima,* then, is of immense value in India, where agricultural lands are routinely fertilized with human excreta, and it might suggest an economical way to reclaim this valuable resource in our own country.

Pheretimas have also been reported to be good fishing bait, although they are seldom raised commercially for this purpose.

Eisenia foetida (brandling worm, red worm, red wiggler, manure worm, red-gold hybrid).   This lumbricid, which grows to a length of two to five inches, cannot live without copious amounts of decaying organic matter, and so it is not found in common garden or farm soils. Rather, it is an inhabitant of compost heaps, decaying logs, manure piles, and other areas of high organic concentration where it can find a diet to its liking.

The brandling worm is easily identified by its transverse rings of yellow and maroon that alternate along the length of its body. Brandlings are prolific breeders but suffer commercially because of their objectionable odor. Much preferred is another red worm species, *Lumbricus rubellus,* which is similar in size and habit, but lacking the odor problem.

Lumbricus rubellus (red worm, red wiggler, hybrid red worm, English red, Georgia red, California red, etc.).   This, another lumbricid, is the most popular earthworm species for commercial production. The red worm is free of objectionable odor, a prolific breeder, and responds well to commercial handling. It can be raised outdoors in all but the very coldest reaches of the United States, and can do well indoors, too. The red worm is of a uniform maroon color, which distinguishes it from the brandling, and it grows to a length of two to five inches. It is very popular as fishing bait because of its active wiggling action under water. Red worms, when introduced to compost or manure piles, will quickly reduce organic refuse to finished compost.

Eudrilus eugeniae (African night crawler, giant tropical worm, Missouri giant, giant red worm, blue worm, purple worm, African red worm, ruby red, giant river worm).   Here is the new glamour star of the commercial earthworm industry. The African night crawler is a member of the subfamily Eudrilinae and is native to western Africa. It is said to have been discovered by anglers along the Mexican gulf coast in the late 1940s, undoubtedly having been imported with plants from Africa. The African night crawler is exclusively a bait worm, and has become commercially successful because it combines some of the best features of the native night crawler and the red worm. It is a large species, like the native night crawler, averaging 5 or 6 inches at maturity, and sometimes growing to 12 inches or more. Like the red worm, the African night crawler is a prolific breeder and can be raised in pits with not too much difficulty. The African night crawler is of no agricultural importance in North America, since it cannot exist in our crop-growing lands. The very few sections of southernmost Florida that are hospitable to this heat-loving species are not agricultural lands. Further, red worms are more efficient compost makers and organic refuse reducers, and so the African night crawler can find no role here, either. For bait purposes, however, it is very popular, and appears to be gaining a larger share of this market with each passing year.

Other earthworm species.   There are many other earthworm species to be found in North America. However, little broad-scale research has been conducted in an attempt to sample, identify, and classify them, and to give any broad estimate of their populations. Most of the little-known species live in nonagricultural lands—forests, wetlands, and other areas where there is little economic justification for such research. Yet, the little-known species perform useful work in reducing organic matter and preparing the soil for the growth of native plants. These plants, in turn, support our broad range of wildlife which we treasure so highly.

No one knows how many different species of earthworms are to be found living in North American soils. Estimates have ranged from 30 to 70, with no confidence expressed in any of the estimates. The number might well be far greater, since many exotic species are perfectly able to adapt to our soil conditions, and it is difficult to know how many of these have already been introduced accidentally with plant shipments. Even foreign plant shipments cleared by federal inspectors, and seeming to carry no earthworms with them, can be host to numerous cocoons that will hatch at a later time. Most of our important earthworm species are peregrines (coming from abroad) and there is every reason to believe that new species of importance will be introduced, or are at this very time making footholds in scattered parts of the country.

Among the genera known to have established populations in certain North American soils are:

Several members of the family Megascolecidae (occurring widely in the Southern Hemisphere, and only in the southern part of North America);

Eukerria and *Ocnerodrilus,* members of the family Ocnerodrilidae, found in lower California;

a few members of the family Acanthodrilidae, including *Plutellus* (found in scattered parts of the continent) and *Pontodrilus,* which is found in some coastal areas and offshore islands;

Dichogaster, found in California, and one species of *Megascolides,* both of the family Octochaetidae;

a few freshwater forms of genera in the family Glossoscolecidae;

the genus *Sparganophilus,* from the subfamily Sparganophilinae; and

within the family Lumbricidae, species of *Eiseniella, Dendrobaena, Bimastos,* and *Octolasium,* as well as the more popular *Lumbricus, Eisenia, and Allolobophora.*

Earthworm surveys. There have been a few earthworm surveys conducted, which we shall examine now. Together, they should give us some idea of the species groups and families that our North American lands support. But more than that, they will add further impetus to the crying need for more research in this area.

●*Arkansas.* The following survey is interesting, first in that it is one of very few such projects undertaken in recent times, and second in that its findings might well be typical for a sizable segment of the country. David Causey of the University of Arkansas undertook the survey, reporting it in the Journal Series, University of Arkansas (Research Paper No. 1035). He makes no attempt to estimate populations of any of the discovered species, but the names of the species in themselves will be of interest to many in Arkansas and in at least ten nearby states.

Causey located 17 earthworm species in all, scattered

among 9 genera. He regards 6 of the species as native to the United States, 8 as introduced European species, and 3 of Asiatic origin.

The 17 species located by Causey include:

Allolobophora caliginosa (the field worm; two forms, found in cultivated soils, lawns, and woodlots).

Bimastos beddardi (a native species found in wet areas, decaying logs, stumps, moss, wooded areas, and other places where millipedes are common).

B. longicinctus (a native species, found in garden soils and prairie regions).

B. parvus (a native species found in the wooded north side of a hill).

Dendrobaena octaedra (a European species, located in a wooded area, formerly cultivated).

Diplocardia communis (a native species, found in garden soils, probably common).

D. riparia (a native species, found along with *Pheretima*, in garden soil).

D. singularis (a native species found in both cultivated soils such as gardens and lawns, and from relatively undisturbed soils in wooded areas; appears to be widespread).

Eisenia foetida (the brandling worm; an introduced European species found in cultivated areas and in decaying logs).

E. rosea (a European introduction, widespread in the United States and no doubt common in Arkansas).

Eiseniella tetraedra (a European form, widespread in the United States).

Lumbricus rubellus (the red worm; a European species, probably widespread in Arkansas).

L. terrestris (the native night crawler; a European species; only one record, received from someone who had purchased night crawlers in order to breed them; should be common in the older cultivated areas of Arkansas).

Octolasium lacteum (a European introduction; found in leaf mold on hillsides).

Pheretima californica (an Asiatic introduction).

P. diffringes (Asiatic).

P. hupeiensis (the third of the genus located in Arkansas; the most widespread species of this genus in the state, according to the author's records).

• *Michigan.*   *Pheretima hawayana,* an Indian peregrine, has been reported in several parts of Michigan. *P. hilgendorfi,* another Indian species, has also been reported in Michigan, in rich and moist soils near lakes. Adults of this species measure as large as nine inches.

• *Washington.*   Several species of *Plutellus,* a genus of the family Acanthodrilidae, have been reported in the moist Pacific Northwest, in western Washington. Included are *P. perrieri, P. altmani, P. kincaidi, P. toutellus,* and *P. macnabi.* Researcher Dorothy McKey-Fender of McMinnville, Oregon, reported these in *Northwest Science* (vol. 44, no. 4, 1970) and also a newly discovered species, *P. hopsonae.* All these species were identified in rugged country on the north side of the Columbia River, in acid soil that supports large stands of Douglas firs.

• *New York.*   Perhaps the most complete local survey on record was conducted by LeRoy C. Stegman of the State University of New York, College of Forestry at Syracuse University. It is so well done, and so interestingly presented, that we will reproduce it in full, not only for the information it conveys but as a model for other studies.

A Preliminary Survey of
Earthworms of the Tully Forest
in Central New York*

Most of the hundreds of articles written about earthworms emphasize their economic or biologic importance in one way or another. Their broad classification is well established, some of the life histories are

*Reprinted with permission of The Soil and Health Foundation, Emmaus, Pa., 1961, from *The Challenge of Earthworm Research*, ed. Robert Rodale, pp. 57–66.

known, and much has been written about their numbers and distribution. We now need detailed ecological studies to determine their real significance in the physical, chemical and biological complex of the soil.

Earthworms are the largest element of the soil fauna, constituting 20 to 80% of its total weight. Bornebusch (1930-31) gives figures showing that the weight of earthworms varies from 95 to 1784 pounds per acre in the soils of Denmark. No weights were taken during this study and no direct comparisons can be made with conditions in Denmark. The numbers collected from the top 6 inches of soil on the Tully Forest showed a wide range of weights and are proof that even their dead bodies contribute a large amount of organic matter to soil. Their biological significance is, however, far greater than their value as fertilizer. Aristotle is said to have called them "The intestines of the earth," and Darwin (1886, p. 813) said, "It may be doubted whether there are many other animals which have played as important a part in the history of the world as have these lowly creatures."

This statement of Darwin may seem exaggerated until we realize that the productivity of the soil determines the plant and animal foods for mankind. Larsen (1956, p. 19) points out that our initial belief that differences in soil were to be explained by the science of geology, that one soil differed from another because of differences in the rocks and sand of which it is composed, has been considerably modified. He says further that plants build soil, and that different plant types build different soil types. Even this statement fails to recognize the important effects of the soil fauna, including earthworms. We are beginning to realize that all of the elements of geology, biology, physiography and climate interact to determine the kind of soil and what and how much it will produce.

The Tully Forest

The Tully Forest is an area of approximately 2000 acres situated about 25 miles south of Syracuse in Cortland County, New York. The general topography is rolling with rounded ridges and U-shaped valleys running generally north and south. The elevation varies from 1380 to 2020 feet above mean sea level. The soils are mostly thin (less than 6 feet) and underlain with shale or sandstone. In certain areas the shale comes almost to the surface and in several such places a heavy moss carpet has developed. Most of the area formerly was used for agriculture but later abandoned because of low fertility, thin soil, topography, or a combination of these.

About one-third of the area consists of transition types varying from recent agricultural fields to brush-grown areas; one-third of conifer plantations of various ages and species composition; and one-third of hardwood forest which varies considerably in species composition, and in age from pole stage to mature sugar bush and beech stands.

Many soil faunal habitats are furnished by these cover types and still more have been created by 3 artificial ponds which were established 5 years ago.

Purpose of Study

This study was carried out to accomplish the following:

1. To determine what species of earthworms are present on the Tully Forest.

2. To determine their distribution and relative numbers.

3. To determine their association with various forest types on the Tully Forest.

4. To secure basic information for more advanced work on the ecology of the soil fauna.

Methods

Samples were collected during the summer of 1955 from the following forest types:

> Old field
> Northern hardwoods
> White pine plantations
> Red pine plantations
> Scotch pine plantations
> White cedar plantations
> Norway spruce plantations

Most of the collections were made during June, July and August. Earthworms were found in all of these types except the Norway spruce. In addition, they were collected from more restricted locations such as creek banks, shores of ponds, beneath loose bark, under stone walls, and other quite generally distributed but special habitats.

All samples to be counted within a forest type were located at least 50 feet inside the boundary of that type to avoid edge effect. The standard sample of soil for qualitative and quantitative information was 2 feet square and 6 inches deep. For each sample, the soil was removed and shaken through a $1/4''$-mesh sieve to expose all earthworms. The samples were distributed at random within the type. Three samples were always taken in each type to make the results more representative. However, when no earthworms were found in 3 samples, others were selected in an attempt to locate worms. Such samples were not taken at random but were intentionally located in areas that seemed most favorable.

Collections for qualitative information only were taken in other habitats without respect to the size of the samples.

All specimens were identified as closely as possible from external characteristics and then sent to Dr. Guy Murchie at Flint College, University of Michigan, Flint, Michigan. He is a competent taxonomist in this group and he made the final taxonomic determinations.

Results

Soils

Soil characteristics are very important in determining the distribution of earthworms. The purposes of this study have been set forth and are general in nature. The following generalized treatment of soils therefore is considered adequate for this first investigation.

The soils of this region are classified under the broad category of gray brown podzolic (forest) soils (Marbut 1935). The soils of the Tully Forest were derived from glacial till. The major soil association found on the forest is the Lordstown-Volusia (Cline 1955). The Lordstown soil is usually characteristic of the steeper slopes and, typically, is shallow, well drained, has a low lime content and lacks a fragipan. The Volusia soil is found on the gently to strongly sloping hills. Here the soil is somewhat poorly drained, the lime content is very low and it also lacks a fragipan.

The texture of the soil was determined in 5 of the types using the Bouyoucos hydrometer method with the following results:

Type	Sand	Silt	Clay
White cedar	18.8	42.0	39.2
Norway spruce	18.4	34.4	47.2
Red pine	20.0	40.8	39.2
Northern hardwood	40.0	41.2	18.8
Old field	32.4	38.4	29.2

The texture of the soil in the white pine plantation was similar to that in the red pine area, and in the Scotch pine the soil was similar to the old field area.

Soil acidity was measured with a Beckman pH meter and was surprisingly constant in the various habitats, not varying sufficiently to account for the presence or absence of the various species of earthworms. The range extended from 4.1 in white cedar to 5.8 in old fields:

White cedar	4.1
Norway spruce	4.7
White pine	4.7
Red pine	4.7
Scotch pine	4.8
Northern hardwood	4.9
Old field	5.8

This relatively low pH places all of the areas on the Tully Forest in an unfavorable category for earthworms according to Murchie (1954) who found that as acidity increases beyond a pH of 6.0 the numbers of species decline. On the other hand Reynolds (1935) checked the occurrence of various species of earthworms with respect to the pH of the soil in sandy coniferous plantations in New York state and found the greatest numbers of species and individuals where the soil had a pH between 5.5 and 4.1. This was also true in this investigation. I believe Murchie's statement indicates that the earthworm populations were lower on the Tully Forest than they would be on deeper, richer, less acid soils.

The moisture content varied from 69% to 7% of the

wet weight. All samples were not tested. However, I believe both extremes were measured.

The organic content of the soil was determined with the loss on ignition method (Wilde and Voight 1959). Thirty cores were taken at random through each type. These were thoroughly mixed and 3 samples were then processed for each collection. The results were as follows:

White cedar	18%
Norway spruce	10%
White pine	17%
Red pine	10%
Scotch pine	10%
Old field	10%
Northern hardwood	16%

Earthworm Species Found

Ten species of earthworms, belonging to 7 genera, were found, and more intensive work should reveal a few additional species. These would be more limited in distribution and probably of less general importance.

The species found are as follows:

Lumbricus terrestris Linnaeus
Lumbricus rubellus Hoffmeister
Lumbricus castaneus (Savigny)
Allolobophora calignosa (Savigny)
Allolobophora chloritica (Savigny)
Eisenia rosea (Savigny)
Octalasium lacteum Orley
Eiseniella tetraedra (Savigny)
Bimastos tenuis (Eisen)
Haplotaxis gordioides Hoffmeister (an aquatic form)

Distribution

Earthworms, like other invertebrates, are not distributed at random. Based upon observations made during the course of this study, the following 2 factors were found to be of great importance: first, the amount and diversity of humus materials present; and second, the amount of moisture present in the soil.

Both the total number of earthworms and the number of different species represented increase with the amount and diversity of humus and raw litter present. Diversity seems to be the more important of these factors, since in pure conifer plantations there was a heavy carpet of raw litter and humus from needles and branches, yet the number of earthworms was very low. This may indicate that decomposing needles are not satisfactory food for earthworms. The distribution of earthworms in such a stand roughly correlates with the amount and diversity of herbaceous ground cover.

In Table I the check marks indicate the presence of earthworms of the species indicated. The question marks show that one of the 3 species of the genus *Lumbricus* was present. Since all were immature, only the generic level could be determined with certainty. *Allolobophora chloritica* was found less than 50 feet from the edge of the old field type and this collection is therefore marginal. The numbers in the last column and on the

Table I   DISTRIBUTION OF EARTHWORM SPECIES

	Al. calignosa	*Ei. rosea*	*Oct. lacteum*	*L. terrestris*	*L. rubellus*	*E. tetraedra*	*Bi. tenuis*	*Al. chloritica*	*L. castaneus*	*H. gordioides*	*No. of Species*
Old Field	√	√	√	√	√		√		√		7
Stream Bank	√	√	√	√	√	√				√	7
No. Hardwood	√	√	√	√			√				5
White Pine	√	√	√	?	?				?		4
Red Pine	√	√	√			√					4
Shores of Ponds	√	√	√								3
White Cedar	√			?	?				?		2
Norway Spruce											
No. of Habitats	7	6	6	4	2	2	2		1	1	

lowest line indicate the numbers of species or habitats in which they were found.

This distribution agrees closely with that found by Murchie (1956) and correlates with the known relative tolerances of the species. Table I therefore reflects the ability of the various species to adapt to different environments.

Numbers and Importance of Earthworms

The number of species of earthworms tends to correlate with the diversity and amount of ground cover in the habitats: the greater the amount and diversity of plant life present, the greater the number of species of earthworms present. These factors seem to outweigh the kind of soil present although soil conditions have much to do with the amount and variety of plants living there.

The number of earthworms found in any cover decreased rapidly after the moisture content dropped below 20-25%. The lowest limit of moisture recorded in which an earthworm was found during this study was 7%. In this case the worm was in a state of aestivation, tightly coiled within a small walled cell. The water content typically was lower in the pure conifer stands than in adjacent mixed cover. Earthworms disappeared from these conifer stands, even in open herb-covered areas, before they did from areas covered with a mixed growth.

The largest number of earthworms was found in the surface layers in the spring when the water table was near the surface. Evidently they were compelled to move upward by the water.

During the summer as the surface soil became dry, the greatest numbers of worms were from 3 to 6 inches beneath the surface. At depths greater than 6 inches the number rapidly decreased and only the larger species were found. The following figures give the number per acre which is the unit used by many other writers dealing with earthworm population studies.

The number of earthworms per acre found in the top 6 inches of soil and their variation between types is very interesting.

Habitat	Maximum	Average
Old field	348,480	151,371
Northern hardwood	196,020	136,125
Red pine	381,150	119,790
Scotch pine	370,260	89,298
White pine	239,580	81,675
Norway spruce	0	0

The Scotch pine plantation was a young plantation in which the trees were under 3 feet in height and the ground cover still consisted principally of grasses and herbs. A Scotch pine plantation in which the crown had closed would present a much different situation.

The variation in number per species per acre is equally interesting, as shown in the following data.

Species	Maximum	Average
Allolobophora calignosa	653,400	90,387
Lumbricus terrestris	196,020	57,172
Octolasium lacteum	185,130	51,183
Eisenia rosea	119,790	46,827
Lumbricus rubellus	217,800	———
Bimastos tenuis	87,120	———
Eiseniella tetraedra	54,450	———

Table II gives 2 sets of figures needed to determine the relative abundance of each species based upon the numbers and distribution. The figures above the diagonal lines are the average numbers of specimens of the species that were found in those samples in which that species occurred. Those below are the frequency indices expressed in percentages.

The relative biological importance will actually differ from these figures for the following reasons:

1. The species differ greatly in size.

2. Their influence upon the environment may be different for different species.

3. Their food, host and parasitic relations may vary greatly between species.

Such a refined evaluation is beyond the scope of this paper.

35

Table II RELATIVE IMPORTANCE OF EARTHWORM SPECIES

	Al. calignosa	*Ei. rosea*	*Oct. lacteum*	*L. terrestris*	*L. rubellus*	*E. tetraedra*	*Bi. tenuis*	*Al. chloritica*	*L. castaneus*	*H. gordioides*
Old Field	7/38	8/25	6/13	4/15	5/10		3/5	2/3	2/3	
Stream Bank	5/77	6/66	4/66	2/22	3/66	1/10				
No. Hardwood	4/33	2/19	2/23	1/36	1/36		5/4		1/36	
White Pine	4/21	3/21	2/14	1/14	1/14				1/14	
Red Pine	5/47	6/7	4/20	2/20	2/20				2/20	
Shores of Ponds	3	4	2	2						
White Cedar	2/33			1/33	1/33				1/33	
Norway Spruce										

The actual number of earthworms present in an area in the top 6 inches of soil was closely correlated with the amount of moisture present. When the soil moisture dropped the number of worms decreased. The present belief is that as soil loses its moisture earthworms burrow to deeper levels. Collections made during this study found a shift from the top inch or two to a depth of 5 or 6 inches but not to deeper levels. The larger, stronger species are believed to go to depths of 6 feet or over (Stephenson 1930). Certain species did wall themselves up at depths to one foot and aestivated or entered a state of torpor until more favorable conditions returned. The digging carried out during this study revealed so few animals at greater depths than one foot that it raises a question about the adequacy of this explanation. A limited amount of migration to more favorable sites was indicated. Moisture content was not determined for all samples and the lowest limit is not definitely known, although it seems to approach 7%.

This study was carried out from June through September, which includes the dry season of the year, when earthworms become scarce or absent in many areas. A similar investigation should be conducted from September to June to complete the picture. I believe the counts would be higher from September to June although the number of species should remain the same.

Discussion

The information collected during this study makes possible a more intelligent evaluation of earthworms as an important group of soil animals on the Tully Forest. We know what species we can expect to find, where, and in what numbers. We now need to know more about their relations to the plants and other animals in the area. To give but a few of these relationships: Earthworms ingest nematodes, fungi, bacteria and protozoa with their food and with the soil they pass through their digestive tracts. Several species in each of these groups are known to be pathogenic to plants or animals. Do the earthworms kill these organisms or simply transport them from the point of ingestion to the point where the castings are released? This may be a considerable distance. If the adults are killed, are any of the nematode eggs, fungal spores, and encysted forms still viable or are they also destroyed? If earthworms are vectors for any of these organisms, how rapidly could they spread the forms concerned by their travels from place to place? How far and how rapidly do earthworms move? Are they important control agents that destroy desirable or undesirable organisms?

One known example may suffice. Bunyea (1931) tells us that earthworms may play an important part in the spread of the roundworm causing gapes in poultry. The infective eggs or the young gapeworms which have hatched in the soil from eggs in the fowls droppings may be eaten by earthworms; they burrow into the body muscles of the earthworm and may remain alive for considerable periods. The earthworm in these cases is not a necessary intermediate host of the parasite; it is merely a mechanical carrier or reservoir, protecting the young gapeworms. They may thus carry the young gapeworms over from one warm season to another. When the earthworm is eaten the gapeworms complete their life cycle in the fowl.

To illustrate another relationship, Barker (1958) considers earthworms biological concentrators of DDT, and, since they constitute an important part of the food of many species of birds and a few species of mammals, their consumption may be lethal to these species where sprays are used even though the dosage of DDT is too small to be effective directly. Earthworms are important food items for many other animals such as frogs, toads, salamanders, shrews and moles. Food chains are very important and need much further investigation.

The direct actions of earthworms not only increase porosity and friability of the soil by their tunnels and castings but they also carry on all metabolic activities. They use oxygen and give off carbon dioxide and other waste products. Some of these waste products are high in nitrogen content and in a form usable by other plants and animals. They reduce raw humus and other substances passed through their digestive systems, both chemically and physically, to smaller units and more simple compounds. The total effect of these processes may not be great for a single worm, but when multiplied by several hundred thousand individuals per acre the effect is considerable.

This general survey has set the stage by telling us what earthworm actors we have on the forest, where they are found and in what numbers. It furnishes information essential in interpreting the importance of earthworms when we know the role they play in relation to other soil flora and fauna.

Dr. James A. Larsen (1956, page 101) makes a statement I should like to quote in conclusion:

"We are, thus, quite familiar with the multitude of species that make up the living world. But we have only begun to study the ways by which plants and animals live as individuals and as part of the world of life. . . . With greater understanding of what happens within the living organism, there will be greater opportunity to understand the relationships existing between the plants and animals—and human beings—that make up the living world."

References

Barker, Roy J. 1958. Notes on some ecological effects of DDT sprayed on elms. J. Wildl. Management *22*: 269-274.

Bornebusch, C. H. 1930-31. The fauna of forest soil. Det forstlige Forsogsvaesen *11*: 1-158.

Bunyea, Hubert. 1931. Diseases and parasites of poultry. U.S.D.A. Farmers Bulletin *1652:* 63.

Cline, Martin G. 1955. Soils and soil associations of New York. Cornell Ext. Bull. *930:* 1-72.

Darwin, Charles. 1896. The formation of vegetable mould, through the action of worms, with observations on their habits. D. Appleton and Company.

Larsen, James A. 1956. Wisconsin's renewable resources. University of Wisconsin Press.

Marbut, C. F. 1935. Soils of the United States. In Atlas of American Agriculture, Part 3. U. S. Dept. of Agric. Bureau of Chem. and Soils. Washington, D.C.

Murchie, Wm. R. 1954. Unpub. thesis. Univ. of Mich. Natural history studies on the earthworms of Michigan.

Stephenson, J. 1930. The Oligochaeta. Oxford, The Clarendon Press.

Wilde, S. A. and G. K. Voigt. 1959. An analysis of soils and plants for foresters and horticulturists. Ann Arbor, Michigan, J. W. Edwards publisher.

LeRoy C. Stegman. State University of New York, College of Forestry, at Syracuse University.

Professional and Amateur Sampling

The sampling of earthworm populations is perhaps best left to the professionals—biologists who have been trained to gather accurate samples and make positive identifications. In this way, the literature of the field will slowly be built up, one piece of data fitting neatly into the other, until we have a complete picture of the earthworms of America. Hundreds of soil scientists have been doing as much for soils—surveying and classifying all the soils of the United States, under a program of the U.S. Geological Survey—and their work is not yet near completion, despite years of intensive efforts. To expect a similar survey of earthworms is almost too much to hope for— and yet, the task must be continued, and it must proceed at a far quicker pace than it has to date.

Where professional activity has been too slow and halting, amateurs have often stepped in, often with gratifying results. The entire organic gardening and farming movement in America has grown and spread by virtue of such amateur experimentation, discovery, and the later acceptance of the resulting principles. Such practices as modern composting, mulching, and companion planting were developed not by professional horticulturists and agricultural scientists, but by backyard gardeners and innovative farmers. So, perhaps, our knowledge of the distribution of earthworm species must be forwarded by informed and willing amateurs. With this thought in mind, we will consider some accepted methods for sampling earthworm populations, and keys to their identification.

Sampling Methods

There are five ways to sample earthworm populations: handsorting, soil washing, electrical methods, chemical methods, and heat extraction. All are explained more fully in Edwards and Lofty's *Biology of Earthworms*.

Handsorting.   This is the traditional method. It involves no more than digging up a soil sample of predetermined dimensions, then carefully separating the soil by hand, removing all the earthworms. The size of the sample is not particularly important, although the larger it is, the more accurate will be the results. Researchers have concluded that 16 samples $1/16$ meter by $1/16$ meter to a depth of 20 centimeters (roughly $2^1/2$ inches by $2^1/2$ inches to a depth of 8 inches) would give an accurate sample for sorting. Some researchers take much larger samples, up to 1 meter (39.37 inches) square. The depth will depend on the species of worms the researcher attempts to sample. For most species, a sample taken to a depth of 8 inches will be sufficient, since most worms live within this depth. But for night crawlers and a few other deep-living species, a soil sample only 8 inches deep would not yield accurate results. It must be remembered also that even top-living species will burrow below their normal depth range in times of drought or unusually warm soil conditions. Any population survey must be adjusted for these factors, as well as for the time of year, which will also influence the number of earthworms present in soils.

Soil washing. In this method, soil samples are taken just as described for handsorting, but the soil is then washed through a series of sieves by a jet of water. One researcher used two sieves, one of 2-millimeter mesh, overlying another of 0.5-millimeter mesh. He then immersed both sieves in a magnesium sulphate solution of specific gravity 1.2, which brought the worms to the surface to be counted. He used soil samples *which he had previously handsorted* and discovered that he had missed fully 48 percent of the worms in the handsorting. These missed worms, however, accounted for only 16 percent of the total earthworm weight, indicating that in handsorting many of the smaller and darker-colored worms will be overlooked, no matter how careful the sorting.

Electrical methods. Anglers have long used electric rods to bring up night crawlers for bait. These rods are still advertised in outdoor magazines. Researchers say that the best specifications for such a device require a steel rod 8 to 10 millimeters (about ⅓ inch) in diameter and 75 centimeters (29½ inches) long, with an insulated handle. The voltage should be 220 to 240 volts at 3 to 5 angstrom units, and the current should be regulated by a variable resistence or by plunging the rod deeper into the soil. The current will be conducted more effectively if the soil is moist.

Electrical sampling is effective in bringing up deep-living specimens. But the final word is one of caution. Children have been killed accidentally by these devices, which should never be used without full knowledge and precautions.

Chemical methods. These involve the preparation of various solutions which are then applied to the soil, bringing earthworms to the surface. Substances used include mercuric chloride, potassium permanganate, Mowrah meal (extracted from seeds of the Bassia tree, *Bassia longifolia,*) and formalin. There are several disadvantages to chemical extraction methods, the major one being that they do not always give accurate samples. Some chemicals, notably potassium permanganate, kill many worms before they can rise to the surface. Then, some earthworm species react more quickly than others to the chemicals, leading again to inaccurate counts. Species with permanent burrows can rise to the surface much more quickly than those which do not maintain burrows. Soil temperature and moisture level will also influence the number of worms which respond to chemical extraction methods.

The English researcher F. Raw, reporting in a 1959 issue of the scientific journal *Nature*, found that a 0.55 percent formalin solution (25 milliliters of 40 percent formalin in 4.56 liters of water applied to a soil sample 0.36 meter square) was most effective of all the chemicals used.

Heat extraction.   This method is not used often, but is helpful in sampling small, surface-dwelling species that might be enmeshed in thickly matted turf. Since handsorting is difficult here, the heat extraction method is sometimes used. Edwards and Lofty describe the method as involving "a container (55 centimeters by 45 centimeters) with a wire sieve 5 centimeters from its bottom. Soil samples (20 centimeters by 20 centimeters by 10 centimeters deep) are placed on the sieve, immersed in water with 14 60-watt light bulbs suspended above, and left for three hours after which worms can be collected from the bottom of the container."

Edwards and Lofty also conclude that handsorting and washing are the most effective sampling methods, but that the formalin method appears to be best for deep-living species.

Identifying Earthworms

Many gardeners and farmers can already tell the difference between a night crawler and a field worm, and those who have purchased worms for fishing bait or composting can distinguish a red worm from either of these. In addition, the brandling worm is easily recognizable by the characteristic maroon and yellow (ranging downward in intensity to brown and buff) stripes running transversely along the length of its body. And perhaps most plant growers and anglers need little more ability than this to identify species. However, if population samples are to be taken by amateurs, then more rigid identification methods will have to be learned and practiced. The one which will be described here is that of David Causey of the University of Arkansas, as reported in the Journal Series, University of Arkansas (Research Paper No. 1035). It is a reliable system, not overly difficult to learn, and relatively inexpensive to put into practice.

The first thing the amateur needs is a *broad field dissecting binocular*. This is a fairly expensive instrument, although not so expensive as many high-powered laboratory microscopes. Its purchase will represent just about the total equipment outlay of the amateur researcher, since very little else is needed. A strong hand lens can be used, but it is difficult to view some of the smaller characteristics such as the spermathecal pores and the tubercula pubertatis without the binocular. In addition, any gardener with any scientific bent at all will be enthralled with the wide range of possibilities offered by the dissecting binocular. All kinds of insects and plant parts can be brought into brilliant magnification, in three dimensions, with the aid of this wonderful instrument.

Rough identification.   Many species can easily be identified by rough characteristics. The size of the specimen is one clue. It is difficult to mistake a 10-inch night crawler for a 4-inch field worm. Size ranges are given in Causey's Tabular Key (see table 1). This invaluable key will also be used to check all other characteristics.

Color is another rough identification characteristic. We have already discussed the stripes of the brandling worm, but there are others not much more difficult to spot. The green worm (*Allolobophora chlorotica*) has a characteristic greenish color and a pinkish clitellum. Field worms are a brownish red, while night crawlers (even if they are of the same size) have a red-maroon-violet hue.

Table 1

Causey's Tabular Key to Earthworms

Name	Clitellum	Tubercula pubertatis	Spermiducal pores	Spermathecal pores
Diplocardia				
D. singularis	13–18 cingulum		19	6/7, 7/8, 8/9
D. communis	13–18 saddle		19	6/7, 7/8, 8/9
D. riparia	13–18 saddle		19	7/8, 8/9
Eisenilla				
E. tetraedra	22, 23–26, 27	23–25, 26	13	9/10, 10/11 (dorsal)
Eisenia				
E. veneta	24, 25, 26, 27, 32, 33	30 and 31	15	9/10, 10/11 (dorsal)
E. lonnbergi	24–30	26–29	15	8/9, 9/10, 10/11 (dorsal)
E. foetida	24, 25, 26–32	28–30, 31	15	9/10, 10/11 (dorsal)
E. rosea	24, 25–32, 33	29–30, 31	15	9/10, 10/11 (dorsal)
Allolobophora				
A. caliginosa	27, 28–34, 35	31 and 33	15	9/10, 10/11
A. longa	27, 28–35	32–34	15	9/10, 10/11
A. chlorotica	29–37	31, 33, 35	15	8/9–10/11
Dendrobaena				
D. subrubicunda	25, 26–31, 32	28–30	15	9/10, 10/11
D. octaedra	27, 28, 29–33, 34	31–33	15	9/10–11/12
Bimastos				
B. palustris	23–28	none	15	none
B. gieseleri	22–29	none	15	none
B. tumidus	22–29	27, 28	15	none
B. parvus	24–30	25, 26–29, 30 indefinite	15	none
B. beddardi	24, 25–31, 32	24, 25–30 indefinite	15	none
B. longicinctus	23–32 or 24–33	none	15	none
B. zeteki	27–37	none	15	none
B. tenuis	26–31	29, 30 indefinite	15	none
Octolasium				
O. lacteum	30–35	31–34	15	9/10, 10/11
Lumbricus				
L. rubellus	27–32	28–31	15	9/10 and 10/11
L. castaneus	28–33	29–32	15	9/10 and 10/11
L. terrestris	31, 32–37	33–36	15	9/10 and 10/11
Pheretima				
P. californica	14–16		18	7/8, 8/9
P. hupeiensis	14–16		18	7, 8, 9
P. diffringes	14–16 (all cingula)		18	5/6–8/9

Sperm sacs	Setae	First dorsal pore	Number of somites	Length in cm.
9, 12	wide	7/8	90–120	18–30
9, 12	wide	7/8	125–160	18–30
9, 12	wide	10/11	135–160	20–27
9–12	close	4/5	80–100	4–6
9, 11, 12	wide	5/6	80–120	3.5–5
9, 11, 12	close	7/8	188	9.6
			75–125	5–15
9–12	close	4/5		
9–12	close	4/5	120–150	3–8
9–12	close	9/10 usually	100–250	5–20
9–12	close	12/13	160–200	12–16
9–12	close	4/5	80–125	5–7
9, 11, 12	wide	5/6	60–125	5–8
9, 11, 12	wide	4/5	80–95	2.5–4
11 and 12	close	5/6	80–100	7.5
11 and 12	close	5/6	100–110	4–7
11 and 12	close	5/6	40–60	2–5
11 and 12	close	5/6	85–111	2.5–4
11 and 12	close	5/6	70–100	2–6
11 and 12	close	5/6	100–130	7–10
11 and 12	close	5/6	100–140	10–14
11 and 12	wide	5/6	90–110	4–8
9–12	wide	8/9, 9/10 or 10/11	100–170	5–16
9, 11, and 12	close	7/8	90–150	7–15
9, 11, and 12	close	6/7	90	3–5
9, 11, and 12	close	7/8	100–175	10–30
11 and 12	all	11/12	105–112	5–12.5
11 and 12	peri-	11/12–12/13	119–132	4.5–12
11 and 12	chaet.	11/12	90–113	4.5–17

(*continued*)

Name	Color antero-dorsal	Notes
Diplocardia		
D. singularis	flesh	Garden soil, leaves, hillsides
D. communis	pale flesh	Garden soil
D. riparia	dark brown	Garden soil
Eisenilla		
E. tetraedra	brown	Water-soaked banks of streams, ponds, etc.
Eisenia		
E. veneta		Stream banks
E. lonnbergi	brownish violet	
E. foetida	brown and buff bands	Manure and compost heaps, decaying logs, etc.
E. rosea	pale red	
Allolobophora		
A. caliginosa	rose or brown red	Garden and woodland soil, river-bottom land.
A. longa		
A. chlorotica	greenish	
Dendrobaena		
D. subrubicunda	red	Wet soil with sewage contamination
D. octaedra	violet brown	
Bimastos		
B. palustris	pale red	Wet banks of streams and ponds
B. gieseleri	brown red	Decayed leaves, rotten logs, etc.
B. tumidus	reddish brown	Decayed leaves
B. parvus	brown red	
B. beddardi	reddish brown	Wet areas, decaying logs, etc.
B. longicinctus	rose red	Lawns and woodlands
B. zeteki	purplish brown	Decaying logs, leaf mold
B. tenuis	rose red	Decayed leaf mold and logs
Octolasium		
O. lacteum	pale pink	Under logs, leaf mold, etc.
Lumbricus		
L. rubellus	reddish brown	Debris along shores
L. castaneus	brown violet	
L. terrestris	brown violet	Lawn and garden soil
Pheretima		
P. californica	brownish	
P. hupeiensis	dark cream	Garden soil, etc.
P. diffringes	brownish	Damp soil along stream

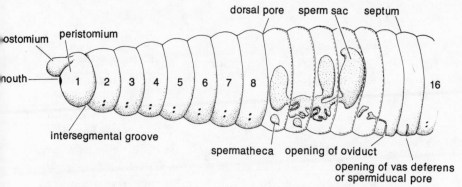

Diagram of anterior end of *Lumbricus*. Somites are numbered 1-16. Testes are represented in 10 and 11, and the ovary in 13, but they are not labeled.

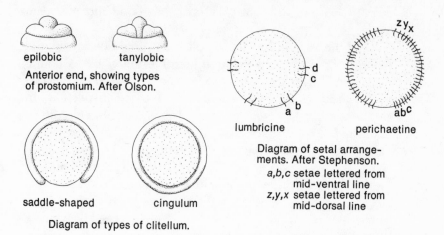

epilobic   tanylobic

Anterior end, showing types of prostomium. After Olson.

lumbricine   perichaetine

Diagram of setal arrangements. After Stephenson.

a,b,c setae lettered from mid-ventral line

z,y,x setae lettered from mid-dorsal line

saddle-shaped   cingulum

Diagram of types of clitellum.

Explanation: The numbers in each column represent the particular segments (or somites) at which each characteristic (in the heading) will be found. Somites are numbered consecutively, starting at the anterior and proceeding toward the rear of the worm. For example, the clitellum of *Diplocardia singularis* is located at segments 13 through 18; its spermiducal pores are on segment 19; its spermathecal pores are between segments 6 and 7, 7 and 8, and 8 and 9; sperm sacs are located on segments 9 and 12; etc.

Source: Causey, David, *The Earthworms of Arkansas*, Research Paper No. 1035, Journal Series, Arkansas Academy of Science, University of Arkansas. Reprinted in *The Challenge of Earthworm Research*, ed. Robert Rodale, The Soil and Health Foundation, Emmaus, Pa. (1961)

Behavior can also sometimes be used as a reliable clue. Red worms will squirm actively when handled, as will the *Pheretimas*.

The location of the sample is another good clue. Members of the genus *Eisenia,* including the brandling worm, will be found along stream banks and in places where large concentrations of organic matter are decaying such as in manure piles, compost heaps, and decaying logs, but almost never in garden and agricultural fields. Night crawlers and field worms will be found in crop-growing lands. *Pheretimas* take to garden soils, but will also be found along stream banks.

All the keys to rough identification should be considered before attempting any positive identifications. By so doing, the amateur researcher will save time and can often make a fairly certain identification with no detailed inspection. In cases of doubt, however, or to confirm a suspected identification, the following method should be used.

The earthworm specimens must be killed in order to inspect them carefully for positive identification. Causey's method is to anesthetize them first, in a 50 percent solution of alcohol and water, and when they become motionless to stack them, like cordwood, between two small pieces of window glass. The worms should be placed as straight as possible. After they have died in this straight condition, he replaces the alcohol with a 5 percent formalin solution, which hardens the bodies. (Hardened specimens are easier to handle).

Next, Causey sets up the dissecting binocular, being certain that a good source of artificial light is directed upon the specimen under observation.

Examine the seta first. By doing this, the *Pheretimas* can immediately be distinguished from all other species. (See Causey's Tabular Key to Earthworms, table 1, for explanations of the seta arrangements of different species, as well as for all other characteristics.)

Next, observe the position of the clitellum. Which segments does it encompass? Segments (also called somites) are numbered consecutively, beginning with number one at the prostomium (head end) and proceeding, segment by segment, towards the posterior of the worm. Many species possibilities can be eliminated after the position of the clitellum is ascertained.

Causey next determines the location of the first dorsal pore. (The pores are not difficult to locate with the aid of the dissecting binocular, and are easier to locate if the specimen has been allowed to dry.) This determination will usually make possible a positive identification. But if there is still some doubt, go on to examine the openings of the spermathecal pores and the position of the tubercula pubertatis. Check Causey's Tabular Key to Earthworms with each observation, and make careful notes. (An explanation of the terms used in the key follows table 1.)

Populations and
Distributions of Species

Our knowledge of the populations and distributions of earthworm species is in its infancy. To begin, we have not even come close to identifying all the different species now living in North America. And we have no meaningful data on the populations of those species we know.

Table 2 shows some typical counts of earthworms that have been taken in the United States in the past. From this, you can see that a population of 2,200,000 worms to the acre might be a high population, and that 190,000 might be low, Beyond that, there are few things that such listings can tell us. The species of earthworm, for instance, is not mentioned— and it is important. A million green worms would be of relatively little value in a cultivated field, while a million field worms would be a valuable asset to any farmer. Then, there is no mention of weight (biomass). Scientific counts of earthworm populations usually include both numbers and biomass, in order to present a more complete picture of total activity in any area. A million *Diplocardia*, for instance, will easily be outweighed and outperformed by a tenth as many field worms or night crawlers.

Table 2

Earthworms at Various Locations

Location	Earthworms to a 7-inch Depth	
	Per Square Foot (number)	Per Acre (number)
Marcellus, N.Y.	38	1,600,000
Geneva, N.Y.	28	1,200,000
Ithaca, N.Y.	4	190,000
New Brunswick, N.J.........	28	1,200,000
Frederick, Md	50	2,200,000
Beltsville, Md	8	350,000
Morgantown, W. Va.........	28	1,200,000
Zanesville, Ohio	37	1,600,000
Coshocton, Ohio............	5	220,000
Wooster, Ohio	30	1,300,000
Holgate, Ohio	14	600,000
Lansing, Mich..............	13	570,000
Dixon Springs, Ill	20	870,000
LaCrosse, Wisc.............	39	1,700,000
Mayaquez, P. R.	6	260,000

Source: USDA, Henry Hopp

Also important is the time of year that the counts are taken. As the research of Henry Hopp has shown, a large percentage of adult worms will be found in the spring, while a larger number of immature individuals will be found in the late summer and early fall. Unless biomass is included in the estimate, counts of simple populations will not give an accurate measure of earthworm activity.

There are many other factors that influence population counts and distribution estimates. The acidity of the soil might change from one field to another, depending upon methods of fertilization, or it might even change within a much smaller area because of the variation in plants growing there. Earthworms, since they are very sensitive to soil acidity, will respond to acidity by an increase or decrease in their populations. Rainfall, temperature, and available organic matter all have a part in determining populations in any given area. Because of all these limiting factors, any attempt to estimate earthworm populations should include samples taken from scattered spots within an area.

Vertical distributions. Then there is the matter of vertical distributions. Each species, under ideal or near-ideal conditions, occupies a certain depth of the soil. The native night crawler is the deepest penetrating species, commonly going down as far as three or four feet. The field worm operates most efficiently in the top 12 inches of soil, although it is not a surface feeder and will not emerge unless forced to, such as by heavy rains. However, either dry soil conditions or cold temperatures will force these species into greater depths. The native night crawler will burrow as deeply as 15 feet in order to find cool and moist conditions, while the field worm will always go at least beneath the frost line in winter, and that can be four feet and more. Population counts must take into account these environmental and seasonal variations.

Species associations. Earthworm species with similar environmental requirements will usually be found together. Brandling and red worms, for instance, will be found commonly together in manure piles, but not in agricultural fields. Native night crawlers and field worms will similarly be found together in fields, to the exclusion of brandling and red worms.

Studies in England have indicated that, in pasture lands, night crawlers, field worms, and *Allolobophora longa* are commonly found together. In peat soils, only four species of small worms were found. In woodland mull soils, researchers found *A. rosea*, *A. longa*, *A caliginosa* (field worm), *A.*

chlorotica (green worm), *O. cyaneum, L. castaneus, L. terrestris* (native night crawler), and *L. rubellus* (red worm). Michigan researchers found *Dendrobaena rubida* and *Bimastos zeteki* closely associated in woodlands there.

Researchers have found also that the agricultural history of a piece of land is an important determining factor in the populations of various species to be found there. In Scotland, an old permanent pasture was found to contain many *A. nocturna* and relatively few *A. caliginosa* (field worms), whereas fresh plowing and reseeding of that pasture increased the numbers of *A. rosea*. Often, *A. chlorotica* (the green worm) will be the dominant species in a field until it is reseeded with grass, after which it will be replaced by more common pasture species such as the field worm and night crawler.

Is There a Hybrid Earthworm?

Many advertisements for earthworms offer "hybrid" varieties, sometimes labeled "hybrid red worms," "hybrid wigglers," "hybrid red-golds," or other similar names. Most of the breeders of these worms will freely admit that they have absolutely no idea whether or not the species they sell as hybrids are really hybrids. But it has become an accepted practice in the trade to use such designations, and no one seems to care very much whether the claims are true or false. They generally fall under the category of advertising puffery.

Most scientists today do not believe that there is a hybrid earthworm. Henry Hopp has said that the claim of breeders in offering a cross between a manure worm and one of the field worms "is groundless as far as we can determine." Hopp examined shipments of these "hybrid" worms and found them to be ordinary brandling worms.

The concept of a hybrid earthworm was first popularized by the late Dr. George Sheffield Oliver, a physician who claimed to have crossed a brandling worm with an unnamed "variety of orchard worm" to create a new and superior species. In his book *Our Friend the Earthworm*, first published in 1937, Dr. Oliver describes his work:

> The author's first efforts to develop a satisfactory hybrid earthworm were made in 1927. Selected specimens of earthworms found in various sections of the United States were studied, bred and interbred.
>
> Observations, most of them coming under practical conditions and circumstances when the author was engaged in landscape artistry, showed that the brandling possessed many favorable qualities which, if transferred to, and retained by, a hybrid would be very advantageous.
>
> Chief among these favorable qualities was the fact that the brandling never deposited its excretions above the surface of the soil.
>
> This quality has two very important advantages.
>
> First, no mounds are formed on the surface of the soil. Such little hillocks, while they are far from detrimental, cause lawns and golf courses to become uneven, sometimes unsightly, and, in the case of golf courses, ill-suited for the enthusiast of mountain billiards.
>
> Second, by leaving all its castings under the surface of the soil near the root zones, the roots of plants and vegetables have easier access to the chemical and mineral elements pulverized by the earthworm's digestive tract.
>
> Early experiments with the brandling, all recorded in copious notes, showed that it appeared completely contented in a tray, box, or can; that, as long as it was well supplied with food, heavy-laden with any and all sorts of decayed animal matter, it was a prolific breeder.
>
> Another characteristic of the brandling was its habit of living close to the surface of the soil, seldom going below six inches. Such a burrowing earthworm will cultivate the soil only around the upper roots of the plants and vegetables, and while this may produce satisfactory results for some plant life, the author's desire was to develop an earthworm that would penetrate deeper into the soil.
>
> Search for a promising earthworm to mate with the brandling produced no satisfactory results until a variety

of orchard worm was found while matured trees were being transplanted.

This worm was large, and apparently spent much of its time deep in the ground, often down to ten and twelve feet.

A number of these worms were procured, carefully fed and studied. Observations showed that they burrowed as deep in the experimental trays, boxes and cans as they could get.

Being satisfied that this type of orchard worm would make an ideal medium for experimentation in the hope of producing a fertile cross between it and the brandling, healthy specimens of both were selected.

These were placed in a special soil mixture, approximately one-third soil, one-third vegetable humus and one-third decayed animal matter. . . .

In the course of time, the worms having copulated, the egg capsules were extricated from the soil and placed in a separate container. When these hatched and grew to near-maturity, the weaker and less promising were culled out.

During the first six months, about a thousand hybrids which had been selected as breeders were mating and producing fertile eggs.

While this experiment, as it appears here in cold type, seems to have been the personification of simplicity, it should be realized that a full five years were consumed in these experiments. However, the results obtained in orchards, nurseries, gardens and poultry houses have proved that the quintet of years was worth every discouraging set-back. These set-backs were too numerous to be listed here. Suffice it to say that there were times when Nature appeared to be stubbornly antagonizing all plans, figures and calculations.

I call this cross between the orchard and manure worm "Soilution." Its chief features are:

1. A prolific breeder.
2. A free animal, no longer a slave to one environment.
3. Its castings never form objectionable mounds above the surface of the soil.

4. It is not an extensive traveler or migrator.
5. It makes exceptionally good fish bait, for it is lively and lives for many hours when impaled on a fish-hook.

With all due respect to Dr. Oliver, and with eternal thanks for the enormous job he did in calling the attention of untold thousands of Americans to the importance and potential of the earthworm, most researchers doubt that he— or anyone—has ever succeeded in creating a hybrid earthworm. A hybrid is by definition, the offspring of two different species. Scientists doubt seriously that two different earthworm species could effect cross-fertilization, and both experimentation and logic bears them out.

There are, first, serious problems of comparative sizes involved in copulation. In order for an exchange of sperm to take place, two worms must engage in the sexual ritual, interlocking in such a way that the spermathecal openings of each worm come into contact with the clitellar region of the other. A minor difference in size can be accommodated by manipulations of the worm's bodies, but a small worm, such as Dr. Oliver's brandling, and a large orchard worm (presumably a night crawler) could not possibly make the adjustment.

Nor would they seek out each other or be attracted by each other, since the sex-attracting glandular secretions of each species are different. Logic tells us that, further, were worms of different species to intermingle in this way, there would soon be only one earthworm species in any ecosystem. As we have seen, however, species associations tend to be constant while the species remain distinct.

It is likely that Dr. Oliver did develop a superior earthworm group, but that he accomplished this by *selective breeding* rather than *interbreeding*. He says that "the weaker and less promising were culled out," and that "a thousand hybrids which had been selected as breeders were mating and producing fertile eggs." These statements suggest that he was weeding out the smaller and weaker worms while encouraging the large and healthy individuals to reproduce by affording them ideal environmental conditions. All breeders know that, under such conditions, any group of earthworms can be made to grow larger, fatter, and stronger.

Although we do not know exactly which species Dr. Oliver worked with (he never gives their scientific names or describes their structure), it is possible that he ended up with a superior breed of *Eisenia foetida*, the brandling worm. If you will go back to the five characteristics that Dr. Oliver lists for his "Soilution" worm, you will see that a well-raised brandling worm will probably possess numbers 1, 3, 4, and 5. Characteristic number 2—"A free animal, no longer a slave to one environment"—is more of a personal evaluation than an observed characteristic, and it is supported by no evidence.

Chapter 2

The Earthworm
through History

The earthworm has played a paramount role in the building of man's great civilizations. Were it not for this creature, in fact, it is entirely possible that civilization as we know it would never have developed at all, that man would still be subsisting in a primitive, semiprimitive, or squalid state, devoting most of his energies to growing or gathering food and fighting off attackers.

If this statement seems overblown, then consider the evidence.

The French researcher Andre Voisin, in his book *Better Grassland Sward*, considers the growth and spread of man's civilizations in relation to the distribution of *active* earthworm species. And when we speak of active species, we speak of the Lumbricidae (lumbricids), the family which includes the genera *Lumbricus* and *Allolobophora*—the greatest of the soil-working earthworms.

Voisin tells us that the Lumbricidae, immediately after the last Ice Age (approximately 10,000 years ago) were to be found in only one narrow band on the face of the earth, and that this area coincided exactly with the areas where the oldest and greatest of man's civilizations were born and developed—the Indus, Euphrates, and Nile valleys (fig. 5). In these areas, man was presented with a veritable Garden of Eden, where crops grew almost without cultivation in a soil of immense richness.

But could the success of these early civilizations have been due to other factors—favorable climate, for instance? Not likely, according to Voisin, for he also produces evidence

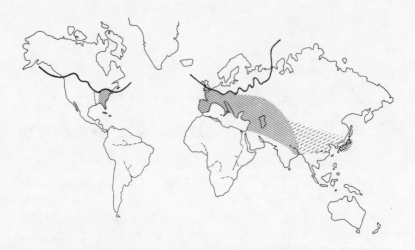

N.B. (1) The continuous line indicates the maximum advance of the Ice Age.
(2) The closeness of the cross-hatching indicates the degree of population by endemic *Lumbricids*.

Figure 5 Distribution of Endemic *Lumbricidae* in the Ice Age (plotted on a present-day geographical map)

Source: Cernosvitov, L., Monographie der Tchechoslovakischen Lumbriciden (Monograph of Czechoslovakian Lumbricids), Prague (1935)

showing that other areas of the earth offered ideal climates and rich soils, too, yet produced no great civilizations.

The greatest of the early civilizations was doubtless that of the Egyptians, who developed a marvelously sophisticated culture and maintained it for *four thousand years*. The Egyptian experience alone is strong indication that a complex civilization cannot develop until the basic agricultural needs of its people are met. There is little time to pursue art and philosophy until bellies are full. The Nile Valley offered the richest agricultural land the world has ever known.

But can the extraordinary soil of the Nile Valley be due not to earthworm activity, but to the annual flooding of the

Nile, which brings continuing renewal of the land by depositing nutrient-rich alluvium?

Again, not likely. The annual alluvial deposits are essential, to be sure, but without the extraordinary earthworm activity of the Nile Valley, even this rich soil would not be so lushly productive. A U.S. Department of Agriculture report of 1949 stated:

> Investigations carried on in the valley of the White Nile in the Sudan indicate that the great fertility of the soil of this valley is due in large part to the work of earthworms. Observations are recorded from which it is estimated that the castings of earthworms on these soils during the six months of active growing season of the year amount to 239,580 pounds (119.79 tons) per acre.

Earthworm casts are the highest grade compost imaginable. As organic and mineral matter pass through the body of the earthworm, many of their nutrients are made available to growing plants. Thus, worm castings constitute a superb organic fertilizer and soil conditioner. Consider, then, the annual incorporation of *120 tons per acre of high-grade organic fertilizer* on Egypt's agricultural fields. This is approximately *ten times* the amount of castings that are deposited on good American and European agricultural lands, and goes far in explaining the unparalleled fertility of the Nile Valley.

There is also evidence that the ancient Egyptians were well aware of the earthworms' contribution to their prosperity. Cleopatra, in fact, decreed the earthworm to be a sacred animal, to be revered and protected by all her subjects—doubtless the only time in history that the earthworm has achieved so elevated a status.

Further evidence of the earthworm's contribution to civilization was offered by E. Huntington of Yale University, who in 1945 listed the world's areas according to the favorability of climate and soil for supporting high living standards for human beings. His world map was comprised of five zones of "favorability"—very high, high, medium, low, and very low (fig. 6).

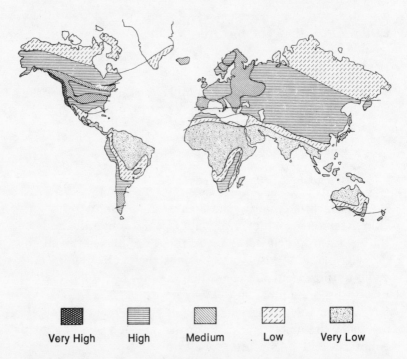

Very High   High   Medium   Low   Very Low

Figure 6 Climatic and Geographical Regions Favorable to the Development of High Living Standards

Source: Huntington, E., *Mainsprings of Civilization*, New York (1945)

Then Huntington drew a second map, this one zoned into areas according to the standards of living that had actually developed in each (fig. 7). There is a strong correlation between the two, as might be expected. The areas where the world's great civilizations have developed, including the Mediterranean basin and Eastern Europe, apparently fulfilled their promise of human development at a high level, aided by favorable climatic and soil conditions.

What is more interesting, however, is that five world areas had *not* fulfilled that promise. They possessed the climatic and soil prerequisites for human development, but remained essentially undeveloped until they were colonized by visitors and invaders from the developed areas, principally Europeans, as late as the beginning of the nineteenth century. These five "unfulfilled" areas are (1) the mouth of the Rio de la Plata in South America; (2) large parts of the United States, including the Atlantic Coast, the Great Lakes Region, and California; (3) a small area of southern Africa; (4) the southeastern tip of Australia, including Melbourne; and (5) all of New Zealand.

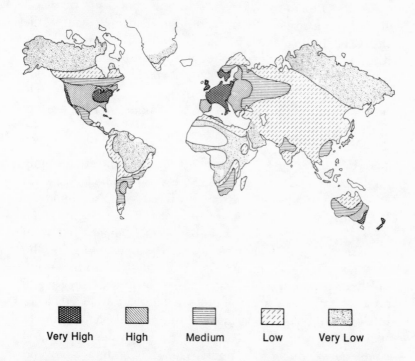

| Very High | High | Medium | Low | Very Low |

Figure 7 Geographical Distribution of Human Progress (zones where groups with a high standard of living have developed)

Source: Huntington, E., *Mainsprings of Civilization*, New York (1945)

Why, when conditions were so favorable, did these five areas fail to support the development of human civilization? Voisin offers a theory, and displays the evidence to back it up. In each of the unfulfilled areas, there were no native lumbricid earthworms, while in the areas of greatest fulfillment, lumbricids were native inhabitants of the soil.

In support of Voisin's theory, we will make a brief examination of the earthworm populations of the United States and New Zealand. In both areas, there is strong evidence that agricultural lands, although possessed of rich soil, were unproductive until the arrival of the European colonists. The Europeans brought with them better agricultural methods, true, but more important they brought with them, unwittingly, *lumbricid earthworms*. In the root balls of plants aboard the European ships were lumbricids. Wedged in the shoes of the colonists' horses were tiny lumbricid egg capsules. These earthworms found soil conditions to their liking in the New World and in New Zealand, and they quickly increased their populations. In so doing, they slowly transformed rich but dormant soils into ones of high fertility and productivity.

The United States. Before European contact, the only lumbricids native to the United States were some lazy species of *Bismatus* and *Eisenia,* essentially worthless as soil builders. We learn this not from the records of the early settlers, who were largely unconcerned with natural science, but from modern geologists who have been able to piece together the evidence. Further, the last Ice Age had stripped the entire northern part of the country of *all* earthworms. Only several hundred years ago, most of our great agricultural lands were totally devoid of earthworms, and supported no agriculture to speak of. In very few areas of the country were agricultural lands rich enough to support even moderately large and flourishing populations of native American Indians.

Since the time of colonial contact with the New World, however, this land—always promising as an area of human development—has fulfilled that promise. The success of agriculture in the United States has grown along with its lumbricid earthworm population.

New Zealand.   The European settlement of New Zealand followed that of the United States by more than a century. It was not until the nineteenth century that good numbers of Europeans were farming that land.

The time of settlement is important in that, by the nineteenth century, the interest in native flora and fauna—including earthworms—had taken hold among Europeans. The early farmers of America took no census of earthworms, while the New Zealand settlers made a careful survey in their reasoned attempt to determine which crops could be grown in that new land. In 1876, New Zealander F. W. Hutton counted and identified 110 species of native earthworms.

By the early part of the twentieth century, New Zealand soil scientists observed that European lumbricids were making vigorous inroads into the New Zealand soils. The lumbricids were replacing the lazy native species, and in so doing were improving the lands. Hill pastures that could barely support a stand of grass gradually became lush and green, even though no fertilizer was applied. Counts of European earthworms ran as high as 4,300,000 per acre, more than *three times* the maximum populations of the same species in their Old World habitats.

More is told of the miraculous transformation of New Zealand agricultural soils in this excerpt from an article by Robert Rodale, which appeared in the January 1961 issue of *Organic Gardening and Farming:*

> There is a tradition in New Zealand, passed from
> father to son by word of mouth, that 50 or 100 years ago
> the soil of that country suddenly became more fertile
> without any fertilizer being added. The grass became
> greener and more luxurious and the yields of all crops
> went up. No one could be absolutely sure of the reason
> for the change, but many suspected that the European

earthworms were doing something that was changing the soil. One farmer in the Raetihi district, Mr. A. S. Ashmore, decided to conduct an experiment that might pin down the reason for the soil improvement. His land was high in an isolated hill district into which the European worms had not yet penetrated. In 1925, he began a persistent program of implanting worms by digging up turfs from fertile valley soils populated by European worms and "planting" them on his hillsides. He continued his worm-moving project until 1945, and by that time Mr. Voisin reports that the results were striking. "The poor hill pastures that had formerly comprised brown top and *Danthonia* (a species found on poor soils) were now transformed into rye-grass-dominant swards," says Mr. Voisin. "Stocking rates and yields per acre had increased enormously parallel to this improvement in composition."

R. L. Nielson of the Rukuhia Soil Research Station came to Ashmore's farm in 1949 to check the results of his experiment. He paid particular attention to a section which had received the worm transplants only recently. This section had a very low population of *Allolobophora caliginosa*, and the grass there still consisted of the old, poor types. It had only one-twentieth as much rye-grass, for example, as the fields with heavy European worm populations. Mr. Nielson concluded that worms were in truth responsible for the tremendous improvement in Mr. Ashmore's pastures.

There is every reason to believe that the same pattern of agricultural improvement has occurred in North America, and that the general agricultural improvement here rests upon the ceaseless work of the superior European lumbricid earthworms. The great wheat fields of Canada, the incredibly rich farmlands of the upper Midwest, and the good, rich soils of the country's eastern region—all due in large part to the accidental introduction of new earthworm species.

In the opening paragraph of this chapter, I said that, were it not for the earthworm, man might never have been able to build great civilizations. Any great civilization must rest on a base of good agriculture, the ability to grow ample supplies of food. It seems that the earthworm—and in particular the lumbricid earthworm—is a key to good agriculture, and therefore a key to the building of civilization. It is no mere coincidence that the growth of great societies has been limited to the geographical limits of the lumbricid, and that, when the lumbricid is introduced to dormant areas of great potential for human development, those areas suddenly develop that potential through improvement of agricultural soils.

Man's Concept
of the Earthworm

Despite the incalculable services which the earthworm has performed for mankind, man has paid scant attention to this creature. There are exceptions in the ancient world, but, in general, references to the earthworm in our literature are slight—and most of these are derogatory.

The Bible. References to the earthworm here are woefully few, and show no understanding of the earthworm's role in soil fertility. Alastair MacKay, in his book *Farming and Gardening in the Bible*, says:

> There are two specific instances where worms damage or destroy plants, the better known being related in Jon. 4:7: "But God prepared a worm when the morning rose the next day, and it smote the gourd that it withered." The other is in Deut. 28:39: "Thou shalt plant vineyards, and dress them, but shalt neither drink of the wine, nor gather the grapes: for the worms shall eat them." The insignificance of the worm is used by several writers to symbolize man's low estate. "But I am a worm and no man," confesses the humiliated David Ps. 22:6. Both the Authorized and Revised Versions fail to do justice to the text of Job 25:6, where two different types of Hebrew worms occur in the original: "How much less man, that is a worm? and the son of man, which is a worm?" The moth larva seems to be designated in Isa. 51:8: "For the moth shall eat them up like a garment, and the worm shall eat them like wool."

Aristotle.   The great Greek philosopher-naturalist (384–322 B.C.) did spend some time in the study of the earthworm. He called it "the intestines of the soil," since it appeared to literally digest the earth. But Aristotle spent relatively little time in the study of this lowly creature, preferring to devote the bulk of his time in examining and classifying shellfish, and in formulating his philosophy. The importance of the earthworm to agriculture apparently did not impress itself upon Aristotle.

The Egyptians.   I have already mentioned that Cleopatra (69–30 B.C.) recognized the earthworm's contribution to the Egyptian agriculture by declaring this animal sacred. Egyptians were not allowed to remove so much as a single worm from the land of Egypt, and even farmers were not allowed to touch an earthworm for fear of offending the god of fertility. It is believed also that certain Egyptian priests devoted their full time to the study of the earthworm and its work. Unfortunately, the results of their efforts have not survived, or have not so far been uncovered for modern man to examine.

From the time of Cleopatra until the eighteenth century, the value of the earthworm was virtually unrecognized. If man paid any attention to the earthworm during this period, then it has either gone unrecorded or been lost in the sands of history. Probably the earliest modern tribute to the earthworm was in the words of the great English naturalist Gilbert White (1720–93) who in 1777 wrote, "Worms seem to be the great promoters of vegetation, which would proceed but lamely without them, by boring, perforating, and loosening the soil, and rendering it pervious to rains and the fibres of plants, by drawing straws and stalks of leaves and twigs into it; and, most of all, by throwing up such infinite numbers of lumps of earth called worm-casts, which, being their excrement, is a fine manure for grain and grass . . . the earth without worms would soon become cold, hard-bound, and void of fermentation, and consequently sterile."

White's assessment is amazingly accurate, all the more so since he apparently had no previous studies to build upon. But White's acute observations merely served as a precursor to Charles Darwin's great work, which began some 60 years after White's words were penned, and culminated in the publication of his classic book of 1881.

Charles Darwin.   In 1837, Darwin, then 28 years old, read a short paper, *On the Formation of Mould* (humus), before the Geological Society of London. His point was that "small fragments of burnt marl, cinders, etc., which had been thickly strewed over the surface of several meadows, were found after a few years lying at the depth of some inches beneath the turf, but still forming a layer." Darwin presented evidence to show that this burying of superficial layers, including stones and man-built structures, was primarily the work of earthworms, which continually bring up fine material and deposit it on the earth's surface. "These castings are sooner or later spread out and cover up any object left on the surface," said Darwin. "I was thus led to conclude that all the vegetable mould over the whole country has passed many times through, and will again pass many times through, the intestinal canals of worms."

For more than 40 years after the presentation of that paper, Darwin continued his careful observations of worms. During this time, also, fellow scientists challenged his work. One critic wrote in 1869, ". . . considering their [earthworms] weakness and their size, the work they are represented to have accomplished is stupendous."

We must remember, too, that during the later years of Darwin's life his theory of evolution was under heavy attack, having drawn far more attention than any theories on earthworms. Perhaps it was largely the attacks on his broader theories concerning the origin of species that led Darwin, shortly before his death, to write his *magnum opus* on the earthworm. In it, he summarized all his past observations and experiments, at one time answering his critics and providing the definitive work on earthworm behavior, never to be surpassed even until the present day.

Darwin's book, issued in 1881 by the London publisher John Murray, was entitled *The Formation of Vegetable Mould through the Action of Worms with Observations on their Habits*. Darwin is remembered chiefly for his classic works *The Origin of Species* and *The Descent of Man*, two books that have never ceased to stir controversy, particularly in religious circles. Yet in its importance to agriculture and human nutrition—and thus human welfare—his modest volume on earthworms may well, in the final analysis, be his greatest work.

This book was published with little fanfare and scant critical reception. In truth, it gathered dust in library stacks for 60 years, being consulted only by a few scholars and students whose major lines of inquiry incidentally touched upon the earthworm. Perhaps part of the problem was that Darwin's work was so thorough, so inclusive, so well documented, that virtually no one thought that further research was necessary or even possible. For decades, scientists writing of geology, soil science, agriculture, or allied subjects merely referred their readers to Darwin's book when the subject turned to earthworms.

Another factor to be considered is the climate of agricultural research that prevailed during the middle and latter parts of the nineteenth century. The Frenchman Boussingault had laid the foundations of agricultural chemistry in 1834, just as Darwin's studies of the earthworm were getting underway. Then, in 1840, the great German scientist Justus von Liebig (1803–73) published his classic monograph on agricultural chemistry. Up until that time, the humus theory had prevailed. It was believed that plants actually ate humus in order to grow. Liebig disproved this theory, demonstrating that plants obtained nourishment from certain chemicals in solution. Since humus was insoluble in water, Liebig dismissed it as a significant factor in plant growth.

Liebig enjoyed a great reputation in his day, his words attracting wide attention and carrying great weight among other teachers and scientists. Sir Albert Howard described Liebig as "a great personality, an investigator of genius endowed with imagination, initiative, and leadership . . . exceptionally well qualified for the scientific side of his task—the application of chemistry to agriculture."

It is small wonder, then, that the course of agricultural practice was increasingly chemical in nature throughout the last 60 years of the nineteenth century, at the very same time that Darwin's earthworm research was proceeding quietly in England. Somehow, the role of the earthworm had no place in Liebig's modern, exciting chemical theories. As we would say today, Darwin's research was not "trendy." On one hand, his work was outdated by Liebig's electric postulations—and on the other, it was decades ahead of its time, not to be considered again until shortly before World War II.

Darwin, of course, was unconcerned with trends. He was a scientist, pure and simple. His book is that of a scientist, making no claims, drawing no overly broad conclusions, pointing to no exciting ramifications. Darwin never expresses his opinions on the potential value of the earthworm to agriculture, never suggests that the tremendous power of the earthworm might be harnessed in order to feed hungry people. He simply records his observations, leaving their applications to others. As a scientist, this was his proper role. Fortunately, his book remained in library collections long enough to be taken up by others of vision, imagination, and understanding—men and women who would, long after Darwin's death, apply his observations to bring the earthworm to its proper status as a benefactor to agriculture and mankind.

Darwin's book was reprinted by Faber and Faber (London) in 1945—64 years after its initial publication by John Murray. In 1945, the last of World War II, food production was of prime concern in Great Britain and throughout Europe and other parts of the world. Sir Albert Howard provided an introduction to the reprinting, giving some of the background of Darwin's work and relating it to modern agricultural research.

The 1945 edition received a far more enthusiastic reception than did the original. The British publication *The New Statesman* said, "No layman could fail to read the calm, clear record of Darwin's studies of these lowly creatures without being fascinated by their story. We all know them; but how many of us know anything about them? Yet they could make or unmake the fertility of a continent."

Darwin's classic is still in print, available from Faber and Faber, Ltd. (24 Russell Square, London), and should be read by anyone who expresses any interest at all in earthworms, farming, or gardening. In seven chapters and 153 pages, Darwin goes into great detail on the habits of worms—the nature of their burrows, their nocturnal wanderings, structure, sensitivity to light, heat, and cold, their diet and manner of eating, how they disguise their burrow entrances, and their distribution throughout the world. He spends much time on the amount of fine earth brought up by worms to the soil surface (this, in part, in answer to past critics) and the part which worms have played in the burial of ancient buildings. Two chapters are devoted to the action of worms in the denudation of the land. He makes no attempt to differentiate among species, but from his descriptions it seems apparent that he studied *Lumbricus terrestris*, the native night crawler.

It is a tribute to Darwin's scientific skill and discipline that today, nearly a hundred years after the publication of his work, scientists still can find no errors of fact or method in it. The only criticism is that Darwin apparently underestimated earthworm populations in his native England, and that is understandable, considering the unsophisticated sampling methods then in use.

To conclude this small section devoted to Charles Darwin, it seems fitting that we should excerpt a part of the last paragraph of his book. Here, he affords himself the rare luxury of a broad, if short, evaluation of the earthworm's role in nature and agriculture. It is perhaps the most often quoted passage from the book:

When we behold a wide, turf-covered expanse, we should remember that its smoothness, on which so much of its beauty depends, is mainly due to all the inequalities having been slowly levelled by worms. It is a marvellous reflection that the whole of the superficial mould over any such expanse has passed, and will again pass, every few years through the bodies of worms. The plough is one of the most ancient and most valuable of man's inventions; but long before he existed the land was in fact regularly ploughed, and still continues to be thus ploughed by earthworms. It may be doubted whether there are many other animals which have played so important a part in the history of the world, as have these lowly organized creatures.

George Sheffield Oliver.   During the 1930s in the United States, the practice of earthworm farming mushroomed with surprising rapidity. The center of the activity took place in southern California, where large numbers of adventurous easterners had migrated, hoping to find the good life through farming or poultry raising in an ideal climate.

The man principally responsible for this new-found interest in the raising of earthworms was Dr. George Sheffield Oliver, originally of Texas, who was a direct descendent of James Oliver, inventor of the steel plow. Around 1906, George Oliver read, quite by chance, Darwin's earthworm book. It was to change his life. Oliver, who was then a successful young physician and surgeon in Fort Worth, saw at once that Darwin had vastly underestimated the earthworm's importance to agriculture. He thereupon set out to correct Darwin's oversight, conducting experiments on the domestic raising of earthworms and their introduction to farm fields. Oliver's own pot experiments indicated quickly that plants grown with earthworms were larger, stronger, and healthier than those grown without.

Soon, Oliver began to raise earthworms on his property—an activity that, at the time, would have been considered positively curious, if not actually suspect. In giving his domesticated worms proper food, soil conditions, and

71

temperatures, he soon had increased his captive populations by millions. He implanted worms and worm capsules in his gardens, orchards, and other spots around the property. Within a short time, his gardens were the talk of Fort Worth and Dallas. His friends were amazed at the vitality of his trees, the profusion and color of his flowers, and the size and luscious flavor of his fruits and vegetables. Oliver did not reveal his secret of success, despite the urging of friends. But before long, he was offered a tempting sum to revitalize the gardens of a friend. Oliver did so, with resounding success, largely through the secret introduction of earthworm capsules. (Oliver was the first to discover that, while implanted worms might die when introduced to new soils, their egg capsules have a far better chance of surviving and establishing a permanent earthworm population.)

One thing led to another, and within two years Oliver had sold his medical practice and set up shop as a landscape engineer, with offices in Fort Worth and Dallas. By accepting lucrative contracts from parks, cemeteries, country clubs, and other large public and private estates, he quickly built up a sizable personal fortune.

By 1920, Oliver's fame as a landscape wizard had spread as far as California, where he was called upon to work his magic at the estates of some Hollywood film stars. He established himself there, and soon was accepting contracts calling for a minimum expenditure of $10,000—all the while concealing the secret of his success—the lowly earthworm.

With the stock market crash of 1929, however, and the resultant agricultural problems of the country, Oliver realized that the earthworm's potential should be realized in the feeding of a nation. Times were hard and people were hungry. He began to publicize his work and promote the earthworm as an answer to crop disease and failure through the improvement of agricultural soils.

It was shortly before this, in 1927, that Oliver first attempted to cross-fertilize different species of earthworms in an attempt to produce a superior hybrid. His efforts, which are detailed earlier in this book, resulted in what he called

"Soilution"—a supposed cross between a night crawler and a manure or brandling worm, which Oliver claimed to possess the best traits of both. The probability that Oliver never did, in fact, interbreed two species of earthworms is less important than his priceless services in promoting the value of the earthworm to agriculture in America. His 1937 publication, *Our Friend the Earthworm,* was one of the first serious treatments of the earthworm since Darwin's, 56 years earlier. Further, Oliver's book appeared at a time when at least a part of the country seemed ready to accept its promise. The dust bowl years of the 1930s provided stark evidence that America's agricultural system was far from perfect, that chemicals were not an agricultural panacea, after all, and that perhaps a closer attention paid to nature's principles was in order.

It was in the late 1930s also that other investigators and researchers were working along similar lines, reaching back to nature's lessons in serious question of our growing reliance on agricultural chemicals. In England, Sir Albert Howard was working on his classic volume, *An Agricultural Testament* (1940), based largely upon his long foreign service in the fields of India. The American industrialist J. I. Rodale, upon reading Howard's work, was so impressed that he set out to buy a farm in Pennsylvania for experimentation of his own, and soon founded a magazine expressing his interests, then called *Organic Farming and Gardening.* Dr. Ehrenfried Pfeiffer, the Dutch wizard of agriculture, was working on his bio-dynamic theories, which stressed the soil as a *living organism* instead of a compound of chemical agents. Soon, Dr. Thomas J. Barrett was heard from, with his patented Earthmaster System of earthworm raising (1942) and his book, *Harnessing the Earthworm* (1947). J. I. Rodale's writings proliferated in the pages of *Organic Farming and Gardening* (later separated into two magazines, then recombined into one—*Organic Gardening and Farming*) as well as in his classic volume, *Pay Dirt* (1945). And there were others—Friend Sykes, the English farmer, inventor, and writer, whose book *Humus and the Farmer* (1946) charted new ways of farming with nature (including the observation that "the worm has perhaps been man's greatest friend for all time"), Lady Eve Balfour, and others. All were pioneers of the organic method in the 1930s and 1940s, and it was at this time that the earthworm was incorporated into the organic method, perhaps to receive its just recognition after countless eons of service to man, animals, and growing plants.

Dr. Thomas J. Barrett.   Dr. Barrett, who was an osteopathic physician as well as, at various times, a printer, reporter, editor, soldier, news photographer, and plant physiologist, was the first to work out a sophisticated system for the large-scale raising of earthworms—the Earthmaster System, which he completed around 1942.

Like Oliver, Barrett possessed a keen scientific mind and a thirst for experimentation. Like Oliver, also, it was Barrett's reading of Darwin's work that set his mind to contemplating the tremendous potential of the earthworm as an agent in agricultural improvement. Barrett saw the earthworm as he saw water power—as a natural resource of great potential, waiting to be harnessed for the benefit of mankind. Darwin had done the long and painstaking spadework. Oliver had proved that earthworms can be raised by the millions with little effort. Now Barrett was determined to go the final step—to develop the perfect system for earthworm raising, and to promote it to the world. He wanted very much to see the tapping of this powerful resource, and he saw himself as the main catalyst.

Dr. Barrett was past 50 when, in the mid-1930s, he began earthworm and soil-building research, establishing the Earthmaster Farms in Roscoe, California, in 1936. He kept in close contact with George Oliver during the last years of Oliver's life.

At one point, Oliver related to Barrett the story of the Ohio farm of his grandfather, George Sheffield, who employed earthworms as a key agent in his continual soil-building program. The 160-acre farm had a 2-acre barnyard in its center, with wide-swinging gates leading into each of the four

40-acre tracts. Thus, the stock could be led into any of the tracts simply by the opening of the appropriate gate. The feature of the barnyard was an enormous compost pit, 50 feet by 150 feet, excavated to a depth of 2 feet. Each morning, the barns would be cleaned and the manure and litter deposited in the compost pit by an ingenious system of buckets, ropes, and pulleys. In this way, literally millions of earthworms thrived in the pit at all times. In spring, the tons of rich compost, along with millions of worms and worm capsules, were distributed on the fields by horse and wagon. Immediately following the spreader was a horse-drawn plow, which turned the material under the soil within minutes, so that the vast majority of the worms would not be killed by the sun or eaten by the flocks of hungry crows that followed closely behind.

In this way, Sheffield's farm flourished from 1830 until 1890—60 years without a single crop failure. Oliver particularly remembers his grandfather's advice concerning earthworms and orchards: "Never disturb the soil under a tree. The earthworm is the best plow for taking care of a tree." There is no doubt that old George Sheffield was fully cognizant of the value of earthworms to his soil, crops, and orchard. It seems ironic that, during all the 40-some years that Darwin was conducting his earthworm observations in England, with little active consideration of their agricultural application, George Sheffield was making nearly perfect use of Darwin's principles on his little-noticed farm in Ohio. Whether Sheffield knew of Darwin's work, we cannot be sure. More likely, he simply considered the earthworm as one more of nature's beneficial agents, like the rain, the sun, and the good Ohio soil. And he was perceptive enough to observe the worms' soil-building actions, and to work with nature in encouraging their multiplication.

The full story of George Sheffield's Ohio farm is related in Barrett's book, *Harnessing the Earthworm*. It is essential reading for anyone concerned with earthworms and organic farming.

The vivid memory of George Sheffield's farm thus inspired not only his grandson's work with earthworms, but also Dr. Barrett's, many years later. It was these two men—Oliver and Barrett—who, from about 1937 until 1950, were most instrumental in convincing thousands of gardeners, farmers, and other agricultural researchers of the value and potential significance of earthworms in agricultural production.

Sir Albert Howard.   Another of the early pioneers of earthworm research was the eminent English agriculturalist Sir Albert Howard (1873–1947). Unlike Oliver and Barrett, who saw the earthworm as paramount in their research activities, Howard found a comfortable place for the earthworm in his broader view of agriculture. Howard, of course, is the father of the organic movement. The son of a Shropshire farmer, he studied agriculture at Cambridge University, then set out on a lifetime of experiment and discovery in the West Indies, India, and England. His *magnum opus, An Agricultural Testament* (1940) set in motion the movement to organic farming and gardening that now is generally accepted throughout most of the United States, England, and many other parts of the world.

Howard had long observed the work of earthworms in his long years of foreign service. Of them, he wrote, in the May 1944 issue of *Organic Gardening:*

> The earthworms condition the food materials needed by the roots of plants. This is accomplished by means of their casts which in garden soil in good condition may exceed 25 tons to the acre in a single year. The casts are manufactured in the alimentary canal of the earthworm from dead vegetable matter and particles of soil. In this passage the food of these creatures is neutralized by constant additions of carbonate of lime from the three pairs of calciferous glands near the gizzard, where it is finely ground prior to digestion. The casts which are left contain everything the crop needs—phosphates, nitrates and potash in abundance and also in just

the condition in which the plant can make use of them. Recent investigations in the United States show that the fresh casts of earthworms are five times richer in available nitrogen, seven times richer in available phosphates, and eleven times richer in available potash than the upper six inches of soil. The earthworm is, therefore, the gardener's manure factory.

Howard also depended on the presence or absence of earthworms as an indication of soil quality, saying, "If, in each spadeful during the autumn digging, one glistening red, active lob worm occurs, about the thickness of a man's little finger, then all is well with the soil and the quality of next season's crop is assured. There will be no need for plant nutrients of any kind: no anxiety need be felt about pests. But if the worms are few, coiled up in balls, or pale in colour and sluggish in their movements, then the next crop will be poor and trouble with pests will be inevitable."

Howard deplored the routine use of agricultural chemicals because, in large part, they destroyed the earthworms that continually aerated, turned, and homogenized the soil, and made nutrients available to growing plants. Like Oliver, Barrett, and others, Howard much admired Darwin's work. He contributed the introduction to the Faber and Faber reprint of Darwin's *The Formation of Vegetable Mould* (1945), in which he said, "No more effective basis for the organic farming and gardening of tomorrow could be found than the long and painstaking investigations described in this volume." Howard also gives much attention to the work of George Sheffield Oliver in this introduction.

J. I. Rodale.   Howard's work provided the chief inspiration for J. I. Rodale, who in the early 1940s became the father of the organic movement in America. For more than 30 years, Rodale experimented, studied, farmed, gardened, wrote, and published, all in a tireless effort to bring his own country back to sane principles of crop growing and nutrition. Through all this, Rodale revered the place of the earthworm in the scheme of organic gardening and farming. Unlike Barrett and Oliver, however, Rodale was of that organic school which believes there is little purpose to the breeding and implanting of earthworms, when the liberal incorporation of compost into the soil will increase their numbers naturally. In his 1945 book, *Pay Dirt*, Rodale says, "To the writer's mind, for general farming purposes, it is more advisable to concentrate one's energies on the production of as much compost as possible. The yearly application of this humus to the soil will encourage earthworms to multiply in great and sufficient numbers. To breed them in such a case would be like taking coals to Newcastle." (This controversy is one that still divides organic gardeners and farmers, and will be considered fully, in chapter 6.)

Robert Rodale. Like his father, Robert Rodale has long recognized the importance and potential of earthworms in farming and gardening. His chief role, however, has been to stimulate serious earthworm research among government and university scientists. To this end, he prompted the publication, in 1961, of a small volume entitled *The Challenge of Earthworm Research*, which was published by the Soil and Health Foundation, associated with Rodale Press. The 12 chapters of this book contain the work of Andre Voisin and various scientific papers of American, English, and Russian researchers.

In his introduction, Rodale says, "Considering that earthworms occupy almost all agricultural soils, it is both remarkable and unfortunate that our knowledge of them is limited. Few attempts have been made to catalog the species of earthworms at work in American soils, and only limited work has been done to explore the effect of various species of earthworms on soil fertility.

"One obstacle to intensive earthworm investigation is the necessity for cooperation between soil specialists and zoologists. The soil scientists have studied the effect of earthworms in general on the soil, and the zoologists have investigated the earthworm as an animal. But only in rare instances have workers in the two specialties combined efforts to elucidate the effects of different species of earthworms on various soil and crop situations."

Robert Rodale's concern for the scientific disregard of the earthworm is well founded, today as well as in 1961. Even now, it is difficult to find a single scientist in government or university research who spends the bulk of his efforts in the study of earthworms.

Dr. Henry Hopp.   One bright exception to Robert Rodale's concern is in the person of Dr. Henry Hopp. In the middle and late 1940s, the U.S. Department of Agriculture sponsored a good bit of earthworm research, nearly all of it the personal product of Dr. Hopp. In the years 1946 to 1949, Dr. Hopp published numerous articles in scientific journals on such subjects as earthworms in fighting erosion, earthworm ecology in cropland, earthworms as a factor in forming soil aggregates, the influence of earthworms on soil productivity, and the effects of various agricultural practices on earthworm populations. During his career at the USDA, Dr. Hopp was undoubtedly the world's leading authority on earthworms, and was responsible for calling the attention of other scientists to the importance of earthworm research as it relates to agricultural practice and productivity. Much of the knowledge we have today in this field can be traced back to the original research of Dr. Henry Hopp.

Even though few researchers have concentrated their efforts on the study of the earthworm, however, many have conducted studies which include it as a central figure. The body of earthworm literature is, in fact, fairly substantial, as indicated by the sizable bibliography at the back of this book.

Other books.   One of the earliest scientific volumes in the field was *Earthworms and Their Allies,* by the Englishman Dr. F. E. Beddard. In the 150 pages of this pocket-sized book, Dr. Beddard details the structure, habits, populations, and distributions of earthworms throughout the world. Much of Dr. Beddard's material is now dated, including his classification system.

The two most recent books of interest to the scientist are *Biology of Earthworms*, by Drs. C. A. Edwards and J. R. Lofty of the Rothamsted Experimental Station, Harpenden, England, and *The Physiology of Earthworms*, by Dr. M. S. Laverack of the Gatty Marine Laboratory, The University, St. Andrews, Fife. The latter of these two books will be largely unintelligible to the layman, although the Edwards and Lofty volume contains a wealth of summary information that any scientifically minded layman can readily appreciate.

But these volumes appear to be oases on a vast desert of scientific neglect. Today, the state of earthworm research remains in a dismal state—fractionalized, uncoordinated, without long-range goals, severely lacking orchestration of any sort. There is little doubt that here is a field of scientific inquiry wide open to exploitation. The scientific appreciation of the earthworm lies in the future.

On the other hand, the commercial raising of earthworms has never been at a higher point in the United States. Thousands of Americans in all parts of the country are raising and selling earthworms, many as a part-time or retirement occupation. The demand for earthworms is at an all-time high, and many believe that the present situation merely represents the threshold of a tremendous future industry, as more uses are found for earthworms in a variety of areas.

The Earthworm's Future

Today, as more and more of us look for new ways to save our environment and improve the general quality of life, we are seeing more and more ways in which the earthworm can find a valuable place in the new scheme of things.

Waste disposal. Earthworms can be valuable assets in the disposal of man's organic wastes, not only in home composting operations but on a municipal scale, as well. North American Bait Farms, probably the world's largest commercial marketer of earthworms, and its president, Ron Gaddie, have been in the forefront in developing these systems. From its base in Ontario, California, North American has proposed a home "ecology box," which, costing just a few dollars, can hold 20,000 worms to take care of an average family's biodegradable waste. North American has also experimented with a large-scale worm plant that, says Gaddie, can handle refuse for any city with less than a million inhabitants. In a pilot program in Ontario (pop. 67,000), Gaddie's worms greatly reduced a ten-ton trash heap within 45 days, leaving nutrient-rich casts where offensive garbage used to be. The trouble with making serious headway with municipal earthworm composting is that great sums of money are needed for experimentation, and that money has not yet been made available. Dennis Wilkins, Ontario's assistant city manager, said in September 1976, that a federal government agency, probably the Environmental Protection Agency, represented the best hope for the supplying of funds for one or several model projects.

Strip-mine reclamation.   Earthworms show great promise in helping to reclaim strip mines. Spoil material on strip-mined lands is made up of rock fragments and lacks organic matter. In order to reestablish vegetation on spoil banks, fast-growing trees such as black locust and European alder are planted. The trees have grown fairly well on the mineral soils; however, decaying leaves remain on the surface for inordinate periods of time. Some method of mixing the organic material into the spoil minerals has been needed.

Dr. John Vimmerstedt, research forester with the Ohio Agricultural Research and Development Center, believed in 1968 that earthworms might be the key to this mixing. The results of his experiment, published in the *Proceedings of the Soil Science Society of America* (vol. 37, no. 3, 1973), were most encouraging. Said Dr. Vimmerstedt and his collaborator, Dr. James R. Finney, "Clearly, earthworms [they used only *Lumbricus terrestris*] can be established on revegetated coal spoil banks, where they promote incorporation of organic matter into the mineral spoil."

In the coming years, as this nation is forced to depend more and more on coal for its short-range energy needs, billions of earthworms might well be called into service to bring about the quick return of coal spoil banks to lush, green areas.

Livestock feed.   The use of earthworms for feeding livestock is hardly a new concept. Some poultry raisers have depended on live worms for feed for many years—and before that, the chickens managed to find their own worms in the barnyard. The practice was more common before World War II than it is now, of course, since poultry raising has become largely the province of giant, computer-oriented agribusiness, but earthworms still offer advantages. They are very high in protein and essential minerals, free from disease, and incur no shipping costs since they can be raised easily on location by the poultry farmer.

Japan is one of the largest foreign markets for earthworms, which are used there for cattle feed. It is believed that, if earthworm production methods can be honed to a point of maximum efficiency, earthworm feed can offer stiff competition to the traditional grains, which will become more expensive as energy and fertilizer shortages occur in years ahead. (Both have been predicted for many years by geologists.)

Monitoring metal pollution.   Dr. Philip Helmke and other soil scientists at the University of Wisconsin have developed methods of using earthworms to monitor heavy metal pollution in soils. "Such pollution," reports the magazine *Catalyst* (V:2, 1977), "can retard plant growth and also poses a serious health hazard by entering food chains through plants or soil organisms.

"Using radioactive tracers, the researchers monitored

both intake and output rates for four heavy metal pollutants passing through the earthworms' bodies: cobalt, cadmium, zinc, and mercury. The worms took up cadmium and mercury most rapidly. . . . The scientists say earthworms may also be useful for monitoring the heavy metal pollutants often present in municipal sewage sludge, which is gaining acceptance as a crop fertilizer."

There are other potential uses for the earthworm—as an aid in erosion and flood control, the holding of river banks and lake shores, the monitoring of environmental quality, and in other areas of environmental improvement—as well as the traditional uses in agriculture, horticulture, and fishing. As valuable as the earthworm has been to us in the past, it would appear that its future is brighter still. If given the chance, the earthworm is able and willing to repair some of the enormous damage we have done to our environment, helping to improve the quality of our lives in many different areas.

Chapter 3

The Earthworm in Its Environment

Like other organisms, the earthworm exists in a complex and incompletely understood ecosystem; the earthworm's presence and actions affect every other soil dweller, while it, in turn, is affected by all the others. But this chain of interaction does not stop at the soil surface, for the actions of the creatures above the soil, including man, have effects— sometimes severe effects—upon the earthworm, and the earthworm has some occasionally surprising effects on these creatures, as well.

The soil is teeming with animal life. In addition to earthworms, which might number several million to the acre on productive agricultural soils, there are insect larvae, ants, spiders, centipedes, wood lice, springtails, mites, millipedes, beetles, and many kinds of bacteria, as well as larger life forms—mice, shrews, moles, snakes, and other tunneling, burrowing, or resting animal forms, all of which interact in some way with the earthworm. Of all these, however, the earthworm is by far the most prevalent, constituting from 20 to 80 percent of total soil fauna, by weight.

By their vigorous tunneling habits, earthworms create convenient access to deeper soil levels for countless smaller creatures which are less able to move the earth, in this way helping to increase the range and populations of these creatures. Since all these living organisms add to the organic matter content of the soil after death, this small service of the earthworm is by no means inconsiderable to man's agricultural endeavors.

Earthworms also are paramount promoters of naturally growing vegetation, by their actions of turning the soil, liberating plant nutrients, creating spaces for air and water movement, moderating soil acidity, and deepening of the top-soil layer by breaking up subsoil and hardpans. Darwin noted that the roots of certain plants eagerly follow earthworm tunnels, benefiting from the rich secretions left behind by the earthworm. This resulting increase of vegetation serves as food for a host of smaller subterranean animal species, as well as for countless wildlife species—both animals and birds—above the ground.

Moles and Other Predators

In a more direct way, earthworms provide food for the larger creatures—moles, shrews, mice, and snakes. All these animals depend upon earthworms for portions of their daily diets, and moles live nearly exclusively on earthworms. The instincts and habits of the mole are particularly attuned to pursuing earthworms, locating their tunnels and burrows with great facility, and making most efficient use of this valuable, high-protein food source. It is known, for instance, that moles will bite off the anterior sections of earthworms, just enough to prevent their regrowth, and then store them in the moles' tunnels as a source of winter food. Peter Farb, in his book *Living Earth*, reports, "In just one mole tunnel, more than 1,000 worm corpses were found, hung on the walls like trophies."

Farb also tells of the following incident, showing just how sharply attuned the mole's instincts are to the location and capture of earthworms:

> G. V. Jacks, Director of Britain's Commonwealth Bureau of Soil Science, once lived near a tennis court where each spring, after the rains and snow had completely washed away the court markings, the lines could still be traced, for mole ridges followed them unerringly. After much detective work, this was shown to be the explanation: the court was built on acid soil; earthworms will not live in very acid conditions, but the chalk used in marking the lines had neutralized the soil underneath. Thus, in the whole expanse of tennis court, the worms were restricted to the earth under the chalk lines. The moles had discovered this, and in their search for worms cut straight swaths under the court.

The lesson for gardeners, perhaps, is that the presence of moles in the garden, far from being a curse, is a solid indication that one's soil is teeming with earthworms—which is an indication that the soil is in good health and perfectly capable of supporting lush plant life of many kinds.

(Moles, incidentally, are not the ravagers of root crops that they are often accused of being. Their teeth are too short to accomplish much damage to roots, rhizomes, and tubers— and besides, they prefer earthworms above all. More likely, the damage seen near mole tunnels has been caused by large-toothed rodents, probably field mice, which avail themselves of the moles' runways.)

How Worms Serve Wasps

The interactions of earthworms with other organisms is still little understood, and what is known has been learned largely by accident, in the study of other areas. An example is reported in a 1969 issue of the *Journal of the Bombay Natural Historical Society*, by researchers A. B. Soans and J. S. Soans. While collecting insect specimens, the two were observing a Sphecid wasp which was hovering over some earthworm casts. The wasp landed on several casts, apparently testing their consistencies. Finally it selected one cast, bit off a part of it, kneaded the mass into a round ball, and carried it away. In about 10 minutes the wasp returned to the casts, again tested several, and settled on the same cast it had used before. It repeated the same kneading procedure and carried away another ball to its nest.

The wasp, which was using the earthworm cast to build its nest, knew that the consistency of the cast was just right for its special purpose. The result was doubtless a stronger nest for the wasp, offering it and its colony a greater measure of protection and contributing to the survival of its species. The wasp, in turn, could very well be instrumental in pollinating important food plants for human beings and other animals.

This minor observation, made completely by accident one day in 1968, in India, adds just one more bit to our vastly incomplete knowledge of the earthworm and its place in the ecosystem. What other services does the earthworm unwittingly perform in the chain of nature? What other parts of the broad ecosystem are dependent on its seemingly simple daily routine? Only time and research will tell, and that research will be conducted not only by trained scientists but by everyday gardeners and farmers who take the time to observe small things around them.

Mystery of the Dying Robins

The springtime caricature of a fat robin pulling tenaciously on a struggling earthworm is based on sharp reality.

Earthworms do, indeed, make up the bulk of the protein food of young robins and some other birds. Baby robins are voracious eaters, as the harassed mother robin knows only too well, and the number of earthworms required to raise a nestful of robins to maturity must be staggering. But the robin's dependence upon the earthworm, when combined with man's chemical activities, can have surprising and dismaying results, as we see in the following account of life and death on an American university campus:

In April of 1959, students and faculty on the lush, green campus of the University of Wisconsin, in Madison, began to notice a disturbing sight. The robins, traditionally numerous on the campus, began to drop from the trees by the dozen. The early morning stroller, walking along Observatory Drive high above majestic Lake Mendota, was likely as not to see an adult, male robin thrashing about on the ground in pitiful tremor, soon to die.

In the following spring, the disconcerting scene was repeated, this time with fewer robins on hand. Obviously, the previous year's death rate had reduced their population, and the trend was apparently continuing in 1960. More dead robins followed in 1961, and by this time wildlife ecologists at the university were more than a little concerned—and watching closely. They estimated that, from the spring of 1959 until that of 1962, more than 340 dead robins had been picked up— the result of DDT poisoning. This is a serious rate of loss, since the normal population in an area such as this is 134 to 198 pairs of robins per 100 acres. Not even counting the robins that had died and were never found, DDT had wiped out the total populations of more than a hundred acres in only three years.

It did not take long for the scientists—notably L. Barrie Hunt—to connect the deaths to the massive DDT spraying on the campus, designed to combat Dutch elm disease. In 1959, the first year of the spraying, 22.5 pounds of DDT per acre were applied, half that dose in 1960 and 1961.

The unwitting vector in this scene was our friend the

earthworm. The robins did not ingest most of the DDT directly, but through the eating of earthworms, which are able to tolerate far higher concentrations of the chemical.

The scenario soon became apparent. The robins migrated to Madison from the South in March. Their fat reserves were, after the long migration, at a seasonal low (especially in the males), meaning that their susceptibility to DDT poisoning was at a seasonal high. (The DDT, instead of being stored in fatty tissues, reached the robins' brains in high concentrations.) Meanwhile, DDT spraying of the elms was going on. The spring rains washed the DDT from the trees and into the ground, where both night crawlers and field worms were feeding. Now, the importance of tolerance comes into play. Sample earthworms collected from beneath the area of the sprayed trees showed 26.4 parts per million of DDT in their tissues. The soil itself contained only 5.3 ppm DDT, indicating that the earthworms were ingesting the DDT and collecting it in their tissues, until their own DDT concentrations were five times as great as those in the soil itself. The robins died with a concentration of less than 10 ppm DDT in their brain tissues. Their feeding habits, which include a high proportion of earthworm food, combined with the earthworms' high tolerance for DDT, led to the robins' doom.

All of this research was going on just before Rachel Carson's electrifying book, *Silent Spring* (1962), awakened the country to the dangers of ill-conceived pesticide usage. In that year, the University of Wisconsin switched from DDT to methoxychlor in its efforts to control the Dutch elm beetle, and the robins returned soon after.

DDT is toxic to earthworms, true, but only in concentrations far higher than those necessary to kill most warm-blooded species of both vertebrate and invertebrate animals. Most research indicates that normal rates of DDT applications do not harm earthworms, although some have found deleterious effects of large doses. Unfortunately, no research has been conducted to discover exactly what levels of DDT *are* toxic to earthworms. In this case, at least, the earthworm's high tolerance to a lethal insecticide, although it helped the earthworm to survive, threatened another of our cherished life forms.

The ecological chain of events does not stop with the death of the robins, however. Robins and other bird species are voracious consumers of insects, some of which are prime destroyers of farm and garden crops. Whenever a bird population is reduced, another biological insect control is diminished. Thus, the DDT that man applied in order to control certain insects was eventually responsible for further insect problems. It is a prime example of man's defeating his own purposes by approaching a problem on a fragmented, rather than an ecological, basis.

Earthworms and Other Pesticides

Much has been said, and many points argued, when it comes to assessing the effects of agricultural chemicals upon earthworm populations. Here again, it appears that controversy continues because research is incomplete. We know that many pesticides and some chemical fertilizers either discourage earthworms or kill them outright, either by affecting their structures directly or by changing the soil's pH, thus making it unattractive or toxic for earthworms. On the other hand, we have seen—in the mystery of the dying robins—that earthworms are tough creatures, able to stand higher concentrations of DDT than can some other animal species. And in a few cases, it has been reported that chemicals have had a beneficial effect upon earthworm populations.

The following is an attempt to summarize some of the more important current knowledge of the effects of major chemical pesticides on earthworms:

Aldicarb. This, like other carbamate insecticides (e.g., carbaryl and carbofuran), is highly toxic to earthworms.

Aldrin.   This insecticide is toxic to earthworms, but not severely so when applied at normal agricultural levels.

Benomyl.   This fungicide, commonly recommended for winter control of apple scab, is very toxic to earthworms, especially to *Lumbricus terrestris* (the native night crawler) and *Allolobophora chlorotica* (the green worm). The loss of the green worm is not especially tragic to orchardists, because they are largely inactive, but the loss of the night crawler is a serious one. The use of benomyl in orchards (and this applies to other earthworm-destroying pesticides, including especially the copper fungicides) is particularly disastrous to night crawler populations because of this worm's feeding habits. When trees are sprayed, most of the spray (from 50 to 80 percent according to researchers Austin Stringer and Clive H. Lyons, writing in *Pesticide Science*, vol. 5, 1974) ends up on and in the soil and not on the trees. This "pesticide fallout" is then consumed more readily by the night crawler, which is a surface feeder, than by other earthworm species which are subsurface feeders. Stringer and Lyons discovered that night crawlers were "virtually eliminated" after only two seasons of spraying with benomyl. Other earthworm species, although severely reduced by the spraying, were able to increase their populations to normal levels after two years without spraying—but the night crawler made no such comeback. In other studies, it was found that orchards treated with benomyl lost 60 to 100 percent of their earthworms after only 14 days.

BHC.   This is another insecticide that is mildly toxic to earthworms when used at normal levels. When used at relatively high levels of application, it will reduce populations, and when applied at high levels—21 pounds per acre—it will eliminate earthworms completely, according to studies conducted at the University of Wisconsin.

BUX.   This insecticide is commonly recommended for the control of corn rootworm. It is toxic to earthworms, reducing their populations by 55.9 percent in Canadian tests reported by A. R. Thompson in the *Bulletin of Environmental Contamination and Toxicology* (vol. 5, no. 6, 1970).

Carbaryl. This carbamate insecticide, sometimes used as a growth regulator, is deadly to earthworms even when applied at very low levels. It causes ulcers to form on their bodies and will soon kill or drive out entire populations. Carbaryl is one of the most common of home garden insecticides, used to control asparagus beetles, leafhoppers, borers, earworms, cucumber beetles, squash bugs, vine borers, flea beetles, fruitworms, hornworms, and grasshoppers.

Carbofuran. This organophosphate insecticide, used for the control of root maggots, is instant death to earthworms. Its use, even at very low levels, will severely reduce or totally eliminate earthworm populations on the farm or in the garden.

Chlordane. This, a persistent organochlorine, is perhaps the most toxic of all chemical pesticides to earthworms. It is, in fact, commonly recommended as an agent of earthworm control on golf courses and athletic fields. Chlordane is commonly recommended for the control of white grubs and wireworms in vegetable gardens.

Chlorfevinphos. This organophosphate insecticide is toxic to earthworms, but not to the degree of carbofuran, heptachlor, chlordane, and some others.

Chloropicrin. Several researchers have reported that chloropicrin is very toxic to earthworms.

Copper fungicides. These chemicals, often used heavily in orchards, are very toxic to earthworms, especially since they tend to accumulate in the soil over time. Several researchers have reported that, when copper fungicides are used routinely in orchards, the soil is nearly devoid of earthworms and the ground beneath the trees is covered with a thick layer of undecomposed organic matter. (Earthworms, if unhindered, will quickly reduce orchard leaf fall, building the organic matter content of the soil, keeping it loose, making nutrients available, aiding aeration and water retention, reducing disease organisms, and in general improving the soil. More about this in chapter 6.)

Dasanit.   This insecticide is commonly recommended for control of root maggots on cabbage and other brassica crops. In the Canadian tests (see BUX, above) it reduced earthworm populations by 78.8 percent, making it nearly as toxic as carbofuran.

DDT.   Most research has indicated that DDT, as has been applied in normal agricultural practice, is not overly harmful to earthworms. There are, however, several studies showing the opposite, including a serial spraying experiment in Louisiana in 1958, in which dieldrin heptachlor and DDT destroyed 80 percent of the local earthworm population. It is probable, however, that the heptachlor was the major offender in this experiment.

Dr. D. E. Greenwood, reporting in a 1945 bulletin of the Connecticut Agricultural Experiment Station, said that his pot experiments showed DDT to be instantly harmful or fatal to earthworms. Other experiments have at times backed up Greenwood's research. Still, the preponderance of evidence shows earthworms to be relatively tolerant of this persistent and powerful insecticide.

As we have seen in the mystery of the dying robins, the earthworm's role in transporting DDT in the natural food chain, made possible by its DDT tolerance, is one case in which the earthworm's toughness has worked to the ultimate detriment of another species in the ecosystem. Fortunately, the use of DDT is—at least at present—severely restricted by federal legislation.

Diazinon. This insecticide, commonly used for the chemical control of black bean aphids, leaf miners, aphids, maggots, thrips, flea beetles, and wireworms, has not been shown to be toxic to earthworms when used at normal rates, although little research has been conducted in this area.

Disulfoton. This organophosphate insecticide is reported to be only slightly toxic to earthworms, although the research here is also slight.

Dodine. This fungicide, commonly used for the control of apple scab and other orchard fungus diseases, has no effect on earthworm populations, according to the limited research conducted thus far.

Dursban. This insecticide, used for the control of cut-worms in tobacco, is moderately toxic to earthworms. In the Canadian tests (see BUX, above), it reduced earthworm populations by 21.2 percent.

Dyfonate. This, another organophosphate insecticide, is moderately toxic to earthworms, according to the research of C. A. Edwards, reporting in the 1970 *Proceedings of the Tenth Weed Control Conference.*

Endrin. This chemical has been found so dangerous to human populations that its use has been severely restricted or eliminated by state and federal action. In this way, it is now in much the same class with DDT and DDD. Endrin, however, appears to be more toxic to earthworms than is DDT—but less toxic than pesticides such as benomyl, chlordane, heptachlor, phornate, carbaryl, carbofuran, and the copper fungicides, all of which are still in wide use. The Canadian tests (see BUX, above) have shown that normal use of endrin will reduce earthworm populations by 52 percent.

Fumigants. These agents, which include D-D, metham sodium, and methyl bromide, are used to control nematodes and soil pathogens. They are extremely toxic to earthworms and can quickly reduce populations to a zero point, even if the earthworms live far beneath the soil surface.

Heptachlor. This compound is related to chlordane and is extremely toxic to earthworms. Heptachlor is not commonly recommended for use in home gardens, and in fact some states have now restricted its use to emergencies or other very special situations.

Lead arsenate. This, and any other lead-containing pesticide, are extremely toxic to earthworms. Fortunately, we have come a long way away from the use of lead in agriculture.

Malathion. This insecticide, commonly recommended for the control of asparagus beetles, aphids, leafhoppers, and thrips, is moderately toxic to earthworms when used at normal levels.

Parathion. This organophosphate insecticide is toxic to earthworms, especially when applied at relatively high levels.

Phorate. This is another organophosphate insecticide that is very toxic to earthworms. In an experiment reported in a 1974 issue of the *Bulletin of Environmental Contamination and Toxicology,* an orchard treated with phorate lost 91.8 percent of its earthworm population.

Stauffer N-2596. This is a relatively new soil insecticide, extremely toxic to earthworms. In the Canadian texts (see BUX, above) it reduced earthworm populations by 85.5 percent—even more so than carbofuran.

Other pesticides.   The research into the toxicity of various pesticides to earthworms is still vastly incomplete. We have little or no knowledge of such effects of many common agricultural and garden chemicals. From the foregoing summary, however, we can reasonably conclude that the routine use of chemical pesticides on farm, garden, and orchard lands will severely reduce or eliminate earthworm populations. Virtually no research has been conducted on the effects of combinations of different pesticides on earthworms, even though such chemicals are used routinely in hundreds of different combinations.

Perhaps more serious, however, is our lack of knowledge in the area of earthworm/pesticide ecology. We do know that earthworms tend to concentrate certain persistent pesticides in their tissues, and that these may thus be passed along to predators of the earthworm, where they are sometimes concentrated still further. But the study of such relationships is still woefully inadequate.

One further example of the sad results of man's infantile understanding of earthworm ecology involves orchard pesticides. A study has shown that fungicides applied to orchards actually contribute to the spread of the disease for which the fungicide was applied to control—all because of the chemical's toxicity to earthworms. In the organic orchard, surface-feeding night crawlers and other species will drag fallen leaves of fruit trees into their burrows and consume them promptly. In so doing, they destroy most of the spores of the offending fungi. A healthy population of night crawlers will commonly consume virtually all fallen leaves by the time the trees bloom the following spring. When toxic fungicides are applied, however, driving out earthworms, the leaves will remain on the ground, harboring the fungi spores and increasing chances for disease the following year.

These few examples of earthworm/pesticide relationships indicate the direction that future research must take, if the earthworm's true place in the food-production system is to be accurately defined. The fragmented approach to agricultural pests and disease, which has brought us many of our present environmental ills, does not attempt to answer the questions posed by these and many other relationships—sometimes very subtle relationships—among agricultural flora, fauna, and man-induced chemical agents.

Earthworms and Chemical Fertilizers

Most chemical fertilizers are relatively benign to earthworm populations, according to the very limited research that has been conducted to date. The glaring exception is ammonium sulphate, which is beyond doubt highly toxic.

Even when chemical fertilizers are chosen with care, however, their total effects upon earthworm populations are apt to be detrimental in the long run, if not the short. Organic methods, on the other hand, will actively encourage the growth and reproduction of earthworms.

As with chemical pesticides, the effects of chemical fertilizers on earthworms are not always direct. For instance, when the German researcher A. Jacob tested the results of nitrogenous fertilizers on earthworms in 1952, he concluded that there was a positive reaction, since the earthworm population had increased from 11.52 per square foot to 15.84 after the addition of the nitrogen. At first glance, it would seem that chemical nitrogen fertilizer was responsible for a 38 percent increase in the earthworm population. Jacob concluded, however, that it was not the nitrogen itself that resulted in the earthworm increase, but "the fact that the nitrogen plots were better shaded as a result of the superior plant growth." In addition, he commented, "the earthworms had a larger quantity of food at their disposal in the form of fallen leaves or dead roots."

In practice, if nitrogen is provided by organic means—by composting in the garden, for instance, or by green manuring with legume crops on the farm—far more organic matter will be provided, soil texture will be greatly enhanced, and the increase in earthworm population will doubtless be far greater.

Ammonium sulphate.   *Farmer's Bulletin* No. 1569 of the U.S. Department of Agriculture says, "The results of three years' application of ammonium sulphate (a high-nitrogen chemical fertilizer) to sod on the experimental farm of the USDA at Arlington, Va., for fertilizing purposes, have shown incidentally that earthworms were eliminated from the plots where this chemical was used. When applied to soils which are naturally neutral or slightly acid in character, this fertilizer creates a strongly acid condition that is distasteful to the worms and they disappear." At least three other studies have since confirmed these findings.

Copper sulphate.   It is known that a copper concentration near the soil surface of 260 parts per million is toxic to earthworms, enough so to reduce populations to a zero point. However, there have been no studies to show the effects of normal applications of copper sulphate, which is commonly used as a pasture dressing.

Nitrogenous fertilizers.   Any artificial nitrogenous fertilizer will wipe out earthworm populations quickly. The damage is done not by nitrogen itself, but by the acid conditions that the fertilizer creates in a very short time, as we saw is true with ammonium sulphate. Whenever a high-nitrogen chemical fertilizer is applied—such as those used for lawns— numerous dead worms will be found on top of the soil soon after. One garden magazine (apparently one that did not hold the earthworm in highest esteem) suggested to readers that the best way to get rid of earthworms is to apply frequent doses of chemical fertilizers.

Superphosphate.   There has been very little research conducted to determine the effects of superphosphate on earthworm populations. A 1950 German study did indicate that populations were increased with the addition of superphosphate, but another study of 1948 indicated the opposite. There have been no recent studies.

There has been virtually no research on other chemical fertilizers. One study in 1953 did conclude that commercial fertilizers had no appreciable influence on earthworm populations at all. Still, the observations of many organic gardeners and farmers lead to the inescapable conclusion that the prolonged use of chemical fertilizers, to the exclusion of organic practices of soil building, leads to a sharp decline in earthworm populations. The observations of Sir Albert Howard, as recounted in his introduction to Darwin's *The Formation of Vegetable Mould,* are typical:

"In following the ploughs in the autumn and spring in the Spalding area, I always found that where heavy dressings of artificials were used every year, with or without organic matter, earthworms were rare. I sometimes walked half a mile after the ploughs and cultivators without seeing one."

The problem with chemicals is not always that they are directly toxic, when applied at normal levels, but that, when used to the exclusion of organic methods, they create a more compact soil, less decaying organic matter that earthworms need for food, and sometimes an unfavorable pH.

Earthworms and Soil Acidity

Earthworms are extremely sensitive to soil acidity (pH). The pH scale, which is the expression of the soil's hydrogen-ion concentration, ranges from 0 to 14, with 7 being the middle or neutral range—neither acid nor alkaline. Numbers above 7 represent increasingly alkaline conditions, whereas numbers below 7 indicate increasing acidity. Most garden soils in the northeast and midwest United States tend to be slightly acid, whereas in large parts of Texas and some other areas, alkalinity is sometimes a major problem. Most food plants prefer moderate acidity.

Most earthworm species prefer a soil that is neutral, or very slightly alkaline, although they will tolerate a moderately acid soil. Many experiments have shown that a moderate application of lime on moderately acid soils will always lead to an increase in earthworm populations.

__*Lumbricus terrestris*__ (the native night crawler) has been reported in soils as acid as 5.4, but will respond more favorably to soils that are more nearly neutral. *Allolobophora caliginosa* (the field worm) has also been reported in acid soils in the 5.4 to 5.2 range, but again will increase in population if such soils are limed and brought nearer to the neutral range.

__*Eisenia foetida*__ (the brandling worm) definitely prefers a neutral-to-alkaline soil with a pH between 7.0 and 8.0, as does *Lumbricus rubellus* (the red worm) which is widely used in commercial breeding.

It has been suggested that earthworms might be sensitive not to soil acidity in itself, but to the low level of available calcium which is present in acid soils. This question has never been resolved, nor is it particularly important to the farmer, gardener, or earthworm breeder, since the addition of lime will both add calcium and raise the pH of any soil or bedding material.

Exactly what happens to earthworms in overly acid conditions? Excess acidity will, first, cause them to go into a state of unnatural dormancy, which zoologists call *diapause*. In diapause, they will neither carry on their soil-improving functions nor attempt to reproduce. If the situation is not corrected, they will eventually die out.

Greater acidity will cause earthworms to flee the immediate environment in an attempt to find more hospitable surroundings.

And, if an earthworm is forced onto the surface of a soil that is severely acid, it will refuse to follow its instinct to burrow into it and will die within 24 hours. An English researcher placed 60 green worms *(Allolobophora chlorotica)* on soil surfaces with acidities between 4.0 and 4.4. The worms at first showed violent reactions, twisting in convoluted fashion and exuding coelomic fluid from their bodies. They then stretched out and crawled around the surface, periodically lifting up their heads and waving them around, almost as if trying to sense an escape route. After 2 hours, they lay motionless, and within 21 hours 58 of the 60 worms were dead. Excess acidity, then, is not just a discomfort to earthworms; it acts much as a violent contact poison, causing convolutions, paralysis, and death.

The last word on earthworms and pH is that earthworms act to neutralize any soil they are in, causing acid soils to become less acid, and alkaline soils to become less alkaline. The reasons for this are not completely understood, but scientists believe that the soil is neutralized by the earthworms' intestinal secretions. This is doubtless a service to agricultural lands, although the impact of the service has never been measured.

Temperature Preferences and Tolerances

Each earthworm species has very definite temperature preferences, and also maximum and minimum temperatures at which it can survive. These vary considerably from species to species, as any breeder of earthworms must soon learn.

Within the tolerable temperature range for each species, all of the earthworm's activities, including metabolism, growth, respiration, and reproduction, are influenced greatly by rising and falling temperatures.

The number of cocoons produced is greatly affected by temperatures. In tests with field worms, researchers found that four times as many cocoons were produced at 16°C (60.8°F) than at 6°C (42.8°F). Further, cocoons hatch much more quickly during warmer temperatures. This phenomenon is probably a survival mechanism among earthworms, since newly hatched worms would stand little chance of survival in very cold temperatures. Some factor within the cocoon, as yet not understood, tells it to wait for warmer weather, much as budding fruit trees may wait out a late spring cold spell.

Warmer temperatures also encourage faster growth among young earthworms. Brandling worms will mature in 9½ weeks at 18°C (64.4°F) but three weeks sooner when the temperature is raised to 28°C (82.4°F).

Among those worms that feed and mate on the soil surface at night (notably *Lumbricus terrestris*, the native night crawler), temperature is critical. Dr. J. E. Satchell, writing in the 1967 volume *Soil Biology*, discovered that the optimum conditions for such activity were (1) soil temperatures below 10°–5°C (50°–41°F); (2) grass-air temperatures above 2°C (35.6°F); and (3) some rainfall during the previous four days. Night crawler hunters will do well to remember these conditions and to plan their hunts when conditions are most favorable.

This nighttime activity of earthworms is responsible for a great amount of leaf litter disposal. Particularly, the native night crawler feeds by dragging leaves into its burrow, where it slowly consumes them and turns them into castings. The English researcher J. R. Lofty found the approximate optimum temperatures for the burying of leaves by earthworms during the four winter months (table 3). No leaves were buried (signifying no earthworm activity) when the temperatures were as low as 0°C (32°F). Yet, there was no smooth correlation between rising temperatures and leaf disposal, nor even any optimum temperature that remained constant from month to month. The most that 20 worms could dispose of in a month was 75 leaves, and that was during March when the temperature was 10°C (50°F). At the same temperature during January, less than half the number of leaves were buried. At 15°C (59°F), 67 leaves were buried in December, but only 30 in January at the same temperature. In all, it seems that the earthworms were most active in their leaf-burying activities during March, when 186 leaves were buried, and least active in January when only 94 were buried.

Table 3

Effect of Temperature on Leaf Burial
(number of leaves buried by 20 worms
in four successive months)

	0°C	5°C	10°C	15°C
December	0	25	35	67
January	0	33	31	30
February	0	53	63	33
March	0	67	75	44
TOTAL	0	178	204	174

Source: Edwards, C. A., and J. R. Lofty, *Biology of Earthworms*, 1972 (based on J. R. Lofty's research)

Earthworms will react to uncomfortable soil temperatures by moving—either up or down. The native night crawler, which prefers cooler temperatures than those of any other common species, will burrow as deeply as it must in order to avoid warm summer soil—and this is why the night crawler is seldom seen during the hot summer months. It will emerge only during the very coolest part of the late night and early dawn in such weather, and then only if it has to.

The German researcher O. Graff, in a 1953 report entitled *Earthworms in Germany,* furnished a chart listing the optimum soil temperatures for the development of different species (table 4). Unfortunately, he did not include the native night crawler in his samples.

Table 4

Optimum Soil Temperatures for the Development
of Different Earthworm Species

| Species | Optimum Soil Temperature | |
	Fahrenheit	Centigrade
Eisenia foetida	77	25
Dendrobaena rubida	64.4–68.0	18–20
Dendrobaena attemsi	64.4–68.0	18–20
Lumbricus rubellus	59.0–64.4	15–18
Octolasium cyaneum	59.0	15
Allolobophora chlorotica	59.0	15
Allolobophora caliginosa	53.6	12
Allolobophora rosea	53.6	12

N.B. The optimum temperature for *Lumbricus terrestris* is not given.

Source: Graff, O., *Die Regenwurmer Deutschlands (Earthworms in Germany)*, Hanover (1953)

Other researchers have reported similar findings. The field worm has been reported to prefer soil temperatures from 10°C (50°F) to 23°C (73.4°F). The brandling worm preferred temperatures from 16°C (60.8°F) to 23°C (73.4°F).

Experiments have also been conducted to determine the highest temperatures that earthworms can stand. The brandling worm's upper limit was calculated at 24.7°C (76.5°F), and the field worm's at 26.3°C (79.3°F). The field worm, it would seem, is a tough character, indeed. It prefers cooler temperatures than the brandling worm (and the red worm, as well) although it can stand both higher and lower temperatures than any other common species in North America. It is also known that the field worm can stand drought better than any other common species.

Unfortunately, there is no similar data for the native night crawler. However, breeders tell us that this species must be kept in temperatures ranging from 1.7°C (35°F) to 12.8°C (55°F) in order to remain in good health.

Earthworms and Moisture

The moisture content of the soil plays a major role in dictating the activities of the earthworm. This creature is, after all, closely related to marine forms. Its skin must be kept moist at all times in order for it to survive, and its body weight is 70 to 95 percent water. Researchers have pointed out that the physical structure and life processes of the earthworm are like those of a fresh-water animal, rather than a terrestrial

As every earthworm grower knows, proper moisture conditions are essential to the activity and reproduction of all earthworms.

105

form. In another sense, the earthworm may be viewed as a marine form which has adapted beautifully to terrestrial life. So well has it adapted, in fact, that earthworms can lose up to 75 percent of their body water and still survive—but also can live for many months completely submerged in water. This is adaptation at its most remarkable, and one reason why the earthworm has thrived for so many centuries in so many parts of the world.

Very dry soil conditions affect earthworms first in reducing their ability to reproduce. Sexual activity slows down as soil conditions become drier, and comes to a halt at a certain moisture level, that level differing for different species. One experiment (Evans and Guild, 1948) indicated that optimum cocoon production occurred when the moisture content of the soil was between 28 and 42 percent. Below 28 percent, sexual activity dropped off with the increasing dryness; above 42 percent, activity slowed down with increasing wetness.

Other research has indicated that the largest numbers of earthworms were found in soils with moisture contents between 12 and 30 percent.

Different species react to moisture changes in different ways. Night crawlers and brandling worms will drive down to deeper soil levels when the soil begins to dry out, but the field worm cannot, or does not. Fortunately, the field worm can withstand dryness to a greater degree than can other species, although it will go into a state of inactivity with increasingly dry conditions.

Every gardener, farmer, and angler has noticed the ground surface littered with earthworms after a particularly heavy rain. It would be easy to conclude from this observation that earthworms cannot stand flooding of their burrows and will risk death to escape inundation. But the case is not quite so simple. True, when most species are given a choice between saturated soil and soil with moderate moisture and plenty of air, they will choose the latter. Still, earthworms have been placed in soil that was completely submerged in water, and they lived for several months. Some species, notably the field worm and the green worm, have been found in waterlogged soils when they could have escaped them. The reactions of earthworms to water are also involved in some migration mysteries—times in which hundreds of thousands—even millions—of worms will simply leave an area *en masse*. This phenomenon is examined in the next chapter of this book.

It is safe to say that scientists have still not come to a satisfactory understanding of the earthworm's reactions to water and soil moisture. We do know that, in most cases, earthworms prefer an environment of moderate moisture. We know also that they can live submerged for up to a year—and yet they will leave their burrows in panic when they are flooded, rising to the surface to be either killed by the ultraviolet rays of the sun (which are deadly to earthworms) or picked off with ease by birds and other predators. These reactions will have to remain mysteries at least for the present.

Earthworms and Organic Matter

Earthworms love organic matter. The presence of a large earthworm population in the soil will testify to its high organic matter content, and the addition of organic matter to the soil will do much to encourage the growth of earthworm populations.

Of course, other factors must be favorable, also. In dense forests where the tree leaves and soil are very acid, earthworms will not be able to take advantage of the abundant organic matter because of the overly acid conditions. This is the reason why many forests have a thick and spongy layer of undisturbed organic litter on their floors. The soil bacteria and other life forms cannot dispose of the litter quickly enough without the aid of earthworms. In contrast, apple orchards in the spring will be nearly devoid of leaf litter if the earthworm population is high. The pH of the apple leaves is to the earthworms' liking, and they will gladly dispose of 90

107

Earthworms and organic matter go together. The kitchen refuse of a family can easily be turned into nutrient-rich compost by a small bin of earthworms.

Table 5

Earthworm Populations in Plots
with and without Manure

Species	Grassland Park Grass, Rothamsted (Satchell, 1955)		Arable land Barnfield, Rothamsted (Lofty, unpublished)	
	Unmanured	Dung	Unmanured	Dung
L. terrestris	13.1	22.5	0.23	10.8
L. castaneus	16.0	59.6	—	—
A. caliginosa	2.9	8.0	0.8	15.4
A. chlorotica	1.6	—	3.2	44.6
A. rosea	10.0	21.3	—	0.23
A. longa	—	—	0.46	1.8
A. nocturna	1.2	18.9	—	—
O. cyaneum	6.9	24.5	—	—
TOTAL	51.8	154.8	4.69	72.83

Source: Edwards, C. A., and J. R. Lofty,
Biology of Earthworms, London (1972)

percent of those leaves by the next time the trees bloom.

Pastures grown to sod support large earthworm populations because of the constantly dying roots and tops of the sod.

The relation between earthworms and organic matter will be discussed in far greater detail in the chapter devoted to earthworms and soil building.

Earthworms and Soil Types

Here is another topic to be discussed in full in the chapter on soil building. Suffice it to say here that earthworms show a preference for light loams, which are the best general

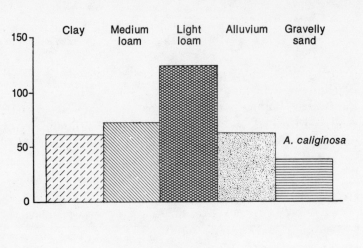

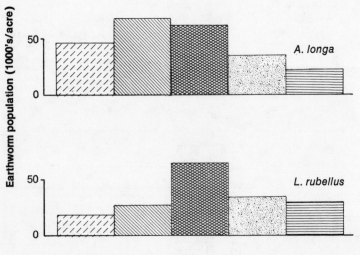

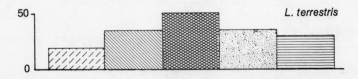

Figure 8 Density of Earthworm Populations (thousands per acre) in Various Soil Types in Scotland

Source: Guild, W. J. Mc. L., Effect of Soil Type on Populations. *Annals of Applied Biology*, 35:2 (1948)

garden soils. Common garden species will also do very well in both medium loams (which contain more clay) and in light sandy soils. As the soils go further into heavy clays or light sand, earthworm populations will drop, although healthy populations can be sustained even by these soils. Perhaps the worst soil for earthworms is acid peat.

In sum, it seems that earthworms prefer good soils to poor ones, but that they will exist in poor soils in good numbers if their basic needs are met and if harmful chemicals are not applied routinely. It has been argued that earthworms cannot be counted upon to help build up poor soils because they will not live in such soils. All the evidence is to the contrary, however. Table 6, for instance, reports samplings of earthworms in various soil types. It will be seen here that a light loam was able to support 256,800 worms per acre, but that even a gravelly loam supported 146,800 and a clay soil supported 163,800.

Table 6

Relations of Soil Type to Earthworm Populations

Soil Type	Population		No. of Species
	(Thousands/acre)	No/m^2	
Light sandy	232.2	57	10
Gravelly loam	146.8	36	9
Light loam	256.8	63	8
Medium loam	226.1	56	9
Clay	163.8	40	9
Alluvium	179.8	44	9
Peaty acid soil	56.6	14	6
Shallow acid peat	24.6	6	5

Source: Guild, W. J. Mc. L., The Distribution and Population Density of Earthworms (Lumbricidae) in Scottish Pasture Fields. *Journal of Animal Ecology,* 20:1 (1951)

Further, there is not much difference among the important species in soil preferences. Both the native night crawler and the field worm prefer a light loam. The field worm shows more tolerance to heavy clay than does the night crawler, but the night crawler shows greater tolerance to gravelly sand, probably because it can retreat to subsoil burrows while the field worm must operate within the top 12 inches of soil.

Earthworms and Soil Minerals

Nitrogen.   Several studies have shown that soil nitrogen is favorable to earthworm growth. Applications of high-nitrogen chemical fertilizers, however, have the opposite effect, quickly reducing earthworm populations. It has been suggested that the beneficial effects of nitrogen come not from the nitrogen itself, but from the increased plant growth which the nitrogen promotes. On the other hand, high-nitrogen chemical fertilizers create acid conditions so quickly that earthworms do not have a chance to adjust to them.Gardeners and farmers, then, can best encourage earthworms by adding nitrogen to the soil through natural practices such as green manuring with legume crops, and by avoiding highly concentrated chemical fertilizers.

Calcium.   Calcium deficiencies in soil have adverse effects on earthworm populations. A 1953 study in New Zealand reported that "only one pasture with a calcium level below 6 parts per 100,000 contained any *Allolobophora caliginosa* (field worms). The exception was on one trial near Eketahuna, where two worms were found near pegs marking the spot where they were originally placed in the soil; in all likelihood they were survivors of those introduced experimentally in 1945, as no more were found either at the pegs or in the surrounding pastures. No soil having a calcium level of 8 parts per 10,000 had a density higher than 10 *A. caliginosa* per square foot, so a higher level than this seems essential if the earthworms are to be expected to thrive. No upper limit for lime is known, as a healthy colony of mixed species was found on a farm near Te Awamutu in soil which contained 36 parts of calcium per 10,000."

The study concluded: "Let the controversy be as it may; it appears to be generally agreed that a moderate dressing of lime on an acid soil poor in calcium favours the development of the majority of active earthworm species."

Potash.   Studies performed by the New Zealand Department of Agriculture showed that the potash level in the soil has no direct effect on earthworms. Indirectly, a low level could restrict plant growth and therefore limit food for earthworms; but there appears to be little direct effect. The researcher R. L. Nielson, writing in the June 1953 issue of *Organic Gardening*, reports, "At low potash levels quite high densities of earthworms have been obtained, whereas in the five places where they failed to establish (but could have been expected to have done so because they were present elsewhere in the vicinity) the test gave medium and high potash values." It would seem, then, that low levels of potash in garden or farm soils will not hinder earthworm development. On the other hand, we cannot depend on earthworms to provide any key to potash depletion in soils. A rich, dark, and crumbly soil, teeming with earthworms, might still yield poor crops (particularly root crops, which feed heavily on potash) because of a deficiency of this mineral.

Phosphorus.   R. L. Nielson found also that phosphorus levels had little effect on earthworm populations. Reported the researcher, "Phosphorus levels ranged between 1 and 5 parts per 100,000, yet high numbers [of earthworms] were obtained at figures lower than 1. On Mr. Ashmore's property, 95 *A. caliginosa* to the square foot were obtained in a pasture with a phosphorus value of 0.9."

Other minerals.   It is well known that high levels of copper have adverse effects on earthworm populations. Of the other trace minerals, however—including cobalt, manganese, iodine, and molybdenum—little is known of their effects on earthworms.

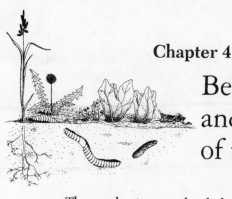

Chapter 4

Behavior and Habits of the Earthworm

The authority on the habits of the earthworm is still Charles Darwin, who spent most of his life in their observation and study.

It was Darwin who discovered, or confirmed scientifically, that earthworms are sightless and deaf, yet have an acute sense of touch that serves them well underground. It was Darwin who concluded that earthworms have only feeble senses of smell and taste, and possess limited but definite intelligence. One can only imagine how many hours the Englishman must have spent in kneeling or lying silently on the ground, watching the worms' construction of burrows, dragging of leaves, and building of casting mounds. He conducted countless experiments indoors, also, taking copious notes at every stage.

How curious, then, that Darwin never mentions the mating habits or reproductive apparatus of the earthworm. Whether this lacuna was a result of scientific disinterest or Victorian propriety, I do not know. (One contemporary cleric did state, disapprovingly, that earthworms "are much addicted to venery.") I do know that it could not have been for lack of notice on Darwin's part, since the native night crawler, with which Darwin was most familiar, is the only common species which mates above ground, and in suitable weather it spends a good portion of its nocturnal activities in this pursuit.

Sex Life of the Earthworm

All earthworms are bisexual—hermaphroditic. However, most are not self-fertilizing. In order to produce offspring,

115

two lumbricid worms must copulate, exchanging sperm cells. Then, each will produce egg capsules which later become fertile and produce one or several infant worms in a matter of weeks. Some species do reproduce without cross-fertilization, but the important lumbricids do not, except in very rare instances.

The mating ritual. There are many references in books and articles to the earthworm's mating during the warm and humid nights of spring, almost as if this creature had an annual mating season. In truth, earthworms will mate at any time when conditions are right. It is true that the warm and humid nights of spring are ideal for this activity—but then so are the warm and humid nights of late summer and early fall, when sexual activity is just as great. Midsummer is a time of low activity, since the hot and dry conditions of the soil tend to reduce earthworm activity in general. In very cold weather, earthworms retreat to their burrows, coil themselves in tight balls to conserve moisture, and think not of sex at all.

Night crawlers mate on the surface, but all other common species, including the common field worm, perform the sexual act underground.

Although the ritual is not identical for all species, that of the night crawler is essentially typical for many of the lumbricids (except that it is performed above ground) and it is also easily observed. The best time to witness the procedure is on a humid night, spring or autumn, when the ground is moist and the temperature is in the 50s. Observation is further enhanced in that earthworms while mating are virtually oblivious to anything else going on around them, even the approach of predators.

A night crawler ready for mating will extend its head end from the burrow after anchoring its submerged posterior with the powerful seta. Cautiously, it will swing its head in a survey of the area, attempting to locate another willing individual. Earthworms ready for mating will issue glandular secretions, by which they are attracted to each other.

After likely partners locate each other, they leave the burrows and embrace. They must be of roughly equal length in order to copulate successfully. Length is important because

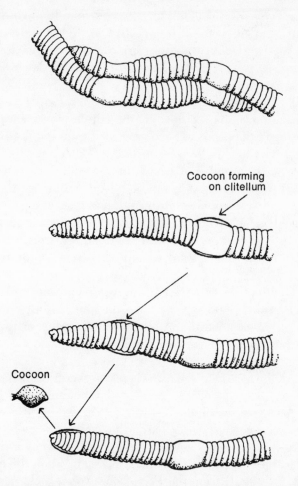

Cocoon forming
on clitellum

Cocoon

Figure 9 Copulation and Stages in Cocoon Production in *Lumbricidae*

Source: Adapted from Tembe, V. B., and P. J. Dubash, The Earthworms: A Review. *Journal of the Bombay Natural History Society,* 58:1 (1961)

the two must lie with the undersides of their bodies together, heads pointing in opposite directions, so that they touch in the region of the spermathecal openings and where the clitellar area of one worm touches the surface of the other (fig. 9). Were the worms of vastly different sizes, successful sperm exchange could not take place.

The two earthworms, after having found each other to be suitable partners, then clasp each other tightly with the seta. Thus locked firmly, they may lie in close embrace for hours, sometimes all night long, until the light of dawn signals a retreat into the burrows.

During copulation, a copious amount of thicker-than-ordinary mucus is secreted by the clitellum of each partner, covering both worms between segment nine and the posterior border of the clitellum. The two slime tubes thus formed cover both worms, but remain apart from each other. This heavy mucus acts first as a protective covering for the sperm that is being mutually transferred, and later as a covering for the eggs. The two pairs of sperm receptacles on each worm receive the several thousand spermatozoa from the glove-shaped seminal vesicles that lie on the worm immediately opposite.

Once the sperm has been expended and received by each partner, the two part from each other. The sperm will be retained in each worm until it is needed for the fertilization of the small, white eggs, which are usually produced after the two worms have parted.

Now, the clitellum produces a secretion which soon hardens over its outer surface—the beginning of the egg cocoon (usually called a capsule). When the surface of the secretion becomes fairly hard, the worm moves backward, slowly sliding the secretion (containing both eggs and sperm) over its body and eventually over its head. When the mass has separated totally from the worm, the two ends close, forming a lemon-shaped capsule. Actual fertilization of the eggs takes place in the sealed capsule. Also included in the capsule is an albuminous fluid which will nuture the incubating young earthworms until they hatch and are able to feed themselves. More egg capsules may be formed immediately by the same worm, until all the stored seminal fluid has been used. Lumbricids which have not mated may still produce capsules, but they will be infertile.

There are from one to twenty fertilized ova in each capsule, but only one or two will hatch. Only *Eisenia foetida* (the brandling worm) commonly bears more than two worms per capsule.

Table 7

Dimensions of the Cocoons of 16 Species
(in millimeters)

Species	Mean Length (L)	Mean Width (W)	L / W
A. caliginosa	3.52	2.74	1.29
A. chlorotica	2.99	2.62	1.14
A. longa	6.20	4.34	1.43
A. nocturna	6.24	4.40	1.42
A. rosea	3.11	2.71	1.15
D. mammalis	2.24	1.96	1.14
D. rubida	2.11	1.75	1.20
D. subrubicunda	2.55	2.26	1.13
E. tetraedra	1.87	1.48	1.26
E. foetida	3.87	3.17	1.22
L. castaneus	2.35	2.06	1.14
L. festivus	3.52	2.88	1.22
L. rubellus	3.18	2.76	1.15
L. terrestris	5.97	4.69	1.28
O. lacteum	3.70	2.58	1.43
O. cyaneum	5.35	3.70	1.43

Source: Evans, A. C., and W. J. Mc. L. Guild, Cocoons of some British Lumbricidae. *Annals of the Magazine of Natural History* (1947)

The young earthworm.   Earthworm eggs will hatch in from 14 to 21 days under favorable conditions—the right temperatures, soil moisture, etc. If conditions are not right, the capsules are amazingly able to hold the fertile eggs until conditions are more favorable. Egg capsules can survive dryness and extreme temperatures that would kill any adult earthworm.

Newly hatched earthworms look like little pieces of white thread, about 1/16 to 1/4 inch long, depending on the species. Within a matter of hours, their color begins to turn darker and within a day resembles that of their parents. They grow very rapidly, reaching sexual maturity in from 80 to 100 days, after which their rate of growth slows considerably.

The mortality rate for young earthworms is very low when conditions are favorable. George Sheffield Oliver conducted an experiment in which he carefully segregated 100 capsules (he did not say which species was involved). They produced 190 young worms. After two months, 185 were accounted for, indicating a mortality rate of only 2.6 percent during the crucial growing period. In the wild, of course, mortality will be much higher because of accidental death from freezing, desiccation, and predation. Still, the low mortality rate is yet another tribute to the perfect evolution of the earthworm.

Rates of reproduction.   It is difficult to estimate the number of progeny an earthworm will produce in a year's time. Much depends on the species of worm, the weather, soil conditions, temperature, and available food. Many estimates appearing in print suggest that the average "domesticated" earthworm (such as *Lumbricus rubellus*, the red worm) can be counted upon to produce from 150 to more than 200 young annually, under good conditions. Oliver gave the "average" estimate of 150, in his book *Our Friend the Earthworm*. Earl B. Shields, a prominent Arkansas earthworm raiser, estimates an average production of 48 capsules annually from a mature breeder, and an average of 4 new worms per capsule, for a total of 192 new worms annually. Many sales offers to would-be earthworm ranchers virtually promise that a starter bed of 1,000 worms will, growing geometrically, expand their numbers to one million by the end of the first year.

Although earthworms are prodigious reproducers, their rate of multiplication is probably not so great as is often believed or stated. Scientific evidence suggests that earthworms, depending upon their species, will produce anywhere from 3 to 106 capsules a year, and that these capsules will rarely produce more than one or two worms per capsule (except for those of the brandling worm). Table 8 shows the number of cocoons produced by one worm in a year, comparing 11 different species, according to 1948 tests conducted by the British researchers A. C. Evans and W. J. Mc. L. Guild. Other tests, reported in 1952 by the German

Table 8

Number of Cocoons Produced Yearly
by One Individual

Species	Year	No. of Cocoons	Species	Year	No. of Cocoons
L. rubellus	1946	79	O. cyaneum	1946	13
L. castaneus	1945	65	E. foetida	1946	11
D. subrubicunda	1946	42	A. rosea	1946	8
A. caliginosa	1946	27	A. longa	1945	8
A. chlorotica	1946	25	A. nocturna	1945	3
D. mammalis	1945	17			

Source: Evans, A. C., and W. J. Mc. L. Guild, Studies on the Relationships between Earthworms and Soil Fertility. IV. On the Life Cycles of Some British Lumbricidae. *Annals of Applied Biology*, 35:4 (1948)

researcher D. E. von Wilcke (table 9) corroborate the findings
of Evans and Guild, with the one exception of *L. rubellus*
(the red worm). Whereas the British researchers found this
species to produce 79 capsules annually, the German study
showed a production of 106. It would seem, then, that the
most productive among the common species are the red
worm and the brandling worm. The latter, although it
produces far fewer capsules annually, is the only species to
commonly issue more than one or two worms from each
capsule.

Table 9

Time of Development for
Some Lumbricid Earthworms

Species	No. of Cocoons per Worm per Year	Incubation Time of Cocoon (weeks)	Period of Growth of Worm (weeks)	Total Time for Development (weeks)
E. foetida	11	11	55	66
D. subrubicunda	42	8½	30	38½
L. rubellus	106	16	37	53
L. castaneus	65	14	24	38
E. rosea				
(A. rosea)	8	17½	55	72½
A. caliginosa	27	19	55	74
A. chlorotica	27	12½	36	48½
A. terrestris				
f. longa	8	10	50	60

Source: Wilcke, D. E. von, On the Domestication of
the "Soilution" Earthworm. *Anz. Schädlingsk*, 25(1952)

There seems to be no similar data for the native night
crawler, *L. terrestris*. However, the reproduction rate for this
species is probably fairly low. Researchers have discovered

that those species which live near the soil surface, and are exposed to a great number of environmental dangers, tend to produce greater numbers of capsules than lower-living species.

In their native habitats, the time of year dictates greatly how many capsules are produced. Fewest capsules are

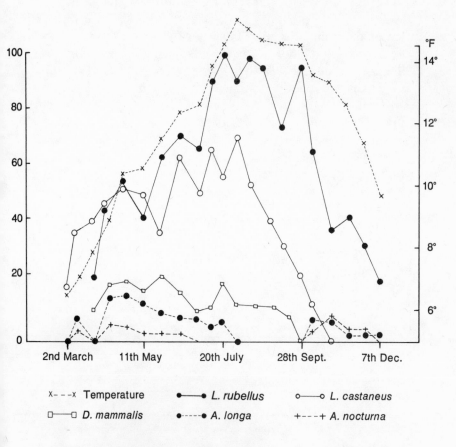

Figure 10 Seasonal Production of Cocoons among Five Species

Source: Adapted from Evans, A. C., and W. J. Mc. L. Guild, Studies on the Relationships between Earthworms and Soil Fertility. IV. On the Life Cycles of Some British Lumbricidae. *Annals of Applied Biology*, 35:4 (1948)

produced in the winter months, and none at all will be produced when temperatures fall below 3°C (37.4°F). In early spring—around February in the middle part of the United States—capsule production begins to increase, and it hits a peak between May and July. After that, however, seasonal production begins to fall off again because of the heat and soil dryness. Evans and Guild have charted the capsule production of five different species throughout the year (fig. 10).

Seasonal populations. How does the seasonal fluctuation of capsule production affect populations? Henry Hopp has done a great deal of work in this area and has found that a high percentage of young worms will be found in the soil during late summer and early fall (the result of heavy capsule production in spring) and that the highest numbers of adult worms are found in the spring (fig. 11). Hopp found that many worms die during the hot and dry conditions of summer and that, in the northern United States, many more are killed by sudden

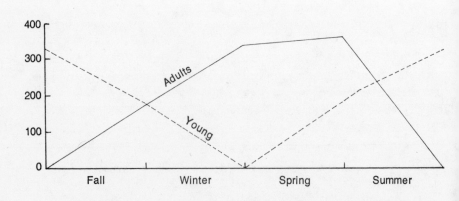

Figure 11 Annual Cycle of Earthworms in Sodland

Source: USDA, Henry Hopp (experiments conducted at the Maryland Agricultural Experiment Station)

autumn frosts, since they cannot retreat in time to escape the effects of the quickly cooling soil. This suggests that farmers and gardeners can encourage earthworm populations by adopting practices that will mitigate these factors—such as mulching, which will help to cool summer soil and protect its moisture content, as well as soften the blow of autumn frosts. This discussion will be developed more fully in chapter 6.

Habitat

Earthworms are found throughout the torrid and temperate regions of the earth, in both forests and grasslands, wherever soil conditions and temperatures will permit their survival. A few hardy species have even been found in the Arctic, Antarctica, and some desert regions.

Most species are found in the top 8 to 12 inches of soil, although extreme heat, cold, or dryness will force them to drive more deeply into the soil. The native night crawler builds more-or-less permanent burrows, which it uses again and again, but most species construct no such burrows, simply moving through the soil as their needs dictate.

Vertical distribution. The native night crawler is the deepest-living species in North America. Its burrows commonly go down as far as 40 inches, but can extend as far as 8 feet or more. Some reports (unconfirmed) have indicated night crawler burrows as deep as 15 feet.

The other important agricultural species—the common field worm—lives much nearer the surface, commonly operating in the top 10 inches of soil. Perhaps the shallowest-living common species in *Allolobophora chlorotica* (the green worm) which is confined to the top 4 inches of soil.

Researchers have confirmed what most anglers have long known—that earthworms live nearer to the surface in spring and fall, when temperatures are moderate and the soil is moist, than in winter or summer.

Burrowing Technique

Earthworms move through the soil in one of two ways: by pushing aside the soil or eating through it. In loose and light soil, the worm will usually push aside the soil, both by using its prostomium (the mouth flap) and by contracting the circular and longitudinal muscles of the body wall (much as the old-time circus strongman would break chains by flexing his biceps). The earthworm also takes advantage of hydraulic lift, since the fluid of its coelomic body cavities, particularly those towards the head end, can be secreted to exert further pressure. If the soil is very heavy and tightly packed, however, the worm may elect to move through it by simply eating its way along. Secretions in the digestive tract soften the earth and make it easier for the worm to move the material through its body. Nevertheless, this mode of transportation is a painfully slow process.

Castings

A question often asked at this point is—if the earthworm is creating burrows in compact soil, where does it leave its castings? The answer is that it usually finds an air space in the soil, or an old burrow (the earth is honeycombed with them), and there deposits about one-third of the contents of its intestine at a time. Night crawlers habitually come to the surface to leave their castings, as do a few other species (notably *Allolobophora longa* and *A. nocturna*), but most species deposit their castings underground. In general, only species which build permanent burrows leave their castings above ground.

Earthworm castings have long been prized by gardeners and other growers of plants, sometimes to a point where almost mystical powers are attributed to them. In some plant shops, they sell for several dollars a pound. In truth, the castings are a compost of the highest grade—but of no greater value than other very high-grade composts. Earthworm castings contain soil particles that the worm has eaten, but these particles are smaller, on the average, than those which entered the worm. Thus, over a long period of time, the soil with a large earthworm population will become finer in texture and more suitable for plant growth. The castings also have about one-third more bacteria than the surrounding soil, and this increased bacterial activity is beneficial to the breakdown of organic matter and liberation of plant nutrients. USDA tests, in fact, have indicated that earthworm castings contain from 5 to 11 times the amounts of the three major plant nutrients (nitrogen, phosphorus, and potassium) as does the soil which contributes to those castings. More about this, in the next chapter.

Earthworms are said to produce their own weight daily in castings. Since they are inactive for long periods, particularly during extremely hot and cold weather, their daily production during favorable conditions probably exceeds this by a good measure. The USDA researcher Henry Hopp estimated that, on good agricultural land, earthworms daily produce about 700 pounds of casts per acre, during favorable periods. Over a year's time, accounting for both favorable and unfavorable periods, earthworms would add 105,000 pounds of castings, or more than 5 percent of the total soil volume to plow depth. It is not difficult, in view of this statistic, to begin to realize the tremendous contribution of the earthworm to soil productivity.

Burrow Construction

As mentioned previously, only a few North American species build and attempt to maintain permanent burrows. Of these, the native night crawler is most prominent.

Charles Darwin spent countless hours in the observation of burrow structure and construction. Here is his description, as set forth in *The Formation of Vegetable Mould:*

> The burrows run down perpendicularly, or more commonly a little obliquely. They are said sometimes to

branch, but as far as I have seen this does not occur, except in recently dug ground and near the surface. They are generally, or as I believe invariably, lined with a thin layer of fine, dark-coloured earth voided by the worms; so that they must at first be made a little wider than their ultimate diameter. I have seen several burrows in undisturbed sand thus lined at a depth of 4 ft. 6 in.; and others close to the surface thus lined in recently dug ground. The walls of fresh burrows are often dotted with little globular pellets of voided earth, still soft and viscid; and these, as it appears, are spread out on all sides by the worm as it travels up or down its burrow. The lining thus formed becomes very compact and smooth when nearly dry, and closely fits the worm's body. The minute reflexed bristles which project in rows on all sides from the body, thus have excellent points of support; and the burrow is rendered well adapted for the rapid movement of the animal. The lining appears also to strengthen the walls, and perhaps saves the worm's body from being scratched. . . .

The burrows which run far down into the ground, generally, or at least often, terminate in a little enlargement or chamber. Here, according to Hoffmeister, one or several worms pass the winter rolled up into a ball. Mr. Lindsay Carnagie informed me (1838) that he had examined many burrows over a stone quarry in Scotland, where the overlying boulder-clay and mould had recently been cleared away, and a little vertical cliff thus left. In several cases the same burrow was a little enlarged at two or three points one beneath the other; and all the burrows terminated in a rather large chamber, at a depth of 7 or 8 feet from the surface. These chambers contained many small sharp bits of stone and husks of flax-seeds. They must also have contained living seeds, for in the following spring Mr. Carnagie saw grass plants sprouting out of some of the intersected chambers.

In more recent times, scientists have discovered that earthworms spend little time in constructing burrows when there is ample food on the ground surface. Other research indicates that the night crawler is a slow builder of burrows, taking from four to six weeks to burrow only eight inches into the soil. The field worm, in the same experiments, burrowed to this depth in only a few days. On the other hand, the field worms's burrows are not permanent, while those of the night crawler will be used for many years, if they are not destroyed by moles and other burrowing animals, or by natural movements of the earth such as in the heaving caused by alternate freezing and thawing. If the night crawler's burrow is damaged, the worm will begin repairs immediately and will complete them in a matter of days or weeks—months, if the damage is extensive.

Protection of Burrows

Night crawlers will go to great lengths to protect and conceal the entrances to their burrows. Said Darwin, "They sometimes work so energetically that Mr. D. F. Simpson, who has a small walled garden where worms abound in Bayswater, informs me that on a calm damp evening he there heard so extraordinary a rustling noise from under a tree from which many leaves had fallen, that he went out with a light and discovered that the noise was caused by many worms dragging the dry leaves and squeezing them into the burrows."

Night crawlers, of course, feed on leaves which they drag into their burrows. But they will drag nonfood objects to the mouths of their burrows, as well. Darwin himself reported having seen burrows plugged with twigs, bits of paper, feathers, tufts of wool, and horsehair. Sometimes they heap little mounds of pebbles on top of the burrow entrance. Using nearly any material at hand, a night crawler will never leave the burrow entrance exposed.

The question arises, then, from what is the night crawler protecting his burrow entrance? Darwin considered this problem at length, and surmised that the worms might be attempting to keep water out of the tunnels, or natural enemies such as Carabus and Staphylinus. He believed also that the plugging of the holes might maintain proper humidity in the burrows and keep out the chilly night air. So far as I know, scientists still have not resolved this question to their complete satisfaction.

Feeding Habits

Earthworms derive their nutrients from organic matter of nearly any kind—animal or vegetable. Although there are one or two references in the literature to earthworm damage to young plants and seedlings, the scientific consensus is that earthworms do not eat living plants but only that organic matter which has begun to decompose. (There is at least one reference to earthworms' destroying young lettuce plants. A possible explanation may be that leaf lettuce will quickly wilt and turn brown at the tips of the leaves if soil conditions are dry. If these brown tips are touching the ground, a night crawler will naturally attempt to drag them into its burrow, since partially decomposed lettuce is one of its favorite foods. To the blind worm, of course, dead lettuce is dead lettuce; it cannot see the green above the brown. But the gardener, upon seeing a lettuce leaf tipped down and pulled into a worm's burrow, might get quite a different picture—and draw a different conclusion.)

Different species of earthworms have different food preferences, and the food available to each species is dependent on its environmental restrictions. The field worm, for instance, which never surfaces voluntarily, is content to absorb the decomposing roots and other matter it finds in the top ten inches of soil. The night crawler, which has a far greater vertical range, can select food on the soil surface or as deeply as its burrow extends, often in subsoil. All earthworm species prefer animal manure to nearly any other food, and some species—notably those living in manure piles—consume nothing else.

The feeding habits of the night crawler have drawn most attention over the years, because they are so interesting and easily observed. At night, this worm emerges from its burrow (always anchoring its tail safely in the burrow) and begins to forage. When it comes upon a leaf or another piece of suitable organic litter, it will grasp the food firmly and drag it into the burrow. Over the years, scientists have marveled at the facility with which night crawlers accomplish this feat. Darwin was the first to observe that night crawlers always grasp leaves by the pointed end; in this way, the leaves are somewhat rolled to form a plug, which fits nicely in the burrow and is convenient to eat in safety, from within the burrow. Darwin cut paper into triangles and offered them to his experimental worms, discovering that they invariably grasped each triangle at its sharpest point. Scientists still do not know how earthworms, with their supposed dim intelligence, can choose the most advantageous point of a leaf for this purpose. Edwards and Lofty, in their 1972 book *Biology of Earthworms*, simply say, "In some unexplained way, worms can discern the best way to drag leaves into their burrows with minimum effort."

Food preferences.   Although earthworms will consume nearly any organic material (assuming it is not too acid or too hard to handle), they do show definite food preferences. The Philippine researcher Pablo T. Tamesis, writing in the December 1967 issue of *Philippine Farms and Gardens,* says that earthworms prefer lettuce and cabbage leaves to all other kinds of food. Dr. Wilhelm Kühnelt, a German researcher, reports in his 1961 book *Soil Biology* that worms show a preference for onions, sea onions (*Scilla maritima*),valerian, phlox, wild cherry, and hornbeam, and a definite dislike for false acacia, sage, thyme, mint, and grasses with thick matted roots, such as *Aira flexuosa*. (Many worms raisers, it should be noted, report that onions introduced into worm beds will drive the earthworms out. The experience of these raisers, however, is largely with red worms, while the scientists probably were studying pasture varieties. The literature concerning food preferences of *different species* is very slim.)

Darwin performed many feeding experiments with his earthworms and found them to like both onions and cabbage (preferring green varieties over red). His worms also showed

131

a preference for celery, carrot leaves, wild cherry leaves, and especially raw meat, including fat. Darwin reported the earthworm's dislike for many strongly flavored plants, including sage, thyme, and mint.

Under cultivation, domestic earthworms thrive on animal manures, treated sewage sludge, poultry mash, various grains, chopped hay, fish meal, tankage, canning factory refuse, and other inexpensive and nutrient-rich materials, along with some more costly additives such as walnut meal, peanut meal, cottonseed meal, soybean meal, etc. Some growers feed occasional doses of liquid vitamin products, especially when worms are being fattened for market—and one Wisconsin raiser likes to give his earthworms ice cream every Saturday night! Much more will be said about domestic earthworm feeds in the later chapters devoted to raising techniques.

Summer and Winter Behavior

As mentioned earlier, earthworms are most active in spring and fall, when the temperatures are moderate and the soil is moist, and tend to become inactive in the heat of midsummer and the cold of winter. Dr. Kühnelt gives us a good description of this seasonal activity in his book *Soil Biology:*

> Of the European earthworms, *Allolobophora longa* and *A. nocturna* withdraw in May or June to a depth of 20 to 40 cm. (8 to 15 inches), construct there a roundish chamber and lie rolled up until September or October. With other species, this dormant period can be induced only by dryness or cold. They withdraw to the dampest parts of the soil, construct a den, the interior wall of which is consolidated by a secretion, roll themselves up into balls and they can remain in this condition for a long time. In this way they can lose up to 50 percent of their weight in water and on being moistened again, they revive. Young animals are found very often in a sleep due to drought, since apparently they cannot dig so deeply as the adults. Young earthworms are also found in groups in the dens. The behaviour of earthworms

in winter is quite analogous. The animals seek out places sufficiently deep and free from frost and there roll themselves up in their self-made holes. They are very susceptible to frost and are killed in a short time by the effect of temperatures between -1.2° and -2°C (30° and 28°F). Hopp and Linder (1947) pointed out that a large proportion of earthworms on fields ploughed annually, die off at the first frosts. Therefore, they recommend covering the soil with straw or other badly heat-conducting material. According to Avel (1928) earthworms which have been kept throughout at a uniform temperature and humidity, nevertheless fall periodically into a resting condition, which resembles the dormancy described as due to dryness or winter.

Surfacing during Rains

Although earthworms can live for a year or more under water, all species will often come to the soil surface during heavy rains, especially if the weather is warm. Thus removed from the safety of the earth, many are quickly killed by ultraviolet light or radiation. Several explanations of this phenomenon have been advanced, none of which is generally accepted by scientists. Harry G. Nelson of the Chicago Field Museum, writing in that institution's *Bulletin* (October 1971), offers this possible explanation: "As the rain tends to saturate the ground and fill all air pockets, the worms move up. They are responding partly to the decreased oxygen supply and increased carbon dioxide supply caused by many soil microorganisms enormously increasing their metabolic activity when water becomes abundant in the soil. The life activities of these bacteria, fungi, protozoans, algae, rotifers, etc., rapidly use up the oxygen not already displaced by the water and in the process release large amounts of carbon dioxide. Further, the liquid nature of the soil at this time greatly slows the movement of all gas particles compared with the action of diffusion when air permeates the soil." Dr. Nelson's explanation seems to be the best offered thus far, although we still have much to learn about this phenomenon.

Mass Migrations

A related phenomenon, reported by many researchers, is that of mass migrations. From time to time—often during damp weather—entire populations of earthworms will emerge from the ground and migrate, often for long distances and to unlikely places. One researcher reported "the abrupt appearance upon the surface of a layer of snow about eight inches thick of an immense congregation of assorted-sized earthworms." A Dutch earthworm researcher reported in 1967 that "Individuals of *Eisenia foetida* (the brandling worm) which were living in the soil in greenhouses, migrated in large numbers up the sides of buildings and even onto roofs, during damp, wet, foggy weather. After a heavy rain, individuals of the same species living in a dung heap migrated to a nearby farmhouse, climbed up the walls onto the roof, and were even found inside the building." Other reports have found migrating earthworms in trees, almost as if, in total panic, they were attempting not only to leave the soil but to get as far from its surface as possible.

Edwards and Lofty say, "The suggested cause of these migrations was that hydrogen sulphide was produced in the burrows, resulting from anaerobic conditions developing because of poor soil ventilation." Still, the exact causes of the mass migration phenomenon are not fully understood.

Do Earthworms Sing?

One of the more unusual aspects of earthworm behavior is their alleged ability to sing. The German researcher C. Merker, writing in the 1940s, astounded fellow scientists by revealing that earthworms have voices. Not only do they have voices, said Dr. Merker, but their faint sounds are "rarely in a solo number but generally in series marked by a definite and changing rhythm." In other words, the worms were singing.

Dr. Merker claimed to be able to hear the sounds when he was within about 12 feet of the worms, and that they were sounds produced not by chance but by the deliberate opening and closing of the earthworm's mouths.

Darwin reported no such singing phenomenon in his 45 years of earthworm research, even though he kept pots of worms in the house, nor has any other researcher. For now, Dr. Merker's singing earthworms will have to remain a mystery.

Defense Mechanisms

There are few animals on earth more defenseless than an earthworm. This creature cannot fight off attackers, obviously, and yet it has none of the sophisticated mechanisms with which nature has endowed certain other nonaggressive species: quickness, jumping or flying ability, camouflage, poisonous secretions, hard exoskeletons—all have been denied our friend the earthworm.

Yet nature has not left the earthworm totally without means of avoiding or escaping its attackers. Its very habitat is perhaps its best defense. Most species never come to the soil surface voluntarily, and those that do exercise extreme caution during their nocturnal surfacings.

The other hope of the earthworm for defense lies in its acute sense of touch. If a foraging night crawler is touched, it will retreat quickly into its burrow, probably not to come out again that night. If the worm is grasped violently, it will dig the seta of its tail area firmly into its burrow, hanging on for dear life. Often it will break in two before allowing itself to be pulled from the burrow. Other species will thrash about vigorously when grasped, thus perhaps shaking loose from a bird or other attacker. Still other species eject coelomic fluid from the dorsal pores when touched. Most worms will voluntarily break off portions of their posterior ends when grasped, even if the grasp is not particularly violent. They can regenerate this portion of their bodies quite easily, although the anterior part of the worm will not react in this manner, since a break near the head would likely result in the worm's death.

135

Chapter 5

The Earthworm
as Soil Builder

Earthworms are soil builders. Through their constant burrowing and voiding of casts, they aerate the soil, improve its water-holding capacity, keep it loose, improve its texture, bring up mineral elements from the subsoil, counteract leaching, break up hardpans, homogenize soil elements, create fertile channels for plant roots, liberate essential plant nutrients into soluble form, neutralize soils that are too acid or too alkaline for plants, and in general enhance the soil's environment for growing plants of all kinds.

The preponderance of evidence supporting these claims is now overwhelming. Yet, since the time of Darwin—and continuing to the present day—there have always been detractors, agricultural scientists and others who claim that earthworms do nothing to improve the soil for growing plants. Their arguments usually fall into three main categories:

1. That earthworms are found only in rich and productive soils, and that therefore it is the rich soil that aids earthworms and not vice versa.

2. That the amount of "tilling" earthworms accomplish is insignificant when compared to the capacity of man's machines.

3. That the nutrient content of earthworm castings is actually low, when compared to that of chemical fertilizers.

Some of the detractors go beyond these basic arguments, occasionally all the way to incredulity. R. Milton Carleton, writing in the summer 1976 issue of the *American*

Horticulturist, maintains that earthworms actually *consume* fertility, leaving the soil poorer than before. (He does not explain where the fertility goes, after the earthworms have consumed it.)

The answering of the three basic arguments is not difficult, and will serve as a starting point in appreciating the contribution of earthworms to soil.

1. Earthworms are found not only in rich and productive soils, as is so often claimed. They are found in soils of all kinds, including stiff clays and sands, so long as there is sufficient moisture present. Edwards and Lofty, in their book *Biology of Earthworms*, quote a study showing that even a light sandy soil supported 232,200 earthworms per acre, and a clay soil hosted 163,800—both respectable populations.

Earthworm populations, however, are strongly affected by organic matter—i.e., the more organic matter in any soil, the more earthworms will be found there, since organic matter is the earthworms' food. But earthworms derive mineral nutrients even from poor soils with very little organic matter. Thus, earthworm populations will be lower in poorer soils, higher in those soils with greater amounts of organic matter. The work that earthworms do in the soil, then, will depend largely on its organic matter content. This in no way indicates that earthworms "do nothing" for the soil, but shows only that their ability to improve soils is limited by enviromental factors.

2. The amount of tilling and mixing of the soil accomplished by earthworms is tremendous. Henry Hopp, the USDA researcher active in the late 1940s, estimated that, on an average agricultural soil, earthworms turn more than 50 tons of soil per acre, annually, into earthworm casts. This amounts to more than 5 percent of an acre plow layer per year. And, the amount of soil *actually eaten* by earthworms represents only a small percentage of the soil which they

move and mix, since earthworms push aside far more soil than they actually consume.

Aside from the actual amount of soil that earthworms turn, they offer further benefits in soil tillage, not to be lightly regarded: Earthworms till the soil continually, for most of the year, at no cost to the gardener and farmer, using none of our precious energy reserves, calling for no machinery or labor costs. John Steinhart, an energy expert at the University of Wisconsin, has calculated that, *for the first time in the history of mankind, we in America are now expending more energy to produce and deliver food than we are receiving from it, in terms of calories.* This is a significant statement, one that bodes ill for the future of mankind in consideration of expanding food needs and shrinking energy reserves. In view of the long-range problems before us, which makes more sense—to increase our dependence on machines for soil tillage, or to encourage earthworms to do this tilling at no cost to us in energy or labor?

In addition to the *amount* of soil that earthworms till, it is important to realize that they till in a way that no machine can duplicate. As we shall see, later in this chapter, the castings that earthworms distribute in their tillage contribute to long-lasting soil structure improvement, while machine tillage offers short-term aid, at best.

3. The last of the three basic antiearthworm arguments—that their castings are low in nutrients compared with commercial fertilizers—is a specious one. Confirmed tests have indicated that earthworm castings, when compared to the soil in which the earthworms worked, contain about 5 times the available nitrogen, 7 times the phosphorus, 3 times the magnesium, 11 times the potassium, and $1\frac{1}{2}$ times the calcium. This is so because earthworms, in passing soil and organic matter through their digestive tracts, liberate minerals for use by growing plants. Still, earthworm castings cannot be compared to a bag of 5-10-5 fertilizer—nor should they be.

The contribution of earthworm castings—50 tons per acre annually—is tremendous, in the aggregate. But the nutrient value of these castings is only a fraction of their total benefits to soil. To say that earthworms are valueless because their castings cannot match the NPK values of a chemical formula is like saying that food is valueless to human nutrition because it cannot match the nutrient value of vitamin tablets.

What Plants Need

Earthworms are not essential to growing plants. In fact, even *soil* is not essential to growing plants. Many of the tomatoes that we buy in supermarkets are grown in large fields of cinder particles, covered with black plastic and pumped with moisture and chemical fertilizers. Of course, this method does not produce the best-quality tomatoes, as supermarket shoppers know—and neither will the highest quality crops of any kind be grown without living soil and the services of earthworms.

For adequate growth, plants have only three critical soil requirements: (1) sufficient moisture; (2) an adequate supply of essential mineral nutrients in available form; and (3) enough air spaces for proper root development. Crops of nearly any kind can be grown in pure sand—or in plastic pellets, for that matter—so long as adequate supplies of water and nutrients are made available.

Soil, of course, is the best natural medium we have for growing plants. Soil receives moisture from the skies and mineral nutrients from its constituent organic matter and parent rock, and can offer adequate air spaces because of the presence of rock particles and that mixture of sand and clay which forms what soil scientists call "aggregate crumb structure." Still, few soils are perfect for the raising of specific or general plants. A soil may be too compact to offer adequate air spaces for root development, or too low in organic matter to offer adequate nutrient supplies, or too light to hold moisture sufficiently.

When a soil is not capable of providing a good environment for plant growth, we then try to improve that soil by correcting its deficiencies, whatever they might be. And this is where earthworms come into the picture. Earthworms are not essential to plant growth—*but they are our best tool for correcting soil structural deficiencies and for maintaining soil at a high level of productivity.* We may still till the earth to mix its constituent materials and provide air spaces; we may still irrigate dry fields and water our gardens; we may add fertilizer to the soil where deficiencies occur. But earthworms will do all of this for us, on a continuing and never-ending basis, year after year, generation after generation. We may choose to improve the soil initially or occasionally by mechanical means, because earthworms might take too long to do the job to suit our needs. But the encouragement of earthworms will ease our burdens in caring for and improving the soil, and, at a certain level of improvement, earthworms will gladly do the bulk of the work for us.

Let us take a closer look at the services earthworms perform for the soil.

Bringing Up
Soil and Minerals

Darwin's major interest in earthworms was in the amount of fine earth which they brought up to the surface. A large portion of his classic book, *The Formation of Vegetable Mould,* is devoted to this phenomenon, as was his first major paper on earthworms, delivered in 1837. He records cases in which layers of cinders and man-made walls were completely covered by the earth particles brought to the surface by earthworms, and he carried out an experiment of his own which yielded results only after 29 years:

> A quantity of broken chalk was spread, on 20th December 1842, over a part of a field near my house, which had existed as pasture certainly for thirty, probably for twice or thrice as many years. The chalk was laid on the land for the sake of observing at some future

period to what depth it would become buried. At the end of November 1871, that is after an interval of 29 years, a trench was dug across this part of the field; and a line of white nodules could be traced on both sides of the trench, at a depth of 7 inches from the surface. The mould, therefore (excluding the turf), had here been thrown up at an average rate of .22 inch per year.

In another part of his book, Darwin says, "Archaeologists ought to be grateful to worms, as they protect and preserve for an indefinitely long period every object, not liable to decay, which is dropped on the surface of the land, by burying it beneath their castings."

Well and good for archaeologists. But how does this habit of earthworms improve soil productivity? It does so in two major ways. First, by digging into the subsoil, loosening it, and threading it with tunnels, earthworms gradually deepen the topsoil layer. Second, by bringing up fine mineral particles from the subsoil and depositing them, as castings, on or near the soil surface, earthworms are constantly adding nutrients to the zone in which plant roots feed. Earthworms, then, not only help to liberate soil nutrients for growing plants, but actually deliver mineral substances that otherwise would remain largely unavailable to most plants.

Increasing Moisture
Absorption and Stability

Soils with a high percentage of clay and silt are often too compact to support passages for water to enter. Even when rainfall is adequate, most of the water on these soils will run off and drought conditions will occur. Earthworms create channels that allow rainwater to enter the soil and be absorbed by it.

The USDA researcher Henry Hopp conducted experiments on silt loam soil. Without worms, the soil had an initial absorption rate of .2 inches of rainfall per minute. The same soil, after earthworms had been introduced and allowed to work for a month, increased its initial absorption rate to .9 inches per minute—an increase of 350 percent. The honeycomb of tunnels and burrows created by earthworms offers easy access to rainwater. Of course, there are other agents that act in this way, including plant roots, ants, and some other soil fauna which create channels. But earthworms are the most important for most farm and garden soils.

Table 10

Influence of Earthworms, Sod, and Mulch
on the Infiltration Capacity of a Clay Soil

| Cover | Relative Rate of Infiltration | |
	Without Earthworms (inches/minute)	With Earthworms (inches/minute)
None	0.0	0.0
Fertilized sod	0.2	0.8
Mulch	0.0	1.5

Source: USDA, Henry Hopp

Not only do earthworms increase the number of entrances for water, but their casts are vitally important in developing *water stability*, that property of soil which enables it to remain loose and to accept and retain moisture for growing crops. A poor soil, even after it has been loosened mechanically by tilling, will lose its water stability after the first few rains. When wet, poor soil will clump together like so much clay; and when dry, the same soil will form hard lumps, antagonistic to root growth.

Henry Hopp tells us that "water stability comes from the cementing of the soil particles together by sticky materials. These materials, once dried, do not redissolve in water. They are produced by the life in the soil, such as earthworms and certain micro-organisms." The difference between earthworm tillage and tillage by machines is that the work of the earthworm is a lasting one; its effects become part of the soil structure itself, while mechanical tillage is a temporary treatment, lasting only a short time if the soil is basically poor in structure. Mechanical tilling is comparable to our taking an aspirin for a headache, instead of searching for the cause of the headache and removing it. And the difference between earthworm tillage and mechanical tillage is yet another answer to detractors who say that the earthworm's work is minimal when compared to the great power of man's machines.

Says Dr. Hopp, "Pick up a few earthworm casts from a garden either from the surface or below ground. Then select a clod that does not consist of casts and break it into pieces of about the same size as the casts. Drop some of both in water. The earthworm casts stay whole for some time while the pieces of clod quickly break apart in the water. The difference in water stability illustrates why earthworm casts help keep soil loose when it becomes wet."

Several chapters back, we learned of wasps which spend much of their time in searching for earthworm casts to use as material in building their nests. The same quality of earthworm casts, so important to the wasps in building stable nests, is equally important to farmers and gardeners in building water-stable soils. The organic farmer or gardener who occasionally delights in kneeling down and picking up a handful of rich, dark, friable soil, knows that his soil will retain its loose structure through rain and drought because it is rich in organic matter and teeming with life. He knows, too, that earthworms are the key to *permanent* soil structure, making frequent tillage unnecessary.

Some years back, Dr. Hopp conducted an experiment which indicated that, after only *one week* of action by earthworms, the water stability of soils was improved by an average of nearly 50 percent. The results of his test, shown in Table 11, give good indication of just how quickly soil structure can be improved through the introduction or encouragement of earthworms. The building of earthworm populations—and the reaping of their benefits—does not have to take years, or even months. Many tests indicate that earthworms go to work immediately when introduced to soils, and that their benefits begin on *day one*.

Table 11

The Effect of Earthworms in One Week on the
Water Stability of Soil Taken from Different Places,
as Found in Controlled Laboratory Tests

Soil Type	Description of Soil	Water Stability of the Soil without Earthworms (percent)	with Earthworms (percent)
Evesboro loamy sand	Eroded bank	2.5	14.4
	Same, with organic debris added	12.9	32.3
	Another eroded bank, with organic debris added	6.6	15.0
	Abandoned brushy field	18.2	45.5
Sunnyside fine sandy loam	Eroded field, with organic debris added	4.7	10.3
	Clover meadow	73.2	79.5
Leonardtown silt loam	Eroded bank	1.3	4.8
	Same, with organic debris added	4.2	8.4
	Young hardwood forest	74.8	80.4
Christiana silt loam	Lespedeza meadow .	4.5	15.7
Paulding clay	Continuous cornfield	19.8	24.5
	Rotation cornfield . .	31.1	39.2
Average of all tests		21.2	30.8

Source: USDA, Henry Hopp

Improving Soil Aeration

Roots do not actually grow "in" soil. They grow primarily in the spaces *between* soil particles, and they have limited capacity to push soil aside to make progress. Air spaces in the soil, therefore, are essential to good root growth. Air is also vital to the growth and important work of soil microorganisms, and to the oxidation of mineral matter for plant use. A soil with insufficient air spaces will be hard, dense, compact, and inhospitable to plant growth of any kind. Of course, air spaces hold water, when water enters the soil, and will later fill with air again as the water is absorbed by the surrounding soil. The tunnels and castings of earthworms thus serve both to aerate the soil and to increase its water-holding capacity. It is this service that makes earthworms valuable not only to gardeners and farmers, but to landscape engineers who seek to control erosion in many situations.

Counteracting Leaching

By the downward movement of water, many soluble mineral nutrients are lost to plant roots. This leaching is, in some measure, counteracted by the actions of earthworms, which will—especially if the nutrients are in organic form—consume them and return them to the upper levels of the soil layer, where they are deposited in the form of castings.

Liberating Nutrients

One of the greatest services earthworms perform is the liberation of essential plant nutrients into soluble forms that can be used by plants. There is no shortage of mineral nutrients in most soils—only shortages of *available* nutrients. It is the earthworm's function to consume unavailable mineral nutrients and, by the actions of enzymes in its digestive tract, make them water soluble. In soluble form, the nutrients can be absorbed by roots and carried to every cell of the plant,

145

where they help it to carry on all its life processes.

Herbert A. Lunt and G. M. Jacobson, writing in *Soil Science* (vol. 58, 1944), reported the results of their comparisons of earthworm castings to the surrounding soil. The castings contained 40 percent more available calcium, 204 percent more magnesium, 366 percent more nitrogen, 644 percent more phosphorus, and 1,019 percent more potassium than the soil from which the castings were made (table 12).

Table 12

Properties of Earthworm Casts and
of Soil from Cultivated Fields

	Casts	Soil 0"—6"	Soil 8"—16"
Total nitrogen (%)	0.353	0.246	0.081
Organic carbon (%)	5.17	3.35	1.11
Carbon: nitrogen	14.7	13.8	13.8
Nitrate nitrogen (ppm)	21.9	4.7	1.7
Available phosphorus (ppm)	150.0	20.8	8.3
Exchangeable calcium (ppm)	2,793.0	1,993.0	481.0
Exchangeable magnesium (ppm)	492.0	162.0	69.0
Total calcium (%)	1.19	0.88	0.91
Total magnesium (%)	0.545	0.511	0.548
Exchangeable potassium (ppm)	358.0	32.0	27.0
Percent saturation	92.9	74.1	55.5
pH	7.0	6.36	6.05
Moisture equivalent (%)	31.4	27.4	21.1

Source: Lunt, H. A., and G. M. Jacobson, The Chemical Composition of Earthworm Casts. *Soil Science*, 58:5 (1944) (Values given are means of six samples. Table is not reproduced here in its entirety.)

Some agricultural scientists maintain that earthworms are unimportant in this regard, that they consume only organic matter, and that this would eventually be broken down by bacteria, anyway. In truth, earthworms consume large amounts of soil, even when ample organic matter is at hand, and by mixing the organic matter with the soil, a rich humus is created, perfect in texture and far richer in available nutrients than the materials from which it was made.

Improving Structure

In good garden and farm soils, the individual particles of sand, clay, and silt will naturally group together into larger units, called *granules* or *aggregates*. The formation of a large number of aggregates in a soil will result in good *structure* or *crumb structure*. Aggregates resist water logging, erosion, and compaction, and remain loose when either wet or dry. An aggregate-rich soil stays loose and well aerated, and allows for proper drainage. Good soil structure, in other words, means good garden and farm soil.

Earthworms are vitally important to the increase in the number of soil aggregates, and thus to good soil structure. Their casts contain a far higher percentage of aggregates than is found in the surrounding soil. Henry Hopp introduced earthworms to a test plot and found that, in only three days, the soil with worms contained 12 percent of large aggregates, while the wormless soil contained only 5.9 percent. Scientists are still not certain how aggregates are formed in the digestive tract of the earthworm. Many theories have been advanced, none satisfactory. What is not doubted, however, is the enormous value of this, one more service of the earthworm, to farm and garden soils.

Aiding Drainage

Soils with poor drainage can be improved dramatically if earthworms are introduced and given support. Experiments by Guild (1952), Teotia (1950), and Hopp and Slater (1949) show that soils with earthworms drain from four to ten times faster than those without. This drainage is a result both of the worms' burrows and tunnels and of the improved crumb structure produced by their casts. On the other hand, in light sandy soils where water tends to run straight through to the subsoil, the aggregates produced by earthworm casts act to improve water retention. Earthworms can also break up compacted layers of soil over time, thus improving drainage when hardpans are the problem. Of course, a hardpan which poses a specific problem in a field can be broken up far more quickly by mechanical means, through subsoiling.

Creating Fertile Root Channels

It has already been mentioned that plant roots grow more vigorously in the spaces between soil particles than in compacted soil. Earthworms create tunnels that plant roots apparently follow quite eagerly. More, the earthworm tunnel walls are lined with nutrient-rich digestive secretions, making them far more beneficial to plant roots than air spaces created by other agents. Sir Albert Howard, in his introduction to the 1945 reprinting of Darwin's work, makes the following notes:

> In the course of these green-manure experiments in Lincolnshire I spent some time in studying the earthworms on land similar to Mr. Caudwell's farms but which were regularly dressed with farmyard manure. Here earthworms were abundant and in some of the old tunnels I frequently observed the reaction of the roots of the potato (King Edward) to fresh worm casts. The fine roots often followed these tunnels downwards, but whenever they passed the earthworm casts a fine network of roots was given off laterally which penetrated the casts in all directions. Obviously the potato was making full use of these accumulations.

Darwin himself says, "They [worm burrows] also greatly facilitate the downward passage of roots of moderate size; and these will be nourished by the humus with which the burrows are lined."

Neutralizing Soil

The castings of earthworms are always more neutral than the soil from which the castings are formed. Thus, over time, an army of earthworms works to keep the soil in the neutral range of the pH scale, neither too acid nor alkaline for the optimum growth of most plants. Just how earthworms accomplish this is another scientific mystery, although it is suspected that the soil, in passing through the worm's intestine, is neutralized by its secretions and by the ammonia which the worm also secretes. No one has ever calculated the exact extent to which earthworms are capable of mitigating soil pH, but the influence must be considerable over a long period of time.

Increasing Crop Yields

With all these beneficial effects on soils, it is not surprising that earthworms have a concomitant beneficial effect on crop yields. Any organic farmer or gardener will testify that earthworms seem to improve yields of any and all crops, that a rich and friable soil, replete with large amounts of organic matter and earthworms, will produce bumper crops no matter what is planted. It is an axiomatic connection which seems to need no explanation or further investigation. Certainly, good soils produce good crops, and earthworms are a part of good soils.

Yet, there are those scientists who doubt that earthworms have any power to affect crop yields, and their doubts rest upon the same misinformation and shaky reasoning presented at the beginning of this chapter. Representative are the following comments by a USDA soil scientist, R. R. Robinson, which appeared in a USDA pamphlet (CA–41–1), dated February 1964.

Large earthworm populations have long been associated with good soils. Undoubtedly this observation has contributed to the widespread belief that earthworms are highly beneficial in improving crop yields. There is little evidence, however, to support this belief. . . . Field studies of the effect of earthworms on crops are not conclusive. Early trials, in which earthworms were added to the soil, did not make allowance for the nutrient elements contained in the worms. The problem is further complicated because, if soil conditions are favorable, earthworms are usually abundant anyway. If soil conditions are not favorable, the addition of earthworms is of little value because they do not survive.

Sound familiar? It is the same old song of the earthworm detractors, a heavy and repetitive melody with unsupportable lyrics. With the single exception of Dr. Henry Hopp, the attitude of USDA scientists, along with many of their associated colleagues in state universities, has traditionally been a negative one. They have long begun with the assumption that earthworms are just one more facet of the "unscientific" cult of organic gardening and farming, and that this method of growing crops is antithetical to the "modern" methods of agriculture, including its principles of heavy chemical treatment, monocropping, and other facets of maximum-profit agribusiness. The earthworm thus judged guilty by reason of association (with organic methods), the USDA has long discouraged serious investigation into the possible benefits of earthworms in agriculture, and has even gone so far as to denegrate or ignore the work of other researchers who have revealed such benefits. Since the USDA has either conducted or influenced the great bulk of agricultural research in this country during the present century, its position on any facet of agriculture or horticulture has broad, far-reaching, and determining effects on both scientific direction and public attitudes.

In recent years, of course, organic methods have become more widely accepted than ever before, first in gardening and then, more slowly, in farming operations. This broad-based move toward organic methods has been led by the public, by gardeners and farmers themselves, with the USDA dragging along behind—not kicking and screaming, actually, but tight lipped and grim faced. The USDA still sponsors no significant earthworm research, and its long tradition of ignorance is the chief reason why we know so little about earthworms, and why we have failed to utilize their power throughout the present century.

For solid indication that earthworms do, indeed, increase crop yields, we have only to search the literature. Edwards and Lofty, in their book *Biology of Earthworms*, mention some of the scientific studies which, together, prove beyond reasonable doubt the power of earthworms in this regard:

J. A. van Rhee (1965) found that, when large numbers of earthworms were added to the soil, the yield of spring wheat was doubled, grass yields increased four times, and clover ten times.

H. G. Kahsnitz (1922) added a large quantity of live earthworms to garden soil and increased pea yields by 70 percent.

Hopp and Slater (1948, 1949) conducted several tests that included the addition of dead worms as a control measure (thus answering critics' claims that it is the nutritive value of the worms, rather than the work they do, which aids crops). They grew herbage plants in poorly structured soil and found that earthworms (along with supporting organic matter) increased yields more than ten times over the same soil in which dead earthworms were added. Hopp and Slater, in other tests, discovered that the addition of live earthworms increased yields of millet, lima beans, soybeans, and hay—all at considerably higher percentages than those achieved by the addition of dead earthworms. From the results of these experiments, and many similar ones, it is certain that it is not merely the nutrient elements contained in the worms that account for crop yield increases, but the actions of the worms themselves.

151

The New Zealand researcher R. A. S. Waters, in 1951, introduced field worms (*Allolobophora caliginosa*) to soil containing manure and found that the earthworms, after working for eight weeks, doubled rye grass yields. This is only one of dozens of studies conducted in New Zealand, confirming earthworms' effects on crop yields. In one study, colonies of 25 earthworms were added to scattered parts of a sown pasture. After four years, the grass around each inoculation point was greener and more densely covered. After four more years, the individual colonies of worms had spread as far as 328 feet from the original inoculation point. There is no doubt that earthworms can live in, and improve, poor soils. The process will be speeded up, however, if more worms are added and if they are supplied with sufficient amounts of manure or other organic food. The scientific researcher can refer to several papers (listed in this volume's bibliography) in order to learn more of the New Zealand experience: Hamblyn and Dingwall (1945), Richards (1955), Stockdill (1959), Waters (1955), Stockdill and Cossens (1966), and Nielson (1953).

There are many other experiments which confirm scientifically that earthworms, by their actions in the soil, directly increase the yields of crops. Oak seedlings grew 26 percent faster when earthworms were added in pot experiments, and green ash seedlings increased in growth by 37 percent over control plants. Crops of California orange trees were increased significantly when earthworms were introduced to groves.

In general, crop yields are increased by earthworms largely because of the worms' positive effects on soil structure. Thus, yields on soil with poor structure can be increased very quickly and greatly by the introduction of earthworms and supporting organic material. Increases on soil that already has good structure will be far less dramatic, since in these cases the benefits will be largely a result of the earthworms' chemical actions, in releasing nutrients and improving pH.

Also, earthworms will have the greatest effects upon those crops that are very sensitive to soil structure. On the farm, these will include pasture grass, soybeans, wheat, millet, and hay, among others. In the home garden, nearly all vegetables are very sensitive to soil structure, and thus the actions of earthworms are vitally important to both good soil and high yields.

In sum, earthworms must be seen not as a "miracle pill," a panacea for better soil and crop yields, but as an integral part of intelligent organic soil management practices. As earthworms are dependent upon organic matter for food, and mulches for protection from heat, cold, and drought, so do growing plants depend upon the earthworm, in combination with bacteria and other microorganisms, to maintain and improve soil structure and fertility. When earthworms are seen as part of a living soil, existing in and contributing to a vital ecosystem, then the question of "whether earthworms create good soil, or good soil creates earthworms" becomes essentially meaningless. Our aim is to improve our soils and grow higher yields of healthy crops, not to banter about academic questions. In this pursuit, the earthworm has—beyond doubt—found a treasured place in the organic scheme of gardening and farming.

Chapter 6

Earthworms for Gardeners, Farmers, and Orchardists

Earthworms are instrumental in building better gardens, farms, orchards, and lawns. Earthworms may even be said to be the *key* to building soils and growing better crops. But earthworms can perform no unsupported miracles, and the gardener or farmer who buys earthworms to correct poor soils may be in for bitter disappointment.

Earthworms, rather, must be seen as *one factor in a total system of organic soil building.* Crucially important also are organic matter, mulch, mineral nutrients, other soil life forms, tillage practices, pH values, and other factors that go into successful organic soil building. Earthworms are affected by all these factors, and in turn affect many of them. Only the gardener or farmer who adopts the entire system of organic soil building will build large earthworm populations. Then, and only then, will the earthworm perform the miracles of which it is capable.

Check Your Earthworm Population

You probably do not have to conduct any scientific samplings to determine whether your soil has a good population of earthworms. If, in spring digging, a few field worms are turned up with each spadeful of earth, then your soil is very probably in good condition, and the earthworms are doing their job. If, on a cool and moist spring night, you can sneak up on a dozen night crawlers in a small area on your lawn, then you have a pretty good idea that night crawlers are doing a good job not only under your lawn but in your garden,

Earthworms can make a giant contribution to gardens of all kinds. Here, Bob Austin uses earthworm compost to top-dress his flower beds near Madison, Wisconsin.

as well. Of course, you can get far more accurate measurements of earthworm populations by using the scientific sampling methods described in chapter 1. Henry Hopp's method of rough testing involved digging out a square of earth, 12 inches by 12 inches by 7 inches deep. If this sample yielded at least ten earthworms, Hopp considered the population large enough to be a significant factor in soil structure. If, however, only one or two worms were found, then he considered the population insignificant. Most gardeners, however, will not want to put too fine a point on this matter, being content to gain a general idea of their own populations by simple observation in working with the soil.

Gardeners and farmers who seem to have a good earthworm population will want to consider ways in which they can increase that population from good to *excellent*. With all the soil-building services that earthworms perform, it would seem that a little effort expended in this direction—perhaps a little extra care at certain times of the year—would pay rich dividends in better soil and crops. And those whose earthworm populations are wanting will certainly look to discover the cause or causes for those low populations, for a soil which is inhospitable to earthworms is probably inhospitable to good plant growth as well. In this chapter, we will reexamine the factors that control earthworm populations, and look at ways in which farmers and gardeners can influence those factors to increase populations.

The Ideal Population

It is difficult to define an "ideal" earthworm population, except to say that no agricultural land in the world supports such a population, except perhaps for parts of the Nile Valley, in Egypt. Dr. Thomas J. Barrett, author of *Harnessing the Earthworm*, considered a population of from one to two million worms per acre as ideal. To give us some idea of the potential performance of one million adult worms, consider that this number would weigh (at 1/31 ounce each) approximately one ton. Producing their own weight in casts daily, our one million earthworms would then produce one ton of high-grade compost every day, during favorable times of the year, and perhaps somewhat in excess of 100 tons annually. Dr. Barrett liked to visualize one million earthworms as an enormous 2,000-pound dirt-eating animal, roaming a single acre, eating enormous piles of dirt, all the while distributing 2,000 pounds of high-grade compost daily. (For those not accustomed to visualizing an acre of ground for our imaginary giant dirt eater, see it as slightly shorter than an American football field.)

Dr. Hopp estimated that, in the North Atlantic and North Central states, earthworms annually produce a little more than 50 tons of casts per acre. Closer to an ideal population, however, would be found in the Nile Valley's incredibly rich croplands. The USDA estimated that earthworms there produce 120 tons of casts per acre, annually.

But soils are potentially capable of supporting far greater populations than even those found in Egypt. Commercial earthworm growers can maintain 3,000 worms in a cubic foot of soil or bedding. If an acre of land, therefore, were transformed into one enormous earthworm bed, one foot deep, it could support *130 million* worms. Whether plants could grow favorably with this intensity of earthworm activity around their roots is a matter of conjecture. The figure is mentioned, however, in order to set some parameters for evaluating populations. A soil can be so poor as to support no earthworms, or potentially as rich as to support 130 million per acre. A population of 500,000 per acre is considered good, by most experts. But we still have no idea of the "ideal" earthworm population. It is very probably somewhat more than 2 million per acre, meaning that we have a long way to go.

Food for Earthworms

Earthworms, like other animals, have only three basic life requirements: food, water, and protection from harmful agents. Of the three, it is probably the lack of sufficient food that retards the earthworm population in most croplands.

Assuming that other soil factors are favorable, any earthworm population will grow only insofar as additional organic matter is incorporated into the soil. The organic matter may come in the form of compost, manure, decaying plants, or organic wastes of a wide variety. It may be added to the soil and tilled in, or grown in the soil (such as a green manure crop) and then plowed under. Any way it is added, organic matter is essential to encouraging greater numbers of earthworms in the soil. In addition, once an earthworm population has been increased, enough organic matter must be supplied periodically in order to maintain that increase.

When to apply organic matter.   The greatest food needs of earthworms occur, fortunately for the gardener and farmer, at the times when organic matter is usually applied to the soil, anyway—in spring and fall. Earthworm activity is at a peak during both these seasons, requiring large quantities of food to support that activity. In the summer, when it would be more difficult to incorporate organic matter because of growing plants, earthworms are not overly active, often resting in the cool of the soil's lower depths, coming to the surface only occasionally or when forced to because of heavy rains. In the winter, they retreat even further into the ground, coiled together in balls below the frost line.

It is, therefore, the fall and spring during which earthworms do the bulk of their earth turning, cast forming, mating, and egg producing. The first cool days of early autumn signal the most active time of the year for earthworms. Many young are hatched during this period, and the need for food is great. Fortunately, it is at this time when both gardeners and farmers are able to add organic matter to the soil most conveniently. Green manure and cover crops can be cut and plowed under. Plant wastes from the garden can be turned under. Roots of cut flowers and vegetables begin to decay. Compost heaps, building up all summer, can be spread on the land and tilled in.

Table 13

Change in Body Weight of the Common Field Worm (*Allolobophora caliginosa*) when Fed Different Kinds of Organic Matter together with a Silt Loam Topsoil

Kind of Organic Material	Change in Body Weight Gain (percent)	Loss (percent)
Lespedeza leaf litter	21.5	. . . .
Fresh cow manure	10.7	. . . .
Green clover leaves	7.8	. . . .
Brown soybean leaves	5.6	. . . .
Dead bromesedge leaves	. . . .	0.5
Weathered corn leaves	. . . .	5.2
None	. . . .	13.4
Wheat straw	. . . .	14.1
Sawdust	. . . .	18.2

Source: USDA, Henry Hopp

In spring, the other peak period, manure piles can be leveled and added to the soil, providing a rich feast for millions of worms stirring into renewed activity. During the summer, the reduced food needs of earthworms can easily be met by the materials which were added the previous spring, and by mulches that will slowly decompose at the ground surface. On cool nights, the night crawler will gladly come to the surface and pull some of this mulch into his burrow. During the summer, also, manure teas and organic side dressings will be received eagerly.

Food preferences. Earthworms prefer organic matter that is in the process of decay, rather than that which is well aged or very green. Of course, green matter will soon go into decay once it is incorporated into the soil. Above all, earthworms thrive on animal manure, which they will quickly attack and turn into sweet humus. Very acid materials, such as large quantities of oak leaves or pine needles, should be avoided. Other than that, however, do not worry about the kind of organic matter you supply. Concentrate, rather, on supplying all you can.

Influencing the environment. Henry Hopp and others have discovered that, although earthworms act upon seasonal changes, their activities are controlled by their immediate environment, and not by some biological time clock as those of some animals and plants are. If, for instance, the weather were moderate and humid all year around, earthworms would then remain active continuously—as they do in some favored areas of the world and in indoor breeding beds where temperature and moisture are controlled artificially. To the gardener, this means that, if he keeps his soil cool and moist in summer, by use of a heavy mulch, he will encourage far greater earthworm activity and a quicker increase in the earthworm population. Mulching is critically important to earthworms, as we shall soon see.

How much food? No estimates have been made regarding the exact amount of organic matter needed to support earthworm populations of any given size. We do know that earthworms prefer organic matter to soil and mineral particles and will consume large quantities of it, if it is available. We know also that they can get by with relatively little organic matter when it is unavailable or in short supply. But I know of no studies relating percentages of soil organic matter to earthworm populations, no studies measuring earthworm population increases after measured amounts of organic matter had been applied to the soil. This is one more area where

A heavy summer mulch will keep the soil moist and cool, helping to encourage earthworms to thrive and increase their populations.

scientific researchers seem to have their work cut out for them.

In any case, the gardener or farmer need not worry about supplying so many tons of organic matter per acre, in order to support his earthworm family. Rather, he should concentrate on incorporating all the organic matter he can, letting the earthworms decide for themselves what level of population density this organic matter can support.

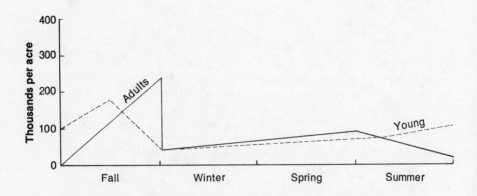

Figure 12 Earthworm Cycle in a Cornfield (Most of the earthworms are killed in the late fall or early winter, and do not build back up to former population levels until the following fall.)

Source: USDA, Henry Hopp

Autumn Mulching
for Earthworms

Protected from harmful agents, an individual earthworm may be expected to live for some years, contributing to the soil all the while. Freezing temperatures in the autumn, however, constitute one of the most harmful agents of all, killing off surprising numbers of adult worms each year. On unprotected soils during a sudden fall freeze, the earthworm population can easily be decimated in a single day, not to build itself back up to previous levels for another year.

Field species of earthworms can adapt to freezing temperatures, and in fact can survive the winter in soils that are actually frozen. However, they build up this tolerance slowly. As cooler temperatures begin to appear in early and midautumn, the worms gradually tunnel deeper into the earth, coming up to feed only to a point where temperatures are bearable. As temperatures grow progressively colder, the worms burrow more deeply into the soil until, by the time winter sets in, they have adapted to freezing temperatures. But that sudden cold snap in October, unless the soil is protected, can be disastrous in northern areas. In the South, the Southwest, and lower California, of course, the chief killer of earthworms is not autumn frost. More likely, populations will be limited in these areas because of heat, dryness, and unsuitable soil conditions.

The obvious lesson for northern gardeners and farmers, however, is to keep the soil protected at all times. As we have already seen, a mulch in summer keeps the soil cool and moist, encouraging activity among earthworms even during hot weather. An autumn mulch is even more important, since it can save the lives of millions of worms and help to insure a building population for future years.

After the growing season, gardens should be treated to copious amounts of organic matter, to serve as food for earthworms (then at a peak of activity) and at the same time should be mulched heavily in order to meliorate autumn temperatures. On farm acreages, some sort of winter cover should be provided, not to be plowed under until spring. Earthworm populations are traditionally high on permanent pastures and sod lands not only because of the food provided by constantly dying roots and top growth, but largely because the earthworms are protected against autumn freezes. Some

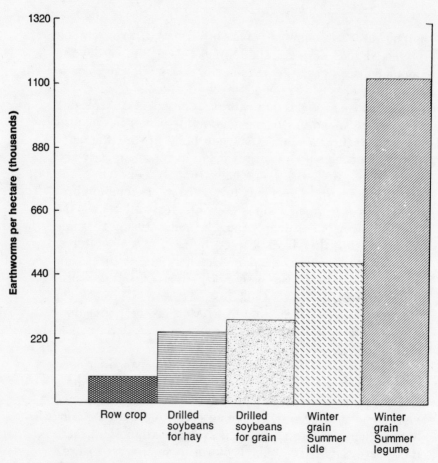

Figure 13 Earthworm Counts in February 1946 under Different Kinds of Annual Cultures

Source: Hopp, Henry, Earthworms Fight Erosion Too. *Soil Conservation*, 11 (1946)

years ago, Earl Kroth, an agronomist at the University of Missouri, planted corn in fescue sod. The thick, fluffy fescue slowed erosion, kept the soil loose, and held moisture. Besides producing good corn yields (155 bushels per acre), the fescue-covered sod provided a good earthworm environment. When Kroth pulled the fescue aside, he found the ground latticed with piles of rich earthworm castings.

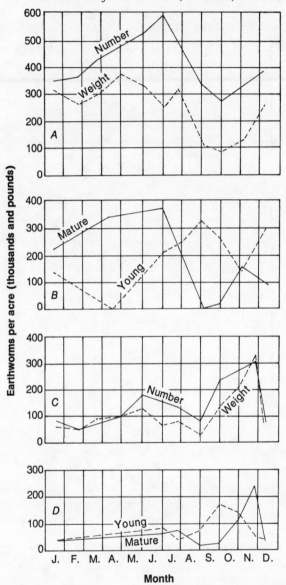

Figure 14 Annual Earthworm Cycle in a Field at College Park, Maryland (On sod ground—A and B—the mature earthworms reproduced and died during the summer; on cultivated ground that had insufficient protection in the late fall—C and D—the earthworms for the most part died in the early part of the winter.)

Source: Hopp, Henry, and Clarence S. Slater, *Journal of Agricultural Research*, 78:10 (1949)

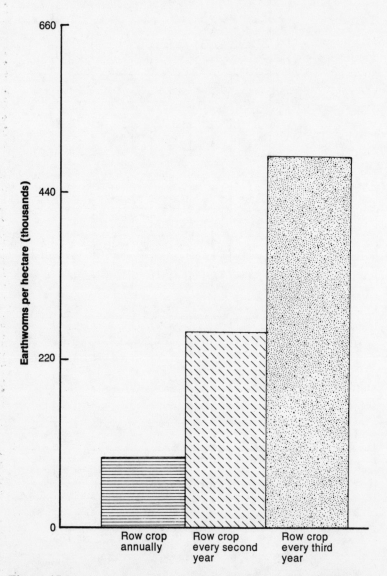

Figure 15 Earthworm Count in February 1946 after Row Cropping in 1945 (Plots were planted to row crops annually, every second year, and every third year.)

Source: Hopp, Henry, Earthworms Fight Erosion Too. *Soil Conservation*, 11 (1946)

Table 14

Earthworms and Soil Physical Properties in Tilled Land Covered over Winter, Compared with Uncovered Tilled Land and Adjacent Sod Land (Measurements were made in the spring, the average of three localities in Ohio and Maryland.)

| Soil Property | Tilled Land in Young Wheat: | | |
	Covered over Winter	Uncovered over Winter	Sod land
Relative infiltration (in./min.)	0.31	0.10	0.36
Large spaces (percent)	7.0	3.9	10.5
Water stability (percent) . . .	59	44	79
Earthworms (no./sq. ft.) . . .	52	10	24

Source: USDA, Henry Hopp

Table 15

Earthworms, Erosion, and Runoff in Comparable Plots at Ithaca, New York (Erosion and runoff data are 10-year averages.)

Treatment for the prior 10 Years	Earthworms per Acre (thousands)	Erosion Annually (tons/acre)	Runoff Annually (inches/acre)
Continuous	0	30	1.77
Three-year rotation	94	5	.40
Continuous meadow	314	0	.18
Idle	813	0	.29

Source: USDA, information supplied by Dr. John Lamb, Jr., to Henry Hopp

Contrast this to traditional clean-cultivation row cropping of corn, in which earthworm populations drop to near zero in the late fall.

Of course, growing crops in sod is not the only way to protect earthworms. Almost any winter soil covering will do the job, including chopped corn stover, wheat straw, or—perhaps best of all—a cover crop such as ryegrass.

It is not surprising that a good earthworm population, supported by sound soil management practices, will reduce or eliminate soil erosion and runoff. Tables 14 and 15 show the importance of providing winter soil cover of some kind, its effects on earthworm populations, and their combined effects on both erosion and runoff. The lessons are clear, and the earthworm—again—is a key factor in the beneficial chain of events.

Soil Acidity

As mentioned before in these pages, earthworms are capable of neutralizing soil, making acid soil less acid, and alkaline soil less alkaline. They work constantly to bring the soil in towards the neutral 7.0 range of the pH scale.

However, despite their neutralizing abilities, earthworms are very sensitive to soil pH values. Neither night crawlers nor field worms can survive in soils with a pH of less than 5.4, and at this very acid range earthworm populations will be held down drastically. As the soil becomes less acid, the environment for earthworms becomes progressively improved and populations are free to increase. Even a soil pH of 6.0 will be less hospitable to earthworm growth and reproduction than one in the 7.0 range.

If you want to provide the best environment for earthworms, then, keep a steady eye on your soil's pH. A simple test should be made every year. On the farm, every field should be tested annually. This habitual testing, of course, will benefit not only earthworms but also all crops, each of which has its own pH preferences, all of which will do nicely in the neutral range.

Nitrogen Lawn Fertilizers

The farmer or gardener who seeks to build his earthworm population will avoid chemical pesticides and fertilizers, and will especially disdain those which are highly toxic to earthworms. Chapter 3 of this book discusses these toxins in detail. I will repeat one note of caution here, however, and that involves the use of high-nitrogen chemical lawn fertilizers. Nearly all of the commercial brands contain high levels of nitrogen in the form of ammonia. These will destroy earthworm populations in the lawn by creating highly acid conditions in a very short time—too short to allow earthworms to adjust to them or to escape to lower soil depths. Many home owners, who somehow have been led to believe that a lawn should look like the top of a billiards table, overfertilize the grass, cut it much too short, spend much time and money in watering and "thatching"—and then wonder why their lawns turn brown with the first summer heat wave. The lack of earthworms under the lawn is the major reason for the rock-hard soil that cannot possibly support a good stand of grass, and all their thatching would be unnecessary if they encouraged earthworms to drag that thatch under the ground and turn it into lawn-supporting humus.

Correcting Basic Flaws

Some gardeners and farmers are faced with drainage problems caused by a hardpan horizon, a layer of subsoil whose pores have been filled in with fine clay particles, eventually forming a cementlike substance impervious to water. The subsoil under the hardpan might be perfectly good and well drained, but the water never gets past the hardpan.

The result is constantly poor drainage. The topsoil puddles readily during rains, and the puddles are slow to disappear. The topsoil, which is likely to have a high percentage of clay, is apt to be dank and sour, unfit for most desirable plants.

In time—perhaps a very long time—earthworms might break up this hardpan horizon. But a subsoiler (a special plow that breaks up the layer but does not bring it to the surface) can do the job in a matter of hours. In doing this, the topsoil will soon become well drained and more suitable for earthworms to live and work in. The earthworms, in turn, will become far more effective in breaking up the hardpan soil, perhaps getting rid of it once and for all.

A heavy clay soil, in addition, should receive copious amounts of organic matter to which some sand has been added. Some gardeners and farmers find it beneficial to take such land out of production for a season or two and simply grow as many green manure crops as possible on it, plowing under and tilling in each one. A halfway measure involves strip composting, in which the plot is divided into strips, perhaps three feet wide, running the entire length of the plot. Alternate strips are used for green manuring, or for sheet composting, in which all collected organic matter is put onto these strips and tilled under periodically—perhaps once a month during the growing season. The final tilling is done in the fall, and the land is left in rough condition so that some heaving will take place during winter's freezes and thaws. The following year, the composted or green-manured strips are used for planting and the alternate strips are used for composting. In this way, half of the plot is planted each year, while the soil is gradually improved throughout.

A light sandy soil can also be improved for the support of larger earthworm populations, simply by the addition of all the organic matter that can possibly be found. Suggested materials include sewage sludge from treatment plants, wastes from canning factories, manure, compost, leaf mold from city dumping sites, sawdust from mills, spoiled hay, brewer's grains, and nearly any other organic material that is plentiful and free for the hauling. Green manuring and strip composting are also effective for the building up of such soils.

If basic soil flaws are attacked in this way, earthworm populations will increase at a much faster rate, and they will be able to do much more to bring about a soil of good health and productivity. It is a self-reflexive principle, where the improved soil helps the earthworms, and the earthworms in turn help the soil to improve still further. As in all selfreflexive actions, progress will seem slow, at first, but will increase geometrically, until at some point the soil seems to be improving so quickly that it is hard to believe. Earthworms are the key to improving basic flaws—but again, they can perform no unsupported miracles.

Is Implanting Necessary?

Can the farmer or gardener achieve better crop results by implanting earthworms? Is it worthwhile to buy earthworms for this purpose? Should earthworms be raised at home for implantation in garden and farm soils?

The answers to these questions are not easy. If they were, the debate over implanting would not have been going on for more than 30 years, as indeed it has.

Those opposed to earthworm implanting seem to fit into two groups: (1) those who feel that earthworms are not very beneficial in any case, and (2) those who recognize the value of earthworms but who feel that, if proper soil conditions are offered, the worms will appear, multiply, and be fruitful without our carrying them from place to place. To the first group belong many government agricultural scientists, including most who write government publications on gardening and farming. It is important, in reading the publications of this group, to recognize the attitude toward earthworms that has long pervaded the USDA. When the authors of such publications say that it is unnecessary to implant earthworms, they say it from a belief that earthworms are not important in any case.

The second group—those who value earthworms but feel that it is simply not productive to implant them—is typified by the writings of J. I. Rodale, who suggested that farmers devote their energies to increasing the organic matter content of the soil rather than raising and implanting earthworms, since adding earthworms to compost-rich soil would be like "taking coals to Newcastle."

Those who believe in the benefits of implanting earthworms cite the writings of George Sheffield Oliver and Thomas J. Barrett, both of whom recommended the practice.

Barrett said, "In the unhurried process of nature it might require from 40 to 50 years for native earthworms to spread slowly from a single breeding colony and fully impregnate an acre of ground." He believed, then, that the best approach is to incorporate quantities of organic materials into the soil, and also to impregnate it with earthworms in order to build the population as quickly as possible. Oliver was similar in his attitude towards this question, except that he believed it was better to inoculate the soil with egg capsules rather than adult earthworms, since newly hatched worms can better adapt to varying soil conditions, while adults may suffer shock of one kind or another (temperature, moisture, pH, and other differences).

There is one situation in which there is a clear case for the implantation of earthworms. That is in a soil of potential productivity, totally lacking productive species of earthworms. Even if copious amounts of manure and plant residues are added to a soil, earthworms will not multiply if there are no earthworms present. Such was the case in New Zealand, where the productivity of soils was turned around completely by the introduction of English earthworm species. This fascinating account was relayed by Sir Albert Howard, writing in the April 1946 issue of *Organic Gardening*:

> Mr. Ashmore farms 864 acres of hill country where the sward consists mostly of dry danthonia and browntop with much moss, and the surface is dry and firm. The

worm population is almost nil. But some eighteen to twenty years ago Mr. Ashmore noticed a green patch in his orchard which stood out in striking contrast to the typical dry herbage which surrounded it. Each year this patch increased and extended until it went beyond the orchard on to an adjoining hill paddock. Here an earlier growth was noticeable and the sward was greener and more vigorous. Strong fresh browntop with rye grass and clover appeared in place of the old harsh dry danthonia and browntop, and moss. A more intimate inspection revealed that the soil here was spongy and moist. Moreover it contained large numbers of a small light-coloured worm, whose casts covered the surface throughout the winter and spring.

The changes wrought by these lowly creatures and the speed with which they spread made a deep impression on Mr. Ashmore. He began to collect the worms and to introduce them into other portions of the land. Later he practised an "inoculation" of different areas by taking out small sods containing the worms and placing them in selected places on his farm. This work was most successful when carried out between June and October, when the worms were most active. At first the sods were selected simply from areas which showed numerous worm casts, but observations soon indicated a difference in the value of various species of earthworms. Certain kinds thrived and multiplied much more rapidly, and so by their quick increase and numerous casts were better fitted for the soil-conditioning work Mr. Ashmore expected of them. Two or three years were needed for the worms to become well established. Thereafter they began to work out in all directions.

For the past fifteen years a systematic planting of paddocks with sods containing worms has been practised. By 1945 about 700 acres had been so treated and the good work of Mr. Ashmore's vast unpaid labour force in arresting deterioration of the pastures and improving their stock-carrying capacity was evident. The number of breeding ewes has been doubled: the wool clip has increased from 10,000 lb. in 1930 to 14,560 lb. in 1943–44.

In 1930 officers of the New Zealand Department of Agriculture became interested in this pioneering method of land reclamation. A specimen of the species of earthworm considered by Mr. Ashmore to be most effective was identified by Sir W. B. Benham of Dunedin as *Allolobophora jasseyensis*, a species common in southeastern Europe, but little known in New Zealand. How it reached the southern hemisphere and the Raetihi farm is not known.

There is no doubt that, in areas where no active earthworms are present, implantation is highly beneficial, providing that the soil is potentially capable of supporting earthworms. But how about here in North America? It was not difficult to find zero populations here in the eighteenth century, or even well into the nineteenth. But today, when the continent's productive agricultural soils have nearly all been staked out and put into production, there are precious few areas where the native night crawler and the common field worm (our two most important species) are not already established. In these areas, the improvement of soil conditions will lead to increasing earthworm populations without implanting.

But perhaps it is not this simple, after all. Considering the increasing number of corporate megafarms, on which heavy chemical applications have killed off all earthworms, it would not be surprising today to find literally thousands of contiguous acres, in production, without a single earthworm. Any organic farmer seeking to reclaim such a field with organic methods might well see the wisdom of implanting earthworms as part of the reclamation process.

There are some areas of the United States in which earthworms are still not common soil inhabitants. Notable among these is Alaska. Even though the milder sections of the state are climatically suited for vegetable growing, the soil is evidently too shallow to offer worms winter protection. These areas, which feature shallow solum overlying gravel and bedrock, could be improved vastly with the aid of earthworms. Both field worms and night crawlers can survive freezing soils, so long as they do not freeze too quickly in the autumn.

Could the implantation of these earthworm species, supported by a heavy winter mulch, be the beginning of Alaska's soil improvement? So far, the only earthworm species recorded in Alaska is *Bismastos tenuis,* a small worm of little agricultural importance. It would be interesting to see Alaska's gardeners experiment with the implantation of *Allolobophora caliginosa* and *Lumbricus terrestris,* to see whether permanent populations can be established in that rugged land.

And what of the Pheretimas? These Indian peregrine earthworms have thus far made serious stands only in the southern and eastern border regions of the United States, although they have been reported as far north as Michigan. Although no significant research has been conducted to determine their potential contributions to croplands, it does appear that they might surpass even the night crawler and the field worm in soil-building activity. If studies prove the potential of which they are suspected, then implantation of this species would make a great deal of sense. Then, we would suddenly find ourselves in the position of nineteenth-century New Zealand, wanting a desirable species of earthworm that might not spread naturally for many, many years.

Commercial species.   Red worms, brandling worms, and African night crawlers—the three species that comprise essentially the entire commercial market—are not suitable for implanting in farm and garden soils, because these soils cannot support them. The first two mentioned can live only in bedding which is mostly organic in construction—which no farmlands or gardens are. The African night crawler cannot exist outdoors except in the tropics.

The important agricultural species—night crawlers, field worms, and the Pheretimas—are not often raised commercially because they breed too slowly and are too difficult to maintain in beds and pits. Therefore, the gardener or farmer who wants to buy earthworms to implant might have a difficult time in finding desirable species on the market.

Implanting from manure pits.   Implanting can perhaps best be done in combination with composting—which is treated fully in the next chapter—or by adopting some variation of George Sheffield Oliver's grandfather's annual routine. You will remember (chapter 2) that old George Sheffield maintained an enormous manure pit in the center of his barnyard which supported the growth and reproduction of millions of earthworms annually. Each spring, he cleaned out the pit, except for a thin bottom layer, and spread the manure on his fields, following quickly with a plow. In this way, he inoculated the fields each year with millions of worms and worm capsules, which he turned under the surface immediately, before the birds could eat them. We have no idea of what species these were. In all probability, however, they were either red worms or brandling worms—manure-living types. If so, then they could not be expected to flourish permanently in the fields. However, even these species will survive so long as the decaying manure lasts, and up until the soil freezes solidly—probably in December or January, in his part of Ohio. He would get a good deal of action from these manure-type worms, then, from early spring until after the autumn harvest, and he would start the process over again the following spring. When the worms died, their nutrient-rich bodies would add further benefits to the soil. In addition, the field species (night crawlers and field worms) would gain great benefits from the added manure, and would in time consume the bodies of the dead and decaying manure worms, turning them, too, into humus and liberating the nutrients they had concentrated in their bodies.

Many modern organic farmers can emulate Sheffield's routine, which is explained fully in Barrett's *Harnessing the Earthworm*. Gardeners, who perhaps have no enormous manure pit, can adapt the system as best they can, with available resources. If a good source of manure can be found (perhaps at a horse stable or cattle feeding lot), it can be trucked home every month or so, and can be augmented with plant wastes or some form of organic refuse from outside sources.

Implanting by machine.   In New Zealand, where the agricultural benefits of earthworms are well recognized, there are still many areas of fertile land which are devoid of beneficial earthworms. The common field worm, prized most highly, is not native to New Zealand, and is a slow migrator. It is not surprising, then, that New Zealand agricultural scientists have attempted to develop a mechanized earthworm implanter.

The success of such attempts was reported in the *New Zealand Journal of Agriculture* (January 1976). Drs. G. A. Martin and S. M. J. Stockdill, of the New Zealand Ministry of Agriculture and Fisheries, have developed a machine that cuts blocks of turf, containing earthworms, which can then be placed in earthworm-deficient fields. Following are some excerpts from the Martin and Stockdill article, describing the process in detail:

> Several methods of introducing earthworms to unpopulated areas have been tried in the past, but the one which has gained the greatest degree of acceptance involves cutting square spade turfs, 75 mm [nearly 3 inches] deep, from an earthworm-rich source area and laying these down on a ten-metre [approximately 33-foot] grid on the unpopulated area. This should be done when recent rain has drawn the worm population to the surface and when a dry or freezing-cold period after introduction is unlikely.
>
> Previously, turfs were hand-cut with a spade, but this job can now be done by the tractor-drawn machine. . . . It consists of a bladed wheel for transverse cuts, plough skeiths for longitudinal cuts, and a horizontal blade for lifting out. The machine may be mounted on the three-point linkage of a medium-size tractor, and operating speed can be up to 8 km/hr [5 miles per hour].
>
> Placing of turfs containing the earthworms involves applying 0.5 kg [1 pound, 2 ounces] of lime to an area of one square metre [1.2 square yards] at each point on a ten-metre [33-foot] grid and laying the turfs, grass side down, in the middle of the limed areas. The lime encourages initial development, and after a period of three to four years, when the worms have populated the area close to the blocks, a broadcast application of lime will

encourage their further spread in soils where calcium levels would otherwise be too low.

Large numbers of these machines are not required and, as commercial production is not warranted, we have made available a standard construction plan. Copies of this plan may be obtained by writing to Mr. G. A. Martin, New Zealand Agricultural Engineering Institute, Lincoln College, Canterbury, New Zealand.

Earthworms
in the Orchard

Earthworms find a special role in helping to maintain orchards in a peak of health. The important species here is *Lumbricus terrestris*, the native night crawler, which not only works soil that plows and tillers cannot go near (for fear of causing tree root damage), but also helps to reduce fungus-type diseases.

As old George Sheffield warned, "Never disturb the soil under a tree. The earthworm is the best plow for taking care of a tree." Barrett tells of a California citrus orchardist who increased yields by stopping all cultivation and encouraging earthworms to do the cultivating for him. He raked his leaves out towards the drip line of each tree, where they would remain moist and be more attractive to the earthworms. In a short time, the worms had eliminated plow sole (the hardpan layer which often forms as the plow blade slides through heavy soil) and made the soil porous and mellow. Trees which he once felt had reached their growth potential began to grow again, and to sport larger and healthier-looking leaves; in time, they more than doubled their former yields.

We cannot expect this kind of miracle in every orchard. But there is no doubt that earthworms do improve the soil in the area of roots, where plows and tillers cannot be used, and can lead to healthier trees and greater yields if they are encouraged to work to their full capacity.

<u>**Earthworms against fungus disease.**</u>   Fallen leaves and twigs are breeding grounds for the development of widespread fungus-type diseases. When these materials are encouraged to decompose quickly, however, the chances for disease are reduced proportionally. Earthworms—particularly the night crawler—are instrumental in this decomposition process, and thus they stand in the first ranks as a defense against fungus diseases.

When left undisturbed, earthworms will reduce virtually the entire season's leaf fall by the time the trees blossom the following spring. Many chemical sprays used in orchards, however, reduce earthworm populations, thus increasing the chances for the spread of disease unless continuing and greater amounts of chemicals are used. The organic orchardist, who wants to avoid such sprays while growing disease-free fruit, will encourage his earthworm population by the periodic incorporation of manure, by sodding the orchard, and by the strict avoidance of earthworm-killing chemicals such as benomyl and the copper fungicides. The toxic chemical sprays are doubly harmful to earthworms, since they tend to fall to the soil along the trees' drip lines, in precisely the area where earthworms are likely to be concentrated because of favorable moisture conditions.

Implanting Earthworms

Ordinarily, there will be no need to implant earthworms in orchards, since most will have at least some population of productive species which can be increased by organic practices. In the case of orchards undergoing transformation from chemical to organic methods, however, there might be a case for implanting. Assuming that sufficient time has elapsed to allow toxic chemicals to leach out of the soil, the area might still be devoid of earthworms because of past chemical practices. In these cases, it might take several years—perhaps many years—for beneficial species to reestablish themselves. The native night crawler is king of the orchard underworld, and it is a species that reproduces slowly. Therefore, in these cases, night crawlers can be introduced to the soil with great benefit. Once more, however—do not attempt to buy red worms or brandling worms for this purpose. They will not survive for long, and they are not effective in reducing orchard litter, in any case. The native night crawler—*Lumbricus terrestris*—is needed. There are a few commercial sources for this species, but be certain that you do not get the African night crawler (*Eudrilus eugeniae*) instead. It is not inconceivable that the latter may be sold, perhaps unknowingly, for the native night crawler. The African night crawler cannot survive in American croplands and orchards.

Collecting native night crawlers.   Probably the best way to obtain night crawlers for implantation is to collect them in the way that anglers do—on the lawn, during the evening. Choose a night when the temperature is in the 50s and the lawn grass is moist. There should have been some rain during the previous several days. If it is raining at the time, so much the better. Cover the end of a flashlight with red cellophane or plastic, get a bucket half-filled with moist soil, and walk quietly. When you see a night crawler extended from its burrow, grasp it gently but firmly near the soil surface. If it has anchored its tail in the burrow, do not attempt to pull it forcefully from the hole, for it will then likely break in two. Instead, wait for a few seconds, until the worm's rippling muscular movement flows back to the tail end, at which time the worm will momentarily loosen its grip in the burrow. At that instant, it can be pulled from the ground without trouble or injury to the worm. With any luck, you will be able to collect several hundred night crawlers in an evening.

If you cannot implant the worms immediately, then store them in a tub or some large container. Mix some compost or manure (so long as it is not hot) with soil, and fill the container to within six or eight inches of the top. Cover with a layer of lawn sod or wet burlap bags. Remember, however, that night crawlers—unlike red worms and brandling worms—might not like the storage container, and might well decide to leave without notice. Therefore, it is best not to plan on a long storage period. It will do no harm to cover the container with window screening, weighted down with boards, to keep the worms in and the hungry moles, shrews, and mice out. In this way, if the soil is kept moist but not soggy, and its temperature is not allowed to rise much above 60°F, the night crawlers can be kept for several weeks.

Implanting technique. When implanting, dig holes around the drip line of each tree, perhaps a foot in diameter and about as deep. Place six to ten worms in the bottom of each hole, on top of perhaps an inch of the soil/manure mix, and fill the rest of the hole with the mixture. Tamp it lightly and go on to the next hole. For an adult apple or peach tree, from six to eight such holes will provide the nucleus of a healthy and permanent earthworm colony.

The same method can be used for implanting earthworms in farm and garden soils, although in these cases field worms as well as night crawlers can be used, and also Pheretimas, if they are available. Since field worms do not come to the surface at night, as night crawlers do, they can be collected in digging up garden or field soils in more favorable locations. If this is done during the day, be especially careful to avoid exposing them to heat and light. Do not use a metal bucket, which can be overheated by the sun very quickly, but get a wooden fruit box or similar wooden container, and cover it with burlap or wet newspapers. Implant field worms the same day you dig them, or store them for no more than a few days. The same caution applies to Pheretimas. Field worms should be implanted no more than six inches deep.

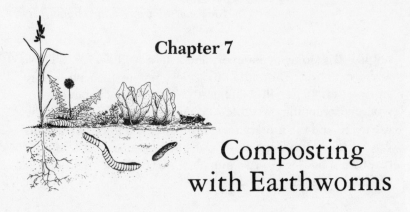

Chapter 7

Composting with Earthworms

Earthworms can produce more compost, in a shorter time, with less effort, than any other tool known to the gardener or farmer. Furthermore, the compost which is produced by earthworms is of the highest grade, containing not only greater amounts of mineral nutrients in soluble form, but also containing a high percentage of castings that help to form soil aggregates, leading to a permanent improvement in soil structure.

The affinity of earthworms for compost is not difficult to see. In fact, it is difficult to keep earthworms *away* from an outdoor compost heap. Most of us, knowing this through experience, see earthworms as a welcome natural addition to our composting efforts, and also as affirmation that we are doing things right. But how much better would our composting efforts be if we saw earthworms as *a necessary component of the composting process?* This will require a slight shift in the point of view we have long held—but an important one. We have learned, through experience or reading, that successful compost requires (1) undecayed or partially decayed organic matter, (2) living soil, or some other bacterial agent, (3) water, (4) air, and (5) proper construction. The earthworms which appear after these factors have been supplied aid the process, we know, but they have served mainly to assure us that we supplied the five major factors.

Now, we are going to see earthworms not as an adjunct to compost making, or as a welcome aftereffect, but as a *sixth ingredient*, just as important as the other five. The result—

See earthworms as the sixth essential ingredient in compost making, and make better compost in less time.

guaranteed—will be better compost, in less time, with less effort on our part. We will let the earthworms do much of the
work for us. In return, we will have to learn to build compost
with the earthworm's needs in mind, and discover which
species of worms are suitable for various composting situations.

We know, of course, that compost can be made without
air and without earthworms. Anaerobic methods necessarily
exclude earthworms, which cannot live in such conditions,
and anaerobic bacteria can produce fine compost. Fill a black
plastic leaf bag with manure and plant residues, tie it shut
tightly, and put it behind the toolshed. Come back for it in six

months and you will find a bag full of sweet-smelling compost, anaerobically produced. It will be good compost, but not as high in soluble mineral nutrients, and lacking the soil aggregate building material that earthworm casts offer. In this chapter, we will disregard anaerobic methods—not because they are without value, but because the earthworm has no place in them.

The Right Worm

Before going further, with practical suggestions and case histories, it is important to remind ourselves again what different species of earthworms can, and cannot, do. Keep well in mind the following points, and they will help you to evaluate all the information available to you, not only in this book but in anything you read or hear about earthworms, compost, and soil building. There is, unfortunately, a good bit of misinformation spread about in print, especially in some advertising literature. Keep these few points in mind, and you will not be misled:

1. Red worms (*Lumbricus rubellus*) and brandling worms (*Eisenia foetida*), the two species most commonly offered for sale by commercial breeders, cannot survive in ordinary garden and farm soils for very long. They will thrive and multiply in compost heaps and manure piles, but even there, many will be killed off or driven away when the organic matter begins to heat up through intense bacterial action.

2. Field worms (*Allolobophora caliginosa*) and night crawlers (*Lumbricus terrestris*) will attack compost heaps and manure piles from the bottom, but prefer to retreat into the soil after having done so. They will not thrive in active compost, and will be killed by the heating process more easily than red worms and brandling worms. Night crawlers, especially, which demand cool soil temperatures, will not inhabit compost and manure piles. If they are thrust into active compost, they will simply die and melt.

3. The data on the Pheretimas are still incomplete. However, it appears that their requirements are similar to those of the field worm and the night crawler. They are soil-living species.

The lesson is obvious. *Always be sure to get the right worm for the right purpose.*

Earthworms in the Indore Method

The Indore method of composting, developed by Sir Albert Howard during his long years of agricultural research in India, is the basic method from which all others spring. Whether organic materials are composted above ground or below, in bins, boxes, bags, or garbage cans, in strips, in sheets, in trenches, in 14 months or 14 days, indoors or outdoors, all methods are derived from Howard's Indore method.

In brief, a pit is dug in the earth, at least 4 feet wide, 6 feet long, and 12 to 18 inches deep. The soil is heaped aside for later addition to the pile. A one-foot layer of brush is laid in the bottom of the pit, to provide drainage. Next, a six-inch layer of green matter—usually weeds, leaves, and plant wastes—is placed on top of the brush, followed by a two-inch layer of manure, a sprinkling of topsoil, and some powdered limestone. These layers—green matter, manure, topsoil, and limestone—are repeated, until the heap reaches about five feet in height. After that, the heap is watered regularly so that it remains damp but not soggy. In a few days, it should begin to heat from bacterial action, and in four to six weeks the interior of the heap should have turned to rich humus, no longer hot. At this time, the heap is turned by forking, so that most of the outer materials are placed in the interior of the heap, also to undergo heating and quick decomposition. After another four to six weeks, the entire heap should have turned into finished compost, brown, crumbly, and ready for use.

Since Howard's time, many improvements have been made in the composting system. We have shortened the time required, by shredding materials. We have developed bins and boxes to retain heat and aid quicker bacterial action. Farmers have developed sheet composting, where materials are applied directly to the soil and allowed to decompose there before being turned under. Often, cover crops are grown for the sole purpose of being cut for sheet composting. Trenches can be dug to receive organic materials in the method known as strip composting, where part of the land is used for crop production while the other part is being

Earthworms are attracted naturally to a compost heap. Manure-type species will inhabit the entire heap—temperatures permitting—but field species will limit their activities to the lower ranges, from which they can quickly return to the soil.

improved. Even gardeners with very little land can maintain indoor compost bins, boxes, and cans where all kitchen refuse can be turned into rich compost for vegetables, flowers, and houseplants. In all these methods, ways can be found to make improvements through the intelligent use of the earthworm.

Earthworms will naturally be attracted to an Indore compost heap, attacking it from the bottom. The base layer of brush will soon become reduced in bulk and filled in with finer debris, and will quickly be infiltrated by field worms and night crawlers, which will turn and mix the earth with the organic matter. The worms, thus supported in this area, will reproduce quickly and increase their population many times over. If the heap is maintained for a year or more in one location, the earth below it will become incredibly rich, friable, and loaded with earthworms. With each rain, some of the nutrients from the compost will leach into the soil, carrying down for many feet and also spreading out somewhat from the actual dimensions of the heap. Earthworms will mix these nutrients into the soil and stabilize them for growing plants. There are several cases in which gardeners began compost heaps beneath sickly trees and soon saw a remarkable recovery of the trees. The combination of the composted nutrients, increased bacterial and fungal action, and the actions of earthworms were undoubtedly the prescription for the trees' recovery.

This enrichment of the soil beneath the heap is also a good reason for changing the location of the heap every year or so. Any prized plants grown there will flourish beyond reasonable expectations.

As the organic materials in the heap decompose to a point where they begin to lose their identity, i.e., as the character of the heap turns more to humus, the field worms will advance further up into the heap. Still, they will not flood the entire heap as the manure-living species will. The limiting factor here is the temperature, which is simply too high in any compost heap—even an inactive one, above ground—to remain attractive to field-living species. Night crawlers will gladly feed at the bottom of the heap, but will not advance even so far as field worms will, since they require even cooler temperatures. In autumn, and in early spring, they will go fairly far into a well-advanced heap—but when the heap has gone this far, it should be used for soil improvement, anyway.

Red worms and brandling worms can be used to great advantage in the Indore heap. They can greatly reduce the time required for composting, and they can completely eliminate turning the heap. This last point will draw a loud "hurrah!" from any gardener who has spent a few back-breaking hours in turning a large heap with a garden fork.

Red worms and brandlers are the kinds commonly advertised in garden and outdoor magazines for fish bait, under names such as red wigglers, hybrid reds, California reds, Georgia reds, banded reds, red-and-golds, etc. Any name that suggests a red-and-gold or banded worm is likely to be a brandling worm. The others are probably red worms. Either is eminently suitable for composting purposes.

Although manure-type worms can work at higher temperatures than field-living species, even they will be killed in the intense heat of a working compost heap, where temperatures can reach 150°F. Therefore, do not introduce them until the interior of the pile has cooled down to the outside temperature. Normally, in a well-constructed heap, this will be in about three weeks after the last materials have been added. At this point, dig holes in the heap, at various points, and drop 50 to 100 worms in each. About a thousand worms (a convenient number for ordering purposes) will serve to inoculate a four- by six-foot pile. If manure-type worms and their castings are already well supplied by the manure that went into the heap, then there will be no need to inoculate with worms from an outside source.

In a matter of days, the manure worms will be working away furiously, consuming the organic matter, leaving rich castings wherever they go, and—important—reproducing at a maximum rate. In a well-tended compost heap, a thousand reds or brandlers can increase to a million in one or two years.

This means, of course, that if you do things right, you will never have to buy worms again. In fact, you can easily recoup the original cost by selling excess worms to others. For northern gardeners, winter protection is vital, and we will take up that later in this chapter.

One more note: Manure-type worms will do much better in the Indore heap if larger quantities of manure are included in the mixture. Instead of the two-inch layer, traditionally recommended, add four inches, or even six. The more manure added, the happier the worms will be. If no manure at all is used, the worms will still have a good chance to thrive, although their progress will be slower. Home gardeners with no source of manure are urged to call on feeding lots, horse stables, or poultry farms—manure-producing institutions where the manure is perhaps not highly valued. Never bother to ask an organic farmer for large quantities of manure. He knows better.

No-heat Indore composting.   A variation of the Indore method makes it possible to produce compost quickly with very little heating, using earthworms. Construct the heap so that its dimensions are longer and wider than a normal heap, but only 12 to 18 inches high. Shred all materials as finely as possible. Then, introduce manure-type worms immediately. They will go to work right away, reducing materials, and the heap will never heat up greatly because its surface area is too large; the center of the heap is too close to the cooling effects of the outside air. This method is closer to nature's own than is the traditional Indore heap, and it works well. The major disadvantages are that it takes up more ground surface area, and the shredding of materials takes time and requires fossil energy to operate a gasoline-powered shredder or rotary mower. The great advantage is that, if the composting is done right in the garden, the finished compost may easily be spread out and plowed or tilled right into the soil, with no hauling required.

Maintaining the earthworm population.   When removing finished compost for use on garden plots or farm fields, be certain to save a good number of earthworms for future composting operations. There are several ways to do this. The easiest is to remove only half the heap at a time, spreading out the remainder to serve as the base for the new heap. If your manure worm population is not as great as you wish it to be, you can save even more by "scalping" the heap in several steps. As we know, earthworms are repelled by light; if exposed, they will quickly drive down beneath the surface. Remove finished compost from the outer parts of the heap, to a depth where worms are exposed. Wait for about 30 minutes, then take another scalping. Continue in this manner until you have removed as much compost as you want. The earthworms will have been driven into a compact area at the bottom of the heap, in the center. At this point, you may spread out the remaining compost, containing the earthworms, and cover it immediately with new manure and green matter. If, as so often is the case, the outer scalp of the heap has not composted fully (since it is the newest material), then set aside this first scalp and put it back after you have finished the operation. It will be the first material to be attacked in the new heap.

Bins and Pits

An improvement on the Indore method, for gardeners and small-scale farmers, utilizes bins and pits of various kinds. The major advantages of such containers are that they concentrate organic material in a smaller area (since un-contained piles tend to slope on all sides), protect the sides of the heap from outside air, and result in faster heating and quicker compost. In addition, the bins can offer esthetic advantages for backyard gardens, and by the use of removable or hinged lids can keep out insects, dogs, cats, mice, rats, and other animals which tend to dig into the heap for fresh kitchen scraps. A heavy-but-coarse screen on the bottom of the pit

The removable lid on this pit will keep out predators and excess rainfall.
Note the burlap insulation built into the lid.

will keep out moles while allowing the free passage of soil-dwelling earthworms. Manure-type worms will not try to flee the pits into lower soil depths.

Pits offer the added advantage of winter protection for manure-type worms, vitally important in the northern regions of the country. Usually, however, the concepts of bins and pits are combined. The earth is dug out to a depth of 16 to 24 inches, even more in far-north areas, and boards are used to extend the pit into an above-ground bin.

This personal experience of James S. Downs of Jasper, Alabama, related in the July 1968 issue of *Organic Gardening and Farming*, explains one family's use of a simple compost bin, using earthworms:

> My most important use of earthworms is in my compost bins. Every year I get from one to two tons of the richest black soil known to man, starting with nothing but kitchen garbage, leftover meat scraps, coffee grounds, leaves, weeds, sweepings. All this goes into the compost bin for worm food, as do all farm wastes, cow manure, and decayed corn husks. In turn—through the earthworms' work—this makes a perfect topsoil, without a long wait.
>
> My compost bin is about 5 x 8 feet, with movable boards on each side so I can add to it as the compost pile gets higher. There is also enough paper and pasteboard to hold moisture, so I don't need to water except occasionally. As the refuse is eaten by the earthworms, it is enriched by their castings and their endless tunneling.
>
> Usually in the spring each year I take from 8 to 10 inches off the top, as this contains most of the English red wiggler worms and worm eggs. In this is also most of the refuse that has not yet decomposed. After I remove finished compost to start my garden, what I've taken off is put back on the pile. This way, there's no turning or moving the compost except from the bin to the garden.
>
> The ready compost is used in hotbeds and to start off seedlings in spring, as well as to spread in vegetable rows in our family garden, which on an acre and a half feeds my wife and me and our seven children. This compost still has plenty of worms and worm eggs

that keep right on working for me—especially in my "continuous-composting" garden.

From compost making to earthworm raising.   Soon after a gardener builds an earthworm pit, stocks it with red worms or brandling worms, and sees the success of his operation, he sees the possibility of selling off excess worms to anglers or other gardeners. Then there is the question of whether he is about the business of using earthworms to make compost, or *in* the business of raising earthworms, with compost as a by-product. The question need not bother many of us, since one activity often runs naturally into the other. Commercial earthworm raising is covered in chapter 8 of this book, and it involves far more than the multiplication of earthworm populations through compost making. But it is difficult to separate the two, after pits and bins are constructed, as evidenced by the following case history, which was written by A. B. Kennerly and appeared originally in the March 1965 issue of *Organic Gardening and Farming:*

Want plenty of good soil for your organic garden plus a good supply of fishing bait whenever you need it?

Then try growing your own earthworms. You can start in a small way with a couple of tubs and build up to a large system of pits like those run by M. S. Pugh of Rockdale, Texas, who makes as much as $1,500 in a year from just one of his six 4- by 18-foot earthworm pits.

For a starter, try two tubs each two feet wide and 12 to 15 inches deep. This way you use the worms from one tub, leaving the other to build up undisturbed. Each tub should produce 3,000 to 5,000 worms a year—enough to supply fertilizer for your favorite plants.

Your first attempt in earthworm culture doesn't have to take a lot of time, work, and money. You can start out with ordinary 4- by 1-foot boxes, setting them over holes 18 inches deep and slightly smaller than the boxes which sit firmly on the ground covering the hole.

The hole is filled with kitchen garbage and refuse, added in layers, and alternating with ground manure and green matter. The pit should be covered with a burlap bag after each operation, wetted down and covered with a board to avoid odors and pest problems.

It is good practice to work with two box-pit combinations, filling the first pit all the way to the top and allowing it to decompose for five to six weeks while the second pit is filled. This system is practically guaranteed to give you a steady supply of rich, soil-replenishing compost, plus literally thousands of earthworms for general garden use.

If you want plenty of soil-conditioning material, build pits in a rectangular shape. Make them of concrete, and the compost in them stays warmer in winter and cooler in summer. Or you can use treated lumber which withstands moisture. Put coarse gravel in the bottom for drainage, and extend the top of the walls above ground to keep water from draining into the pits.

Compost for the pit is placed about 15 inches deep to start. Pugh prepares the compost by soaking peat moss and mixing it with ground peanut hulls or ground corncobs, 2/3 peat moss and 1/3 hulls or cobs. He mixes the compost well and turns it once a week, then he adds three to four inches of compost every couple of weeks or less often if the worms do not consume it.

By itself, the compost would make a fine soil conditioner for any garden. But, in addition, the following materials are fed into the Pugh pits as earthworm fertilizer.

Using a coffee can to measure the feed that goes into his electric grinder, he starts off with one can of ground peanut hulls which carry little plant food but add organic matter to the feeding ration. Next he adds two cans of corn meal for carbohydrates and two cans of alfalfa meal for protein, plus two more cans of cottonseed meal. Finally, three cans of ground corncobs are added for their moisture-holding qualities.

Each night Pugh wets down the top of the pit and, since worms normally come to the surface at night to feed, he tops off the compost with the amount of feed they consume in 24 hours. He warns against over-wetting the compost because it can make the feed sour and cause trouble.

Fifty to 100 worms are sufficient to give you a start for a small bed. The Texas A.&M. specialists recommend feeding the worms such organic material as leaves of celery, cabbage, lettuce, turnips, and other vegetables which are readily taken as food when small amounts are worked into the top of the compost. Another good ration is composed of one part cottonseed meal, and two parts alfalfa meal. Laying mash, which was formerly used, had to be eliminated when manufacturers began using chemicals for worm controls in poultry.

Pugh cleans out his beds once each year and fills them with new compost. Late fall is a good time since this marks the end of summer fishing season, before the worms bed down for the winter. The compost still has a few worms remaining in it to give a new start of worms in the garden.

As you can see, Mr. Pugh clearly crossed the line from compost building into earthworm raising. However, the gardener who is more interested in compost than the earthworm business can learn much from commercial operations such as his, especially when it comes to building and maintaining outdoor pits and bins. For the gardener who seeks to build a compost/earthworm pit for the first time, however, the following instructions should help:

1. Stake off an area three to four feet wide and as long as you wish the pit to be.

2. Excavate the earth from this area to a depth of 16 to 24 inches. (If you live where winter temperatures get to -10°F or colder, make it 24 inches.) Pile the excavated soil to one side, in as compact a heap as possible, for later addition to the pit.

3. Drive two-by-four stakes into the four corners of the pit, if you will be using board construction. (Scrap lumber from old buildings is fine.)

4. Nail boards all around the pit, except for one end which you will keep open in order to work with the material. Loose boards can be held in this area, using further stakes to support them. Add boards on top of each other, leaving about a quarter-inch between each for aeration. Add boards only as

the pile of materials requires them for support. The boards above ground need never be higher than 16 inches above the ground surface; if the pit is 16 inches deep, this will mean a total of 32 inches of vertical board area. (Remember that these earthworms will not work more than six to eight inches below the surface of the heap, no matter how high it is built.)

5. If you elect to use concrete blocks instead of wood, excavate the soil to a depth of one or two blocks, and add no more than two layers of blocks above the ground. At this low height, the blocks can be set in loosely, without mortar. Allow a little space between them for aeration.

Many gardeners find it helpful to divide the pit into two sections, one for new compost and the other for old. As finished compost is removed from one section, the earthworms are transferred into the newer heap on the other side, and a new heap is begun in the just-emptied side. In this way, there is always a ready supply of compost for garden use, and the earthworms are maintained constantly. An ideal setup would comprise two double pits.

Some gardeners outfit their bins with board lids, hinged on one side so that they swing up and open easily. This device keeps out the sun and protects the surface of the heap from excessive heat during the summer, enabling the worms to work nearer to the surface where new material is deposited. It also keeps out predators during the night and conserves moisture during hot and dry periods. When a lid is used, you must keep a constant check on moisture. Add water with bucket or hose as necessary, or—better—open the lid during rainfalls, if moisture is needed. Be certain, however, not to make the lids so tight fitting that they exclude air.

In addition, some bottom protection will be helpful, especially in keeping out moles, which will gladly come up from below to destroy thousands of earthworms in a single evening's feast. A layer of quarter-inch rustproof wire mesh, affixed securely to the bottom of the pit, will solve the mole problem.

Winter protection in the North. In the South, where winter temperatures rarely go below 20°F, red worms and brandling worms can be maintained easily in outdoor pits with a minimum of protection. A few layers of burlap bags and

Winter earthworm composting requires special measures. This open bin will not offer adequate protection for worms past the first light snows of winter.

a mound of straw piled over the beds will offer all the insulation needed, even if they are occasionally covered with snow. In places like Minnesota, Montana, and Vermont, however, where winter temperatures routinely dip to 20 below zero, special protection is a must.

The best winter-protection system I have seen is explained fully in a 46-page booklet, *Let an Earthworm Be Your Garbage Man*, prepared by Home, Farm & Garden Research Associates. It is essential reading for any northern gardener who decides to construct earthworm pits.

Briefly, the booklet suggests, for summer composting, lining an eight-inch-deep pit (which is shallower than commonly recommended) with concrete blocks. Since the blocks are eight inches high, they will come up to the ground surface. Another layer of blocks is placed on top of these. Sixteen such blocks will form a pit 4 feet square and 16 inches deep, enough to hold all the garbage from a small household.

The bottom of the pit is lined with garbage and covered with two or three inches of soil, then with burlap bags. Water is added, if needed. A covering of one- by two-inch mesh "turkey wire" is placed on top of the open pit, weighted down with four concrete blocks to exclude predators. Layers of garbage and soil (the soil which was dug to excavate the pit) are added until the pit is full. In three months of warm weather, the compost in this pit should be finished.

In winter, the experimenters dug the pit twice as deeply—16 inches—and lined the earthen walls with two layers of concrete blocks below ground, with a third layer above ground. The removed soil was piled at the edge of the pit and covered thickly with straw, in order to insulate it and keep it from freezing during the long and cold winter. Cans of kitchen refuse were kept tightly covered in some protected area, where they were not likely to freeze solid. If they do freeze, they can be brought indoors just long enough for the mass to become loosened from the sides. When the can is full, it is carted to the pit. The burlap is removed, the garbage goes in, a layer of soil is added, the burlap goes back on, and back goes the turkey wire and holding blocks. (If any freezing problems occur, remember that straw or spoiled hay is the best insulator, although leaves can be used, also, if they are readily available.)

The Vermont researchers say that, even in 20-below weather, the earthworms keep working and the composting process continues all winter long, albeit more slowly than in summer. By spring, the kitchen refuse added the previous autumn is ready for use in the garden.

Indoor Composting in the Winter

Most people who raise earthworms indoors do so in order to produce earthworms for sale. Especially where ice fishing is popular, earthworms bring a premium price during the winter, when they cannot be collected in the garden. The indoor raising of earthworms for profit will be covered in the next chapter. Here, we will concentrate on using earthworms, indoors, to dispose of family garbage.

Nothing makes more sense than investing in a thousand manure-type worms in order to handle a family's garbage. The alternative is to grind the food scraps in the sink disposal and flush them down the drain. From there, they will be collected in sewage treatment tanks and probably used as landfill. In less sophisticated systems, they might well end up as pollutants in water systems. In few cases will this valuable organic matter be returned to the land. How much better, then, to collect all the family garbage, including newspapers and even dust from the vacuum cleaner bag, let earthworms turn it into rich, crumbly humus, and return it to your own land.

There have been a few family earthworm composting units placed on the market in recent years, including an effective "Ecology Box" by North American Bait Farms of California. But we will begin with a simple homemade system that is both easy and inexpensive. It can be used anywhere, winter or summer, and it can be expanded into as large an operation as you wish.

It is best to begin on a modest scale. Construct a wooden box two feet wide, two feet long, and one foot deep. Or, get a vegetable lug box from your local supermarket and, if it has large spaces between the boards, tack in plastic screening to hold in the earthworm bedding. If you construct your own box, provide for drainage and aeration by drilling a half-dozen $1/8$-inch holes in the bottom, and some more around the sides. A box two feet square, and one foot deep, will accommodate a thousand adult worms (or "breeders," as they are called in the trade).

Order a thousand red worms or brandling worms. You can specify breeders, but a pound of pit-run worms, which are less expensive, will do the job as well. Meanwhile, gather up the materials you will need to greet their arrival: about a bucketful of good garden loam, another of manure, a third of peat moss, and some clean pebbles or small rocks.

Inspect the worms as soon as they arrive. If all or many of them are dead, notify the seller, explain the circumstances, and ask for them to be replaced. Earthworm raisers are almost invariably good about such things. If the worms seem alive and healthy, however, go ahead and prepare the bedding, as follows:

Wet down the peat thoroughly. If the soil and/or manure are dried out, moisten these materials, too. Mix together equal parts of all three, adding some dried grass clippings, hay, or crumbled leaves, if you wish. (Don't use oak or other very acid leaves.) Soak this mixture overnight. Don't worry about the worms; they can stay in their shipping container for a week or more, without harm.

The next day, squeeze out the excess water and fluff up the material (which we will now call bedding). Line the bottom of the earthworm box with a single layer of pebbles or rocks, to allow for quick drainage. Then, place four inches of the bedding material rather loosely on top of the pebbles, and wait for a day to see if any heating takes place. This is important, because if initial bacterial action forces the bedding temperature much above 100°F, all the worms will be killed. Any heating that does occur in a small area such as this, however, will subside within 48 hours—and in the meantime, your worms will be content to remain in their shipping container. Try to keep the container's temperature between 50° and 70°F—certainly not above 85° or below 40°.

When you are satisfied that the bedding will present no serious heating problems, add the worms, including the bedding that they were shipped in, to the box. Simply push aside the bedding material, place the worms in the center, and cover them loosely. Place a burlap bag over the top of the bedding and moisten it with a houseplant sprayer or sprinkling can. Several layers of wet newspapers can also be used, or layers of cheesecloth—anything that will conserve the moisture without excluding the air.

Keep the bedding moist but never soggy. If the container begins to drip from the bottom, as it probably will, arrange some sort of container under the box to catch the drippings. A plastic dishpan is good for this purpose, or an old washtub. Use the drippings to water your houseplants.

Start out by feeding the earthworms cautiously. If you give them more than they will eat in a 24-hour period, the garbage will sour, creating odors and attracting flies, or will heat up, killing the worms. Begin with soft foods that the worms can easily handle. The chances are that they have been "fattened up" before being sent to you (especially if you ordered breeders) and they might take a little time to adjust to the change in diet. Begin with soft foods, such as cooked vegetables, leftover cereal (including the milk), vegetable soup, lettuce, bread scraps, soft leaves of vegetables, even ice cream. A little cornmeal will be appreciated, and coffee grounds can be added at any time. Do not use onions, garlic or other strongly flavored foods.

Place the food on top of the bedding and tamp it gently into the bedding. But do not bury it, or it will begin to heat up.

After a week or two, your earthworms should have adjusted to their new home and should be on a regular feeding schedule. You can help them along, and build better compost, if you add a thin layer of partially decayed manure from time to time (being sure that it is past the heating stage, but not completely composted).

Every two weeks, the bedding in the box should be turned and aerated. Reduce the amount of food after such turnings, since the worms will not come to the surface as readily for a day or two after having been disturbed.

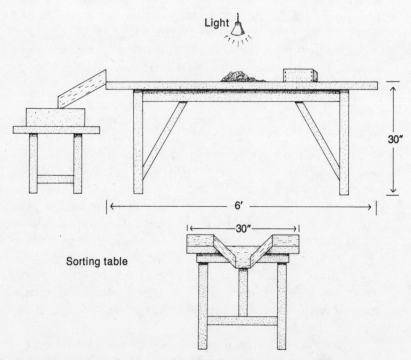

Figure 16 A sorting table is useful for handling materials from box cultures.

After a month, you can add another two inches of bedding material, to handle the increased worm population, and after three months it will be time to start another box, since the first will likely be filled.

When you are ready to divide the box, prepare a second box as you did the first. Then arrange a good-sized table under a 100-watt hanging light, so that the light comes within two feet of the table surface. Lay a plastic sheet on the table. Dump the worms and bedding on the plastic, and heap them into a mound that peaks to within a foot of the light bulb. Pick off the pebbles and return them to the first box. (By this time, you might wonder if the pebble layer is necessary. The answer is that, although it is a good idea, it is not absolutely necessary unless drainage or souring problems are encountered.)

Any worms that have been exposed in turning the box will quickly react to the light by digging towards the center of the mound. This will allow you to scrape much of the bedding (which is now casting-rich compost) into a bucket, to be used for outdoor gardening or houseplant purposes. Wait another 10 minutes for the worms to retreat again from the light, then scrape away another layer of compost. After several such scrapings, all the worms will have driven themselves into a compact ball at the bottom of the mound, where they can easily be divided and put back into fresh bedding in the two boxes. You then proceed as before, perhaps correcting some mistakes you made the first time around.

Of course, one box of earthworms is not going to take care of all your family's garbage, nor is it going to supply great quantities of compost. The first box is a starter, an experiment with which you can hone your techniques. After the third month, you will have started two boxes; after the sixth month, four boxes; after the ninth month, eight boxes; until—one year from your original experiment—you can start sixteen boxes, with confidence that you know what you are doing.

Boxes can be stacked in tiers, by affixing half-inch-square wood strips, 14 inches high, into the four corners of each box.

The strips will support the box on top of it, giving a two-inch space between boxes. Four such boxes, or even six, can form such a tier, thus conserving floor space. They can be watered easily with a small houseplant hose that attaches to the faucet, or with a portable insecticide sprayer that operates with air pressure. The drippings from all but the bottom box will fall into the box beneath it.

How many boxes of worms will you need to handle all your kitchen refuse? A rule of thumb is that one pound of earthworms will eat one pound of garbage in one day, and will produce one pound of compost. You might find that your earthworms eat more, or less, but soon you can make your own calculations based on personal experience, and you can stop expanding the operation when you have enough boxes to handle all the garbage your family produces. Excess worms can be turned into the outdoor compost heap or sold to local anglers.

Earthworm Composting on the Farm

In the 1940s, USDA scientists Henry Hopp and Clarence Slater undertook a notable experiment. They found some very poor clay subsoil, containing no earthworms and virtually no organic matter, and, by adding lime, fertilizers, and manure, grew a modest stand of barley, bluegrass, and lespedeze on two separate plots. On one, they left the growth untouched, while on the other they cut the top growth to form a mulch, and they added some earthworms to the soil.

By the following June, the plot containing earthworms was covered with a rich stand of all three crops, while the section without worms supported almost nothing but weeds. The total vegetation in the wormed plot was *five times* that of the wormless one. The plot with worms also had far better water-absorption and water-holding capacity, and twice as many soil aggregates—all the result of earthworm action.

The lesson learned here is one of which every organic farmer should be keenly aware. No soil should be left unprotected over winter. Large-scale mulching and sheet composting will protect earthworm populations, and the earthworms will improve the soil structure and crop-growing capacity.

A prime case history of sheet composting on heavy clay Texas soil is given in the following report, taken from the April–May 1954 issue of *Crops and Soils* magazine. It was contributed by R. M. Smith and D. O. Thompson of the Temple, Texas Agricultural Experiment Station.

If you live where rainfall is higher than the 30- to 40-inch belt of Texas, you might have thought that earthworms were of no importance this close to the border of the sub-humid West. But when it rains in the Blackland and westward into the Grand Prairie, the earthworms are ready to work.

Five to eight tons of fresh worm casts per acre have been picked up from the soil surface after one good rain on the Texas station. And as much as 25 percent of the plow layer of soil in good condition has been separated out by hand as recognizable worm casts. This amounts to half a million pounds per acre and is what the researchers call big workings in any part of the country.

Heavy grazing puddles this clay soil when it is wet and destroys worms. Overgrazing at any moisture content damages soil structure and prevents worm benefits. A short rest from grazing often brings back the worms in large numbers.

Where a two-foot layer of soil profile was taken off 20 years ago, and the soil seeded to native grass, the worms are busy building new soil. The greatest activity that we have seen is in ungrazed native grassland on the Temple Station. Conditions are evidently ideal for dense populations, and the heavy grass protects all the casts that are formed.

Many worms coil up and rest in the subsoil. They start working when moisture and other conditions are right.

In cotton land, we have found places where they

have coiled and rested at depths of four to five feet. And the worms, themselves, go even deeper than that into the soft marl that lies under many Blackland soils.

Where hard chalk or limestone is found at shallow depths in the Grand Prairie, they coil in the soil above this rock and seem to survive long periods of drought. They are ready to work fast when rains come.

Wherever land is covered with dead crop residues, worm casts soon appear. A part of the reason is the protection that the mulch gives to fresh casts. They are not beaten to fine pieces by rains. The mulch also provides needed food and protects the worms from sun and from being squeezed to death by farm machinery or animal hoofs.

Year after year, much of the Blackland grows row crops, one after another. This is hard on worms.

One of the things that hurts them most is tractor wheels. They just can't stand the strain, especially when the soil is wet. Usually the only worms found in such land are small, like thread or wire. It's a case of the good dying young.

But even so, a few small worms can be found. Short rests from the wheels of machinery let the young grow and reproduce.

Where heavy machinery has never been used, in small runoff plots, the surface soil is riddled with holes and rich in casts, even where corn has been grown every season for 20 years. There is 10 percent or more of quick-draining soil pore space in these plots. Worm action accounts for much of this space, which assures air for crop roots.

Even so, there appear to be more worms where crop rotations include small grain or grass and sweet clover. Going into the second winter with biennial sweet clover on the ground, in 1952, five tons of casts per acre soon appeared. The heavy soil could thus take in lots of water that might have been wasted as runoff, if it had not been for worm openings into the storage rooms of the subsoil.

The size of worm casts varies, but not so much as the size of worms. Most casts are between $1/25$ and $1/10$ of an inch in diameter. When mixed with a small amount of finer particles, this size is excellent for seedbeds. It is also big enough to resist being washed away by sheet erosion.

Pore spaces among aggregates of this size are about one-fourth as big as the unit soil particles. This is enough space for water intake at high rates of several inches per hour. We are not likely to get runoff because of dense soil surface until worm casts have been destroyed.

Worm casts, as well as other soil aggregates, unfortunately, are often destroyed by rain, machinery, or trampling. Tests with Blackland soil have failed to show any greater water-stability for worm casts than for ordinary particles. The type of raw organic matter that the worms eat may influence the stability of the casts.

In each of six comparisons, earthworm casts contained more organic matter than the whole surface soil in which they were found. The average difference was 37 percent of that in the whole soil. The actual organic matter contents were 3.33 percent for the worm casts and 2.43 percent for the whole soil.

Of course, earthworms can't create organic matter. They concentrate it by eating and digesting various crop residues, and by inoculating it with microorganisms. The process is one that may well increase the availability of plant nutrients and favor productivity.

When residues are left at surface by subtillage methods, earthworms appear to thrive. Tractor wheels do less damage when the load is spread by surface straw, stalks, or stubble. These organic materials also feed the worms, and help protect their workings from sun and rain.

We don't know how far trash mulch and worms can go in maintaining or improving the condition of our heavy clay soils, but present results look promising for the future.

Earthworms are here. They penetrate tight soils. They make excellent aggregates. They digest and concentrate organic residues and plant foods. These are things that we are continually trying to do by other means.

Is it possible that we are failing to use one of our best soil-building tools, simply because we are looking for something that has a new name or that comes from far away?

The lessons learned by the researchers Smith and Thompson, more than 20 years ago, in Texas, are vitally important today for farmers in every part of the country, working with all kinds of soil. For a productive soil, rich with hard-working earthworms, protect the land and the worms, particularly in the autumn before the first hard freezes come. The regular use of sheet composting and mulching in a well-considered soil management program will go far in building up a permanently high earthworm population and a more productive soil.

Earthworms and Rabbits

Many rabbit raisers have found a natural ally in earthworms, which can both simplify their operation and provide an extra source of income and high-grade compost.

The idea is to place earthworm bins below the rabbit hutches, so that the rabbit manure and urine, along with wasted food, are dropped automatically into the earthworm pits. The rabbit wastes are all the earthworms need to thrive and multiply, and, in addition, the system eliminates problems of odor, flies, and cleanup of the hutches. The rabbit raiser, further, has a new by-product to sell, in the form of earthworms and earthworm castings, thus increasing the profit of his total operation.

The earthworm pits should be constructed just as any outdoor pits are, from either scrap lumber or concrete blocks. They should be placed directly under the hutches and should be a few inches longer and wider than the hutches in order to catch all droppings.

Care of the earthworm pits is the same as for ordinary pits, except that no food need be added. Keep an eye on the pH of the bedding material, and on its moisture content. If too much manure is dropped, the excess may be taken off and added to a supplementary outdoor earthworm pit.

Excess worms may also be added to poultry litter, where they will both help to break down the litter into more compost and serve as a high-protein supplementary food for the birds. As with using earthworms under rabbit hutches, worms in the henhouse will help to reduce odor and fly problems.

Earthworms and rabbits can be raised together with maximum efficiency. Here, Gretchen Swarthwood gathers whole handfuls of earthworms from under her rabbit cages.

Chapter 8

The Business of Raising Earthworms

The raising and selling of earthworms is a growing industry with a potentially bright future. *Newsweek* magazine (21 June 1976) has estimated that upwards of 90,000 Americans are raising and selling earthworms, and that annual sales amount to $50 million. Further, some efforts are now underway to encourage the use of earthworms in various environment-related projects, from the reclamation of strip mines to the composting of municipal refuse. For now, however, the small-scale grower can hope to sell 90 percent of his product to only four markets: (1) anglers (or bait shops which sell worms to anglers); (2) other people who raise earthworms, or who want to begin raising them; (3) organic gardeners, for composting purposes; and (4) a distributor, who will usually contract for the worms before they are raised. We will survey all these markets, and others, in this chapter.

Where the Money Is

There are a few fortunes being made today in the earthworm business. But these fortunes are being made not by the farmer or backyard grower who sets up a few bins, perhaps relying on the worms' rapid mating habits to produce geometric future profits; but by the *marketers and distributors* of earthworms. Some of the people who have made the most money in earthworms, in fact, no longer raise worms at all, but ply the market by buying and selling earthworms and earthworm contracts.

Earthworm raising is a healthful and profitable business in which the entire family can take part. But don't look this way for quick riches.

Generally, these distributors buy worms from small-scale growers and sell them to new small-scale growers at more than twice their buying price. There is also said to be a market for earthworms in Japan, where they are reportedly used to fatten livestock for slaughter. It is uncertain how large the Japanese market is. What is certain, however, is that marketers or distributors rely heavily on selling worms to first-time growers, offering them also written instructions, personal help along the way in solving problems, and a contract to buy back all the worms that the contract grower manages to raise. There is nothing illegal in this (unless the distributor reneges on his contract), nor is it in any way unethical. The practice is a common one in agribusiness, in the growing and marketing of many crops. The distributor is simply contracting to buy futures, although part of that contract involves the grower's investment in the distributor's "starter package." Still, the novice earthworm raiser should be aware of the structure of the industry, before he invests money and time in what might prove to be a disappointing venture.

Talk to any earthworm distributor, and you will receive a glowing report, full of the promise of easy profits. Here are excerpts from some of the literature of various distributors, sent to people who have expressed an interest in entering the earthworm-raising business:

> Meet Mr. Moneymaker! The earthworm is just about the best natural friend we have in this current trend of reclamation.
>
> The bait industry in the United States is approaching gross sales of one billion dollars per year. . . . The ever-expanding market for earthworms is literally growing daily. Use of the earthworm for today's and the future's ecology is almost limitless. . . . As the demand grows in leaps and bounds, the lack of adequate supply reaches crisis proportions. We have expanded our farm and still cannot meet our quotas, so we ask you to help by becoming one of our contract growers.
>
> Our complete growing instructions should enable you to have a successful and profitable farm. The time in-

volved would be similar to raising a garden.

It's easy to raise earthworms—they require no expensive equipment, and take little space. Earthworms flourish on all kinds of waste organic material such as animal manures, or plant sources. There is no noise, no odor, no disease; raise them anywhere—they make you money day and night.

A man or woman working alone can make a good living raising earthworms. Many families, working together, have become successful in their own business. It is easy, light, interesting work, ideally suited for both men and women—and there is no limit on earnings.

According to the literature, the raising of earthworms is easy and profitable, the demand for worms far exceeds the supply, and the future of the industry is little short of fantastic.

Talk to the earthworm grower, however, and you will get a different picture. In preparing for the writing of this book, I surveyed several hundred earthworm raisers, large and small. Following are some typical comments I received which differ from those of the distributor/promoters:

> We are going to need better prices in the future because of inflation. Yes, inflation has hit the worm industry, too.
>
> There are many untrue "facts" in books and misleading figures. Finding a market is a big problem.
>
> It's too much work. Too many problems in relation to income.
>
> We definitely have mixed emotions about the business. We entered the business with "eyes wide open" after some degree of research (visiting established farms, reading, asking questions, etc.). Based upon our initial 13–14 months experience, we are of the opinion that the business will never return sufficient profit to justify our staying in it. Because of the intense competition in the industry, the price one gets for his product is totally inadequate in view of the cost of feed, labor, containers, advertising, postage, etc. The little producer, in our opinion, *will not survive!*
>
> Unfortunately, the worm business is by nature prey to "fast buck" operators who, as with other small farm

enterprises, overload the market and establish poor trust among growers and potential customers. This, in turn, discourages many of us who through our experience as worm growers and farmers realize there is a good use for the worm as a recycling agent and energy transformer—i.e., waste to food.

Major keys to the earthworm business are the same as to any other business. Hard work is necessary, and, of course, much physical work is often required in this business. Sound management is often learned the hard way—as it was with us. Too many people are in the worm business now, everybody seems to be jumping in, but they don't know the first thing about keeping a worm alive.

I really feel the only way worm growers are going to get the price for their worms is if they join together and make a set price for their worms. Right now we are getting $2.00 a pound for our worms wholesale which I feel is a small price for the time and effort you put out to give your customers top-grade worms.

The keys to success in the earthworm business are hard work, honesty, and willingness to spend money. The major problem is slow sales caused by the exploitation of the worm business by phony contract sellers.

The major key to success in the earthworm business? WORK! We didn't calculate demand properly. Need customers.

There is obviously a disparity between growers and distributors in viewing the earthworm business. The distributor implies that the work is easy, while the grower reports long hours of hard physical labor. The distributor says that the demand for earthworms is "of crisis proportions," that supply is lagging far behind demand, while the grower often reports difficulty in finding a sufficient market for his crop. The distributor, while not promising vast riches, does imply that unlimited profits can be made, simply because earthworms reproduce geometrically, while the grower often reports that, even when working long hours, he still cannot make a decent profit—and he cannot afford to hire help to expand his operation, at current wholesale prices.

Unfortunately, few first-time growers have had a chance to hear the views of disenchanted growers. Their information, too often, comes almost exclusively from the distributor who is attempting to sell a starter package. Typically, this package includes 100,000 worms (enough to stock a 3-foot by 8-foot by 12-inch-deep pit), some compost for bedding, and a contract promising to buy back all worms raised. Literature is included, and often a promise of individual help. The 1977 price for this starter package was typically about $575, with extra lots of 100,000 worms offered at $475 each. The guaranteed buy-back price for adult "bait-sized" worms was $2.00 per thousand. It is not difficult to see that, when the distributor buys worms from his old contract growers at $2.00 per thousand, and sells them to new contract growers at $5.75 per thousand, he is making a decent profit on each exchange, even when allowing for other expenses. Put another way, he is buying back the same worms he sells to his growers—at less than half the price. It is not difficult to see, also, that—by effective promotion—he can induce great numbers of people to become growers, and can keep millions of earthworms "floating" from one grower to another, making a healthy profit on each exchange. In this case, the high-volume earthworm sales never reach their alleged true market (anglers, gardeners, etc.) but simply pass from grower to grower. The pawn in this game is the inexperienced, small-scale grower, who must first invest $575, then put in long hours of hard work in order to recoup his investment and begin to make any profit at all. Many first-time growers drop out of the business in discouragement, while some others see the light and begin to sell to would-be growers, also—in which case they, too, become distributors. The fact is that, under the present market structure, the astute distributors are the ones making large profits in trading earthworms, while the small-scale growers are doing the hard physical work of actually raising them.

Using the *Newsweek* figures, it is easy to see that, if 90,000 growers are producing gross sales of $50 million, then the average annual sales per grower are only $555. And if the large sellers are making large profits, then tens of thousands of small growers are making very, very little—and many are losing money.

The above view, of course, is not a total one. There certainly are growers who are making a profit, including large-scale operators who raise and sell millions of worms a year, and there are many who like the work. If this were not true, there would not be so many people in the business. Most growers believe firmly in the future of the business, convinced that their fortunes will rise as new markets are developed and growers band together to get better prices for their product. Many small-scale growers have established profitable local markets, selling to bait shops and supplying individual customers in fishing areas. Others do well in selling by mail order, through classified ads in gardening and outdoor magazines. And, of course, there are many who do well in growing worms under contract to distributors, despite the seemingly low buy-back prices. If manure is ample and free, and if no large overhead expenses are incurred, the small-scale grower can still make a modest profit in this way. To many, it certainly is preferable to other kinds of available work. Last, earthworm raising fits in nicely with other farming operations, so that it can be viewed as just one more auxiliary farming enterprise.

I do not mean to imply, either, that distributors are unethical in their relations with growers. Most are fully as honest as the people whom they sign up as growers. Their occasional glowing promises can be natural products of honest enthusiasm. In fact, the established distributors are the ones hurt most by the few dishonest ones, those who refuse to honor contracts, or who simply disappear after the worms are delivered and the grower's money is collected. In the worst cases, the worms are never even delivered, and the "distributor" skips town as soon as the investor's check is cashed at the local bank.

The advice to the would-be earthworm raiser, then, is time honored: *Caveat emptor*— let the buyer beware. There are long-established distributors whose credentials are well known, whose reputations are sound. Before signing with any distributor, however, check with your local Better Business Bureau, district attorney, sheriff, county agricultural agent—or all of these. Ask the distributor for a list of nearby people who have signed with them in the past year or two, and take the time to call the contract growers or, if possible, drive out to see their operation firsthand. Ask questions—about profits, time, labor requirements, special problems. Do some serious marketing research before investing, if you would avoid later disappointment.

Earthworm Markets

Bait sales.   The fishing bait market has long supported the commercial earthworm industry. Despite all the talk—and some action—about developing new markets in an increasingly environmentally oriented society, it is still the Saturday angler who is the major support of the earthworm grower. There are an estimated 30 million fishing licenses sold annually in the United States, and doubtless more anglers than that. Not all of them purchase bait, but a good number do. The United States fishing-bait market has been estimated at $26 million annually.

Although the earthworm is not the only live fishing bait, it is by far the most popular. During a few weeks in both spring and fall, night crawlers can be collected easily on nearly any lawn or sodded field. But during the rest of the year, the angler favoring earthworms must buy them. Retailers include gasoline stations, truck stops, tackle shops, sporting lodges and camps, motels, rod and gun clubs, small grocery stores, and even roadside homes. Automatic vending machines have appeared in recent years, providing 24-hour service. The retail bait seller who is open at 5:00 A.M. naturally has the best chance to sell to anglers who hit the road early.

Many bait retailers have taken to raising their own earthworms, in order to lower costs and increase profits. Those who buy their worms often do so by mail order, usually from a reliable grower or wholesaler who consistently supplies lively, large worms at an attractive price. Bait retailers with especially large volume often contract during the previous winter for a whole season's supply.

The small-scale grower can often capture a good share of his local retail bait market by vigorous personal promotion and attractive pricing. He has three advantages over his distant mail-order competitor: First, he is likely to be known personally in the community. Second, he can usually sell for a somewhat lower price, because he can avoid shipping charges. Last, he can deliver worms at any time on short notice, should the retailer suddenly be caught in short supply. Even if he cannot persuade the retailer to buy regularly from him, in fact, he should leave his card (with telephone number) with the retailer, offering to help out in case of a sudden shortage. Many regular retail customers are made in this way.

The disadvantage that the local grower works under, on the other hand, is the problem of changing the retailer's buying habits. Especially if the retailer has been buying worms for several years from a mail-order supplier, and has no cause for complaint, he will then be reluctant to tamper with a satisfactory relationship. Often, however, there will be cause for complaint—and it is seldom the supplier's fault. Many shipments of worms are lost in transit, especially during the hot summer months, because of improper handling along the way. Live earthworms, no matter how well packaged and insulated, can soon become dead earthworms when left standing on a loading dock in full sun for half a day. Suppliers will almost always replace such shipments, but this is of little help to the retailer, who must wait for three or four weeks for another shipment while his regular fishing clientele seek other sources—perhaps ones that will become permanent.

The small-scale grower can also sell directly to anglers in

his community. His costs of marketing will be higher, because of the greater time involved in making individual sales, but then he will get a higher price, also, since he must give the retailer a discount which is not offered to the angler. Often, the children in the family can make extra income by handling individual sales. Roadside stands are sometimes effective, if the road carries many anglers to their destinations and if the stand is open early enough. But more often, the children build up a list of steady customers in the traditional way—by plenty of personal contact, followed by continued good service.

The matter of pricing is entirely a free-market affair. Ascertain the current price of worms in your area, and set your own retail prices at about that level. Then, figure on giving any retailers a 40 percent discount on those prices, in order to allow for their profit margin.

The small-scale grower who has saturated the local market might expand into mail-order sales. The best place to advertise is in the various outdoor magazines—*Field and Stream* and *Outdoor Life* are the largest—and the various fishing magazines. If your state has its own outdoor magazine, advertising there would probably be ideal. You might also get new retailer customers in this way, since the owners of gasoline stations and bait shops are often avid anglers and outdoors people themselves, and will often be readers of the magazines you select for advertising.

The most popular earthworm species for the fishing market is the red worm. Growers point out that red worms are far tougher and more active on the hook than are their field worm or night crawler cousins, even though they are smaller. The African night crawler is another popular bait worm. It is larger than the red worm or brandling worm, although smaller than the native night crawler, and it is attractive to fish. During spring and fall, of course, the grower can supplement his bait stock by collecting native night crawlers on lawns and fields. Placed in clean bedding and properly stored in the refrigerator (between 35° and 45°F), they will last for several weeks in good condition, perhaps to a time

219

when spring fishing is still at a peak, but when the angler can no longer find night crawlers on his home lawn.

The brandling worm is another good bait species, but it is unpopular with anglers because of the unpleasant odor it releases when impaled by a fishing hook.

Sales to other growers.   There is no way to tell what share of the market is taken up by other growers, but it is substantial. It is very possible that earthworm raisers, and would-be earthworm raisers, buy more earthworms than any other segment of the market, including anglers and bait retailers. Of course, the largest share of the grower market is supplied by the larger distributors, who can sell 100,000 worms along with a buy-back contract. Still, there are sales made to small growers by other small growers. These sales will usually be local ones, unless national mail-order advertising is used.

The grower market is one that has not been utilized well by the small-scale grower. Particularly if he depends exclusively upon literature from the promoter/distributor, he might not even think of this market segment as legitimately his. Still, there are many people thinking about going into the earthworm-raising business, and the small-scale grower can supply these people with healthy breeder and pit-run worms just as easily as can the large distributor, and usually at a more attractive price. Of course, the small-scale grower would not offer a buy-back contract, unless his business had grown to a point where the product could easily be turned back on the market, but in any case he should offer the buyer some personal advice on raising earthworms, especially if it is the buyer's first experience in growing worms. In selling to other growers, there is no need to promote "breeding stock," since pit-run worms will probably be more suitable to a new bin, anyway, and are less expensive.

There is also a considerable amount of buying back and forth among established growers. Occasionally, a grower will receive a large order which he cannot supply with his present stock. In this case, he will buy from other growers in order to fill current orders. Prices are negotiated.

Sales to gardeners and farmers.   The market comprised of gardeners and farmers, although much discussed and promoted, is probably not a major one. A few small-scale growers report success with this market, and for some growers it *is* a significant one. But, in terms of the total earthworm market, it probably accounts for less than 10 percent of total sales (although there are no industry figures).

There has been a considerable amount of misinformation given to gardeners and farmers by overzealous earthworm promoters, regarding the services that red worms and brandling worms can be expected to perform for crop-growing soils. Some literature instructs gardeners to implant these species, then to expect them to multiply and thrive permanently in soils. In truth, the red worm can survive for extended periods only so long as copious amounts of manure or other rich organic matter are spread on the soil. The brandling worm is even less suited to agricultural soils, since it can live in virtually nothing but pure organic matter. Sales to gardeners and farmers, then, should be made with the clear understanding that these species can be used in making compost, and that only the red worm can exist in crop soils—and then, only if an intensive sheet composting program is carried out. Even with sufficient organic matter, there is no guarantee that red worms will survive over winter in northern soils. In the far north, they certainly will not.

Other markets.   Much promotional literature stresses other markets for earthworms, including potential sales to fish hatcheries, zoos, laboratories, rabbitries, game bird breeders, poultrymen, and municipal composting authorities. All these market segments, together, add up to nearly nothing. Nearly all fish hatcheries, game bird feeders, and poultry farms rely exclusively on commercial feeds; the few who do use earthworms are probably in a position to raise their own.

Some zoos do use earthworms for a few exotic animal species (notably platypuses and kiwi birds), but they prefer night crawlers. Laboratory suppliers which provide earthworms to schools and experimental labs prefer night crawlers, too, because of their large size—and they often raise their own. Rabbitries *sell* far more earthworms than they purchase, since the combined rabbit/earthworm operation produces far more earthworms than rabbits. And no municipalities are currently using earthworms for refuse reduction, as great as this potential might be.

There certainly is *some* market among these for earthworms. The point is that the market segment is a very small one, and the chances of the small-scale grower tying into it are even smaller.

Starting Out with Earthworms

The first-time earthworm raiser will be well off to begin on a modest scale. No matter how many books are read, or how much information is gained from visits to earthworm farms, the novice grower is certain to kill some worms through oversight, inattention, sheer inexperience, and common mistakes. In beginning, it is better to kill $5 worth of worms than $500 worth.

This chapter is not a complete guide to the commercial raising of earthworms, nor can it hope to be. The subject is worthy of a book in itself—and, fortunately, there are many good books on the market devoted to commercial raising, most written and/or published by Earl B. Shields. These are listed in "The Earthworm Grower's Library," following chapter 9 of this book. The personal case histories in chapter 9 will also offer many good tips. Here, we will skim lightly over many of the factors to be considered in earthworm raising, to acquaint the novice grower with standard practices. All the recommendations that follow apply to the red worm (*Lumbricus rubellus*), which is by far the most popular, useful, and easiest to raise of all commercial species.

Indoor Bins

Earthworm culture is better suited to the outdoors than to basements. Nevertheless, there are some good reasons for growing worms indoors, as well as out. Basement bins can easily transform a family's kitchen refuse into rich compost, as explained in chapter 7 of this book. Small orders may be conveniently filled from auxiliary indoor bins, too, in inclement weather. During winter, northern growers can supply ice fishermen at a time when no other earthworm bait is available. Finally, a stock of worms purchased in the fall can be encouraged to reproduce and multiply over the winter in indoor bins, whereas they would remain largely dormant in outdoor pits.

A good-size indoor wooden box measures 3 feet long, 30 inches wide, and 18 inches high. Using the standard measure of one thousand worms to one square foot of bedding, a bin of this size would hold from six to seven thousand worms. Of course, bins or boxes of nearly any size may be used, depending on the grower's preferences and available materials. Wood is usually used indoors, although cinder blocks or other materials will serve just as well.

The seams of the bin or box should be fitted tightly, or otherwise sealed, to prevent the worms from escaping. A 40-watt light bulb hanging above the pit will discourage worms from climbing out, although a surer device involves a frame covered with hardware cloth, which is hinged on the top of the bin. A screen door hook and eye will keep the lid secure. About a dozen ⅛-inch holes should be drilled in the bottom of the bin, and a piece of copper or plastic window screening should then be tacked to the inside bottom. The holes will provide necessary drainage, while the screening will prevent the worms from leaving the pit. Some sort of a container should be placed beneath the pit to catch the draining liquid, which can then be used to water houseplants. Some growers simply place a tin can beneath each drainage hole, while others use more elaborate devices.

Indoor bins may be constructed in many sizes and of a variety of materials. This cement-block basement bin will present few maintenance problems for many years to come.

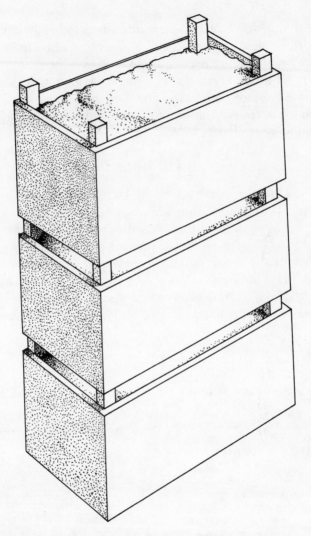

Figure 17 Basement earthworm boxes can be stacked easily if wooden strips are fitted into the corners.

Red worms, brandling worms, and African night crawlers are well suited to indoor culture, since all three can live happily in the temperature range of the average basement. Native night crawlers, field worms, and Pheretimas are not recommended for commercial raising, either indoors or out. African night crawlers are almost always raised indoors, since they cannot tolerate even slight freezes.

The care of earthworms indoors is essentially the same as their outdoor care. Predators will be less of a problem indoors, of course, and temperature and moisture may be more easily controlled.

Outdoor Pits

Outdoor pits may be as large or small as the grower wishes. Generally, they are no more than six feet wide, since it would be difficult to work with a wider pit without stepping into it. Many commercial pits are 100 or more feet long, although these are usually broken up into sections so that worms in different stages of growth can be kept separated.

The first-time grower will perhaps want to begin with a wooden box, about 28 inches by 18 inches by 6 inches, which

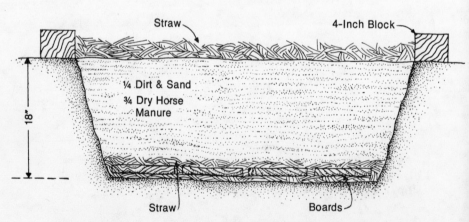

Figure 18 This cross section of a desert-country earthworm pit shows 18 inches of horse manure mixed three-to-one with soil and sand. A straw mulch is on top, with another layer of straw on the bottom, while a layer of scrap wood boards offers a hot-weather refuge for the worms.

Earthworms in backyard bins and pits should
be given added protection at the approach of
the first autumn frosts. Here, a heavy layer of
hay is being added, in anticipation of a cool
night.

will easily hold a thousand adult red worms and give them
room for growth and multiplication. Larger pits may be
constructed as the need arises.

In northern areas, where the ground freezes in winter,
the pit should be sunk into the ground. Chapter 7 of this book
gives clear instructions for building a northern pit.

A layer of alfalfa or other hay should be placed in the bottom of the pit, to provide for some drainage and facilitate the
collecting of the earthworm compost later on. Where moles
are a problem, a board floor is added, often laid over a layer of
gravel.

Fill the pit about two-thirds full with earthworm bedding (no more than eight inches deep) and introduce a thousand red worms or brandling worms. Cover the worms lightly with the bedding material. Cover the bedding with two or three layers of burlap, to help preserve moisture, reduce light, and keep out birds. Sprinkle the pits once or twice a week, according to the weather, keeping the bedding always damp but never soggy.

Protection of Pits

Pits should be protected against strong sunlight, excessive rainfall, and predators. A grove of trees will offer ideal protection from sunlight, and from hard rainfall, also. Some

Outdoor pits may be built to any length, but are seldom more than six feet wide.

A grove of trees offers ideal protection for outdoor pits.

growers build a pit completely around the trunk of a tree, the tree providing protection to the pit while receiving a continuing supply of the richest fertilizer. If no such ideal location is available, however, then some structure must be built above the pits, using stakes and some inexpensive roofing material. Often, on the farm, a ramshackle outbuilding is perfect for the housing of earthworm pits.

Earthworm Bedding

Many long-time commercial growers have developed their own formulas for the bedding they feel works best for their worms. A reliable, basic one, however, is one part stable manure, one part peat moss, and one part good, screened top-soil (based on volume, not weight). Be sure that the manure is past the heating stage, but not completely old.

229

Earl Shields suggests that the topsoil can be eliminated with no loss in bedding quality, using a simple 50-50 manure and peat moss mixture. And, since both red worms and brandling worms are manure-dwelling species, there is much to be said for this preference.

As the season progresses, other organic wastes may be added to provide both bedding and food. Cut weeds, shredded cornstalks, manure scrapings, kitchen refuse—almost anything that would be suitable for an ordinary compost heap will serve as earthworm bedding and food. Do avoid overly acid materials, unless ground limestone is added at the same time, to neutralize them.

The bedding will hold moisture effectively if you soak the peat moss thoroughly, then squeeze out excess moisture before adding it to the other ingredients, but shredded newspapers will serve as a moisture holder, too. The popular Buss Bedding, a good commercial mixture, is made mostly of pulverized newspaper.

Feeding Earthworms

Earthworms prefer manure to other foods, but will live on nearly any organic material that they are capable of swallowing, so long as it is not overly acid or very strongly scented. Avoid onions, garlic, highly spiced foods, and large quantities of citrus refuse or other acid materials. Poultry manure should be introduced cautiously, since it heats up quickly and intensely.

The small-scale grower should have little trouble in getting all the free earthworm food that he needs. The list can begin with manure and kitchen scraps. Coffee grounds and tea leaves are especially favored by the worms. Treated sewage sludge is a particularly good food, although it should be allowed to season for a month or two before it is used.

Fattening worms. Commercially raised worms are usually fattened before they are shipped to buyers, just as cattle

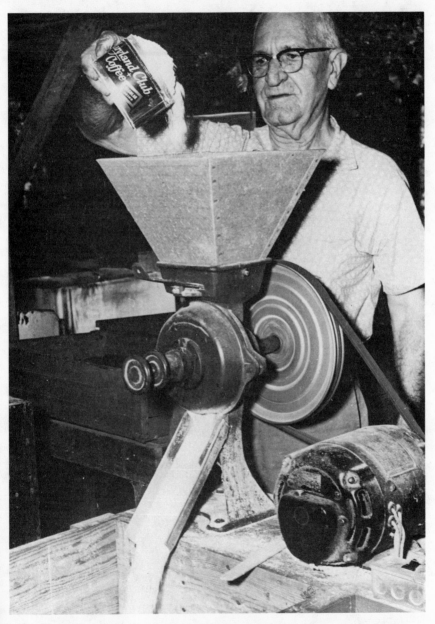

M. S. Pugh, of Rockdale, Texas, prepares his earthworm feed with extreme care, using a mixing mill to ensure accurate measurements of all ingredients.

231

.

are fattened in feedlots. Typically, worms to be fattened are removed and placed in a separate bin, and given the best of bedding and food for about two weeks.

Manure is a good bedding material for the fattening box, although some growers prefer sewage sludge, which they claim is incomparable. Scientists at the University of California at Los Angeles achieved good results by using Buss Bedding, combined with Purina Lab Rabbit Chow, coffee grounds, soil, walnut meal, and peanut oil. Many large-scale growers, who sometimes cannot depend on getting steady supplies of organic waste materials, depend exclusively on sewage sludge for bedding, and various ground livestock feeds—poultry mash, cornmeal, rabbit chow, alfalfa meal, walnut meal, or other highly nutritious feeds. African night crawlers are often fattened in pure peat moss, and are fed heavily for several weeks.

Feeding technique.   Red worms and brandling worms are surface feeders. They do not usually spend much time on the actual bedding surface, but prefer to inhabit the top inch or two of bedding, if it is dark and damp there. All feed should be placed on top of the bedding, or mixed in very shallowly—never buried in the bedding, where it will likely heat up, create acid conditions, and kill worms. Most growers use the trench method, wherein very shallow trenches—perhaps one every foot or 18 inches—are dug along the length of the pit. The feed is poured along the trenches and tamped down very lightly with the back of a shovel. Then the burlap is replaced and the worms are left undisturbed to attack the food. This technique applies both to regular pits and fattening pits, as well as indoor bins and boxes.

How often to feed.   The general rule is to feed earthworms no more than they will eat in a single day. In practice, however, worms in outdoor pits are usually fed once or twice a week. The important consideration is that the food does not turn rancid, which again will create harmful acid conditions. In feeding, as in so many matters, only experience will guide the beginning grower to a sure knowledge of his business. It is one more reason to begin on a modest scale, expanding only when basic problems are solved.

Dividing Bins, Pits, and Boxes

All earthworm containers must be divided periodically, as the worms multiply and turn the food and bedding into compost. The rule of thumb is that bins, pits, and boxes should be divided every three months, during which time the worm population should have doubled. You may find that you should divide more or less frequently, as the need dictates.

The simplest way to divide a container is to separate the entire contents in half, vertically, and to remove one-half to a new container of the same size. Then the material in both containers is spread out evenly, and new bedding and food are placed on top, to about two-thirds of the height of the container. This technique applies to all containers, indoors or out. (If the cutting is made horizontally, the division of earthworms may be vastly unequal, since most of them will be found in the top few inches of bedding during warm weather, and in a lower horizontal level during cool weather.) If you wish to remove castings during the division process, remove the burlap from outdoor pits, exposing the surface to bright sunlight or artificial light. The worms will retreat to lower depths, and the castings may easily be removed from the top.

Harvesting

Both large- and small-scale growers have devised many ingenious schemes for the quick and easy harvesting of earthworms. Still, many growers report that this chore demands more time and work than do most of their operations.

Worms in small boxes may be harvested easily by dumping the box on a table and dangling a 100-watt light bulb over

Adult breeders must be picked and counted by hand—a great job for the kids in the family.

the heap, as described in the last chapter. The worms are driven into a tight ball at the bottom of the heap, where they gather to escape the strong light, and they can then be gathered up easily.

In large outdoor fattening pits and bins, the worms are fed heavily the night before, which brings them to the surface, then are forked into a cart in the morning. The cart is wheeled to a counting and sorting table, where the real chore begins. If adult breeders are to be sold, they must be picked out and counted by hand. Most growers have learned to count quickly, by fives or tens, and are sure to toss in a few extra worms for good measure, rather than taking time to count, one by one, to a thousand or more. Of course, if worms are being sold by the pound, the job is far easier (although the selling price is lower).

A recent invention of North American Bait Farms, Inc., is the "Down to Worms Harvester," which is said to harvest the entire contents of a three- by eight-foot bed in 30 to 40 minutes. Worms and bedding are placed on a slanted conveyer screen which moves upward and vibrates at the same time. Bedding and castings drop into a pile at the lower end, while the worms are carried to the top and dropped into a pile at the other end.

There are many tips for harvesting and packing earthworms in the Shields books, which are listed after chapter 9 of this book.

Preparing Worms
for Market

There are many different kinds of containers suitable for packing earthworms for either local sale or long-distance shipping. We will skip lightly over these, again referring the reader to the Shields books for more detailed information.

For local bait sales, nearly any kind of watertight small food container can be used, including ice cream boxes, the plastic containers that supermarkets use for oysters and chicken livers, even self-locking plastic bags. A half-pint container will easily hold 50 adult worms for bait. Earthworms should not be kept for more than a few days in such containers, however, since they exclude air. Commercial growers usually use specially designed cartons with perforated lids, or "breather"-type paper bags. Suppliers of these, as well as other earthworm-raising equipment, are listed in the *Earthworm Selling and Shipping Guide*, available from Shields.

For long-distance shipping, earthworms should be packed in corrugated cardboard cartons, tied very securely and labeled "LIVE EARTHWORMS—OUTSIDE MAIL." Again, the Shields publications go into shipping instructions in helpful detail.

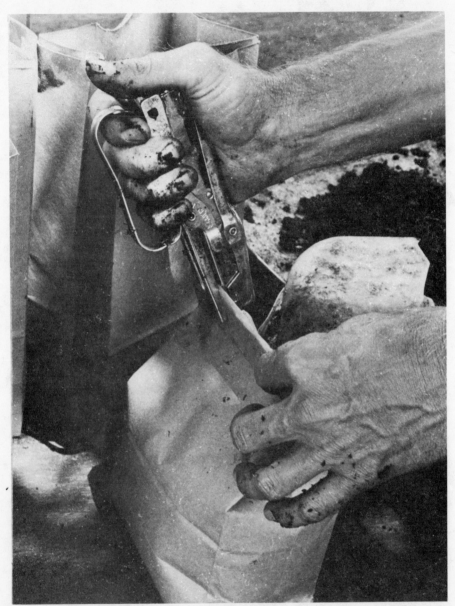

For local sales to fishermen, simply count out the worms, place them in a plastic food bag, and drop that into a paper bag.

Predators and Pests

Earthworms in outdoor pits can be decimated by a small number of moles, which are their number one predator. Many outdoor pits, even if they are constructed with cinder blocks, are outfitted with boards running the length of the floor. A few inches of gravel should be spread beneath the boards, in order to facilitate drainage. The bottom boards are spaced a half inch apart, which will allow for drainage but keep out moles and other burrowing predators. If moles still get into the pits, traps are recommended.

Mice are not the problem that moles are, their gravest offense usually being the eating of grain meant for the earthworms. Unless their numbers are great, mice found in the pits should be no cause for alarm.

Snakes eat earthworms, too, but again pose no major problem for commercial growers. The board flooring will keep them out of the pits.

Ants are often a major problem, not because they injure the worms but because they consume quantities of carbohydrates and fats, which are important in fattening the worms. The best control for ants is to spread a line of pyrethrum (which is nontoxic to warm-blooded animals) on the ground around each pit. Never apply pyrethrum directly in the pits, however, since it does kill earthworms, too. A dusting of steamed bone meal over the pit surface will also repel ants.

Mites, like ants, often become a problem because they consume food meant for earthworms. Earl Shields recommends an occasional light dusting of the beds with sulphur or tobacco dust to control mites. Ants, mites, and other crawling insects can also be discouraged from entering pits by the tacking of a band of sticky roofing paper around the sides of the pit. The insects become mired in the sticky material and perish.

The centipede is one insect which will kill worms. Centipedes seldom show up in large numbers, and many that do appear will be revealed on top of the bedding as soon as the burlap covering is pulled away. Scoop up as many as you can and either crush them or flick them into a can of kerosene or crankcase oil.

In general, insect problems will be reduced if the pH level of the bedding is kept in the neutral range. Since acid conditions tend to increase in pits over time, it is necessary to make periodic pH tests of the bedding, and to add ground limestone or dolomite as necessary. Most insects prefer acid conditions, while earthworms cannot stand them.

Raising the African Night Crawler

The African night crawler (*Eudrilus eugeniae*) has become a popular bait worm in many parts of the country. Because of its size (larger than the red worm), it reminds anglers of the native night crawler, and seemingly for this reason alone it has commanded higher prices than have red worms or brandling worms.

African night crawlers are more difficult to raise than are red worms, chiefly because they cannot tolerate temperatures much below 50°F. Nevertheless, many growers, particularly those in the Deep South, have come to specialize in Africans. The inexperienced grower, however, is advised to become proficient in the raising of red worms before attempting this exotic species.

The recommended bedding temperature for Africans is 70° to 80°F. For this reason, some supplementary heating device is needed for the pits, even in the Deep South. African night crawlers are, in fact, almost never raised outdoors.

The recommended bedding for Africans is composed of equal parts of manure and peat moss, with a pH of from 5.5 to 6.0. Some growers rely solely on peat moss, feeding the worms heavily with commercial livestock feeds. Beds should be stocked at the rate of 20 to 25 worms per square foot. Add one-half inch of bedding material every week or two and wet it down at least once a day.

Africans breed profusely and grow rapidly. Eggs hatch in from one to three weeks, and within six months the worms grow to bait size—about 6 inches. If encouraged, they will continue to grow to about 12 inches.

The feeding requirements for Africans are the same as for red worms, although Africans will eat more. Finely ground poultry mash, rabbit food, and corn are favorite feeds for this species.

Remember, in shipping African night crawlers, their extreme sensitivity to cold. They are best not shipped to northern states before mid-April, or after early October, no matter how well they are packed.

There is a good 53-page book, *Raising the African Night Crawler*, written by Charlie Morgan and available from Earl B. Shields. It is a book highly recommended to anyone considering the commercial or hobby raising of the species.

Auxiliary Income

An earthworm grower who has carefully cultivated an earthworm market might want to consider adding to his income by raising other bait, selling books on raising earthworms to first-time growers, and even marketing earthworm compost to urban houseplant growers.

Other bait.   Depending on the grower's geographic area, and his personal interests, he might consider the raising or collecting of crayfish, fiddler crabs, bloodworms, sandworms, crickets, mealworms, catalpa worms (larvae of the sphinx moth), frogs, salamanders, hellgrammites (larvae of the dobsonfly), minnows, goldfish, or small catfish (including stone cat, madtom, poison cat, and tadpole cat—all members of, or related to, the *Noturus* genus). All are used for bait in various parts of the country, and all have at least a small commercial market. (Do check state restrictions on all of these,

239

since some are outlawed for bait use in certain states.) A good guide to their raising or collecting in the wild is a 22-page pamphlet, *Fish Baits: Their Collection, Care, Preparation, and Propagation,* distributed free by the U.S. Department of the Interior, Fish and Wildlife Service, Bureau of Sport Fisheries and Wildlife, Division of Fish Hatcheries, Washington, D.C. 20240. Ask for Leaflet FL–28.

Earthworm books. All the Shields books are available for marketing by earthworm growers to their customers. Promotional literature, which is available from the Shields people, can result in a good number of profitable auxiliary sales. Discounts for books usually depend on the number of copies purchased at any one time.

Earthworm compost. The best market for earthworm castings or compost is in city flower shops and houseplant centers. Prices vary throughout the country, and so you should check the current prices for a five-pound bag of cow manure or fancy potting soil, then set your price at a somewhat higher figure. You can bag the castings in a double plastic bag, one slipped inside the other for added strength. Between the two bags, where it will not become covered by any casting particles, you can place an attractive printed label. Do not make extravagant claims for the castings, as is sometimes done, but merely promote their true plant-growing properties.

Chapter 9

How We Made It Big (or Small) in Earthworms

Following are case histories, most drawn from the pages of *Organic Gardening and Farming*, of some people who have raised earthworms either for profit or soil-building purposes.

The Story of the Earthworm

by Dorothy Hewett

Little did we realize years ago, when my husband casually dumped the leftovers from a 25-cent carton of fishing worms into a can of dirt "to keep them for the next trip," that they would some day sweep us right into the center of a large earthworm-breeding enterprise.

It transpired that the can soon became cans, and then pails, and then tubs, and then pits, until finally that silent little army threatened to overrun the place and take up billets right in our house, unless we got busy and learned that they weren't just multiplying for the sake of multiplying; that there was work to be done with them—not just sitting and fishing; and that, whether we liked it or not, we would have to learn and teach others how to do that work.

Littler still did we realize that after we did learn how to domesticate them, they'd become so domesticated that we'd actually invite 'em right into our house to stay all winter, right in the middle of our already-crowded utility room and back entryway. We who owned the house, mind you, had to

241

squeeze our way in and out of those places all day long or else go 'round to the front entrance all the time.

But littlest of all did we realize that these creatures would also soon monopolize even our conversation, and that from then on every time George and Dorothy Hewett opened their mouths to speak all they'd ever talk about would be earthworms.

We didn't realize all this was happening to us—but it did; and it will happen to you when you learn to domesticate earthworms, how to raise them in boxes, in your bedroom, bathroom, basement or backyard—or all four put together. A real earthworm enthusiast doesn't quibble over who gets space priority where—the family or the wormery. In fact, the time is already here when no self-respecting house planner will fail to provide a whole wing for the worms. Personally, I'd like to call that wing "the soilarium"—and you might as well make it roomy, for in no time at all it will be the center of attraction of all your family and all your company—take it from us.

If you think we're overly excited about worms, stop to think that they gained and held the attention of the great English scientist, Charles Darwin, for 50 years! And when he got through he concluded: "It may be doubted whether there are many other animals which have played so important a part in the history of the world as have these lowly organized creatures."

To the animal we've been pleased to call "lowly," God apparently assigned the mightiest task in the world—the task of keeping the surface of the earth forever renewed; the task of forever converting back into topsoil humus—every bit of waste matter left over by man and beast, as well as every bit of dead vegetation, so that the earth might forever stay pure—cleaned up—and able to support all the life that lives off it in a condition of health, wealth, and perfect enjoyment.

Now, of course, the earthworm was given helpers to carry out his vast job—helpers in the form of billions upon billions of tiny microorganic creatures who do miraculous preliminary work. But the earthworm seems to be the chief executive, the coordinator, the homogenizer, and the final deodorizer, purifier and vitalizer of the waste; because not until it has been swallowed, digested, and excreted by him in particles that break down to the size of finely ground black pepper, has the waste matter actually become earth again.

One of the greats of our own time and country, Dr. Thomas J. Barrett, who originated the idea of harnessing (domesticating) the earthworm—raising him intensively in boxes or pits full of compost—had this to say in his beautiful book, *Harnessing the Earthworm*: "In contemplative mood, we hold a handful of rich, dark earth—humus. It is without form, yet within it all forms are potential. It is without structure, yet within it all the wonders of civilization sleep. It appears dead, yet within it all life resides . . . . "

This rich, dark earth—this humus he is referring to—is the product of the earthworm.

Now you have another question right on the tip of your tongue. We know this from experience with thousands of tips of thousands of tongues, so you may ask it right now: "But why raise them in boxes or pits? Why not just throw them right in the ground and let it go at that?"

That's the most asked question in earthwormdom, and the answer is: Because it would take you ages to gather in the open ground, excretion by excretion, speck by speck, a handful of such glorious earthworm castings as you could gather up in a second from your box or pit. Besides, why scatter these precious deposits of new-made earth all over the ground when we want them, in concentration, right under our flowers, bulbs, fruits, vegetables, shrubs, and trees—in order to give them vitality and beauty and a flavor literally out of this world?

Do you need any more reasons why you should learn to raise your own earthworms, make your own humus, and enjoy your farms and gardens like you've never enjoyed them before?

The problem of breeding earthworms is a lot like the

problem of keeping babies in a playpen. You want to keep the little angels in one place, so they won't be crawling all over and getting into trouble. Luckily, there's a simple solution (at least with earthworms); just put the things they like in the "pen" and they'll stay there, happy as a lark.

We've found that the "culture box" makes an excellent playpen for earthworms and is also the simplest method for beginning earthworm breeders.

Any good-sized wooden box will work well. Fruit or vegetable lug boxes, approximately 17 by 14 by 6 inches, are fine and can usually be obtained from any food market. You can place the boxes in a corner of the basement, garage or shed, under the house or outside in a sheltered place.

This size box accommodates 500 full-grown breeders, or half a pound of pit-run (mixed sizes), which ordinarily amounts to 800 or so worms from babies to breeders. Since the usual earthworm order is for either 1,000 breeders or one pound of pit-run, you'll need two made-over boxes to start off with.

(Note: This recipe will make enough for just one box.)

Spread a 12-quart pail of finely screened topsoil out on a flat surface (floor or worktable) until it is leveled out to a layer three inches high; similarly spread over this a 12-quart pail of finely ground peat moss that has been thoroughly soaked beforehand in water, for 24 hours, and then drained or squeezed free of dripping water; spread over this a 12-quart pail of crumbled horse, cow, sheep or rabbit manure; sprinkle the whole surface of this layered pile with a mixture of food made by thoroughly mixing a cupful of dry cornmeal with a one- (or two-, if you have it) pound canful of coffee grounds.

(Note: We have purposely omitted advocating chicken manure. It is too hot for indoor culture box purposes, and besides, it is apt to have been contaminated by poisonous poultry-house sprays and insecticides.)

Now with a small trowel, start at one end of the pile and systematically toss, turn, mix and aerate this compost, until you get to the other end of the pile; then go back and forth again—tossing, mixing, fluffing—taking only a little at a time.

The ideal moisture content is reached when you can squeeze a handful of compost in your fist and have it hold together in a wet but not dripping mold. Test your compost now. If it needs more moisture, sprinkle some water over it gently and evenly and let it penetrate through the loose pile. Repeat this whole tossing, mixing and moistening operation once a day for five days.

On the fifth day, before you toss it put your hand down into the heart of the pile to test it for heat. If it is cool to the touch, your work is done; if there is the slightest warmth, keep mixing and moistening once a day until it is thoroughly cooled. Earthworms will crawl out *en masse* if your compost is warm; if they can't escape, they burn up—actually melt and die.

It usually takes the average earthworm hatchery from one to three weeks to fill and ship your order. Find out when you place your order and get your boxes and compost ready ahead of time. We are now going to assume that your worms have arrived and are setting in their containers waiting to be planted in your culture boxes.

1. Toss and fluff up your compost again, just in case it got lumpy or packed while waiting for the worms to arrive. Also test it for moisture and remoisten, if necessary.

2. Lay a piece of burlap, corrugated cardboard, or a few folded sheets of newspaper over the loose-lath false bottom of box.

3. Evenly spread about a half-inch layer of dried lawn clippings, withered small weeds, or crushed dried leaves. (Note: Use no grass that has had weed-killer or chemical fertilizer applied to it. Earthworms are very sensitive to chemicals and won't work in compost that is not to their taste, but will

pile up in bunches along the walls of the box and eventually crawl out.)

4. Fill with compost to within three inches from the top of box.

5. Dump half of your breeders into each box (don't tire them out by trying to count out exactly half—just guess it). Or, if you've purchased pit-run, put half of those (by guess) in each box. If you are stocking your box indoors, turn on a 100-watt light about a foot above the box to make the worms go down into the compost quickly.

If you're working outdoors, the sunlight will accomplish this. Worms don't like being exposed to strong light. If the weather is raw or dark, go inside with this operation. Cold worms scarcely move. Under the right conditions they'll burrow down in 5 to 30 minutes. Any that remain on top after that are usually either cripples or dead. Just ignore them. When you have covered them over with the compost (as per step 6 below), they'll decompose and disappear.

(Note: Most earthworm hatcheries put in enough extra worms to take care of a dozen or two casualties; all guarantee live, healthy delivery; most cover their shipments with both insurance and special handling.)

6. Now fill your box with compost up to within an inch from the top. This gives your worms a depth of six inches of compost to work in, which is their *minimum* requirement.

7. Mix a handful of very dry cornmeal with three handfuls of coffee grounds. (This will be enough to do two boxes.) Sprinkle two handfuls of this in two ridges on top of compost (in each box), keeping two inches away from both the sides and the ends of the box. These open spaces will give the worms a chance to escape from this feed in case it heats up temporarily.

8. Fill box to rim with dried lawn clippings or similar material. Press these into a mat by using a light board, being careful to tuck all the grass inside the walls of the box. Lay a piece of well-soaked burlap over the grass, or any kind of cloth the size of the box, being sure to tuck it in so none of it hangs over the rim. The burlap should be about ½ inch from the upper rim when pressed into place. Worms will crawl along overhanging burlap or grass and get out.

9. Improvise a sprinkler by punching small nail holes in the bottom of a two-pound coffee can. Pour a quart of water into the can and sprinkle your box evenly through the burlap, covering the whole surface. Avoid wetting the outside surface of your box.

The reason we always water through the burlap and grass from now on is to distribute the water evenly and gently, thus causing a minimum of flooding of the channels that the worms have made for themselves down below.

Water your boxes once a week, and keep an eye on those two ridges of cornmeal-coffee mix. After about the third week, your first two culture boxes will need no more special care until it's time to subdivide them into four; so you are ready to stack and store them now.

The first thing to consider when storing your earthworm boxes is that now and then, for reasons of their own, worms—like small boys—take it into their heads to run away from home and see the world. Other times, they leave because they're too dry, too wet, too crowded or too hungry, or just plain TOO. Maybe they get bored. Who knows?

For small boys we leave a light burning in the window and a piece of cake on the table. For the wandering worms we provide another box of compost, called a "trap," down on the floor (where they usually land). They crawl in there, feeling they've gone somewhere different. A good worm man keeps this trap regularly watered, and looks inside about once a week to retrieve the vagabonds and put them back upstairs. If they didn't have this sanctuary to go to, they'd crawl around on the dry floor and be dead next morning.

The box used for the trap is not equipped with a false, loose-lath bottom, nor has it any burlap or corrugated cardboard or paper on the bottom. Rather, its bottom is made of at least three pieces of box material, laid ⅛ inch apart from each other and from the sidewalls of the box, to give the worms all the chance in the world to crawl into the trap from the floor. The trap bottom also has a couple of lath slides on the underside for airspace.

This trap need not be built up to seven inches, like the culture box. It can be left as is, or a shallower box four or five inches can serve, just so its upper rim is of the same dimensions as the boxes that are going to be stacked over it. Also, it need have only four inches of compost in it, because it is only a temporary feeding station, not the permanent home. The trap is a good barometer as to how good your earthworm husbandry is. Learn lessons from it.

Next above the trap comes the spacer. Make yourself a supply of spacers out of two pieces of two-by-two the length of the box and two pieces of lath the width of the box. Nail the laths onto the upper corners of the two-by-twos, *securely*, with three shingle nails in each corner. These spacers provide air circulation between the culture boxes in the stack, and are high enough to permit watering the boxes evenly and completely without lifting them down each time. Considering how heavy the box becomes after awhile (about 40 pounds), the spacer is no negligible device.

So we alternate the spacers and culture boxes until we come to the topmost spacer on the top box in the stack, and there we put a solid wooden cover for general protection from the elements (if you're keeping your stack outside) and from cats, birds—yes, and people.

Caution: Be sure your boxes and spacers are flush with one another, and that vertically the stack is not leaning in any direction, in order to avoid the whole thing tumbling over some day when a cat or a dog or you yourself give it a slight bump. Also, when storing indoors, place your stack several inches away from walls, not only for circulation reasons, but so that the light may penetrate down behind. We advocate keeping a 25-watt night-light over the stack indoors, and, if at all possible, outdoors. The expense is practically nil, compared with the contentment that reigns in the wormery and provides precaution against worm wandering.

The *temperature* of your storage place should get no lower than 50°F, nor higher than 75°, for best results. Worms work best and breed best at 60° to 75°. Below 60° they begin to get sluggish, and at 32° and lower they are completely dormant—merely balling up somewhere to await better conditions. During the colder months we use a simple wafer-type thermostat that turns on a fan-type 650-watt electric heater when the temperature drops to 50°. Our culture box storage room is a well-insulated 6- by 15-foot lean-to on an outbuilding. This economical setup has paid for itself many times over in continuous worm production.

While it is all right to keep your stack outdoors during the milder weather, where it is protected from excessive heat, wind and rain, you must bring it in for the winter if you live in a cold climate. It pays you well. Our boxes are brought in for the winter with a population of 100,000 babies and breeders. By spring they have multiplied into millions!

Except for watering the boxes once a week, your original culture box needs no more attention until it's time to divide each one into two boxes. (It's been conservatively estimated that one earthworm will produce over 200 others in one year—so you can see why subdividing is so necessary and so rewarding.)

Here's a timetable for subdividing culture boxes:

boxes stocked with breeders—divide after 30 days;
boxes stocked with pit-run—divide after 40 days;
boxes stocked with eggs and spawn (babies)—divide after 90 days.

The week you are planning to divide, don't water the

box. The mealier the material, the easier it is to handle the worms. The last operation after dividing will be the usual watering. A good tip when handling worms is to keep a can of dry soil at hand and keep rubbing your palms and fingers in it to keep them from getting gummy.

Dividing a culture box is about a 15-minute job. It should be done in strong sunlight or under a 100-watt light hung about a foot above the box. This encourages the worms to go down quickly into the compost, as they don't like being exposed to strong light.

How to Divide Boxes

1. First, prepare a new culture box similar to the first one you made. Put in about an inch layer of compost, consisting of soil, manure, and peat moss.

2. Remove burlap, grass mat, and the uneaten cornmeal-coffee grounds mix from the top of the original culture box and lay these materials over the inch of compost in the new box. Many baby earthworms will be clinging to these materials, and this is a good place to deposit them.

Expose the surface of the original box to the light for a few minutes until the larger worms have had a chance to go back down to their channels below. Remember, the spawn and capsules are what we're after. These are mostly in the upper two to three inches of the box at dividing time. The lower three to four inches are the headquarters of the breeders; we don't aim to disturb this area any more than necessary.

3. Prop your original box. Quickly and gently start scraping out the compost, with your fingers preferably—or you may use a small garden fork, but not a solid-edged tool which will cut your worms. Let these scrapings fall in a pile in front of you, onto a cardboard or heavy paper. As this collects, empty it into the new box.

Keep scraping—taking a half-inch depth at a time—until

you begin to see the many heads of your breeders sticking up out of their channels. Then stop, turn your box bottom side up, prop it, and similarly go to work on the bottom half until you come to the breeders there. Empty your remaining scrapings into the new box and level them out gently.

4. As you scrape, occasional breeders that failed to get out of the way will show up on your pile. Save them in a can until you're through scraping and then toss them back into the original box.

5. Set your original box down level on the table again. Sprinkle the whole surface lightly with a handful of the corn-meal-coffee grounds mix. Fill the box to one inch from the top with new compost. Lay down the two ridges of cornmeal-coffee mix, top with new grass mat and new burlap, gently water with a quart of water, and store it. Divide this box again in about 30 days—watering and feeding between time as above instructed.

6. Repeat everything you did in paragraph 5 immediately above, in your new culture box, but you'll not have to divide this box for 90 days because it will be all spawn, eggs, and tiny red worms. But watch the level of the compost closely and keep up the full six inches.

Note: You will want to keep a record on each box from now on, to remind you when to feed, inspect, and divide again. We thumbtack a card on each box, using waterproof ink to note on it everything that we do to the box, and the dates we do it. Thus, we keep in touch with the history of our stock from the beginning.

About the fourth month after starting your original boxes, you will notice that the bottom four inches of material (the breeders' home) is getting blacker and blacker, and finely granulated. It will look as different from the original coarse compost as day from night. This is your new, perfect earth, made by Nature's perfect earthmaker, the earthworm. Cherish it! Sometimes this transformation takes a little longer;

sometimes a little shorter. But when it has happened, it's time to separate the breeders from this, their old home, and provide them with a brand-new home in all-new compost.

Again, you will have refrained from watering the culture box during the week you are planning to do this job. After going through the usual steps of scraping down to the breeders, turn the breeders' box upside down onto a cardboard under a strong light. Pile the castings up in a tall, tight cone, and give the worms time to get clear down to the bottom-center of the cone in a solid mass. This should not take more than 20 minutes. Then go back and start lopping off the top of the cone in double handfuls—collecting same in a pail.

Then start cutting in around the base of the cone. Keep these two maneuvers up until you see the boiling mass of worms at the bottom. Lift them up in both hands and immediately plant them in a newly prepared culture box as you did in the beginning, when they first were shipped to you.

In the castings there may still be eggs and white spawn. The eggs you can lift out with a spoon. The spawn will go down and roll up in balls and masses under the light, if given plenty of time, and may be planted in another box.

Branching into Outdoor Pits.

After you've racked up 10 or 15 culture boxes full of worms, you are ready to introduce as many as you want to spare into outdoor pits. Just be sure to remember that the worm works best in the upper six to ten inches. It's folly to throw a pile three to five feet high at him. Rather, make your pit long and shallow.

Plan to plant 500 breeders or 1,000 mixed sizes per cubic foot of compost and they will do their job quickly and well. Be sure to have a solid, or a ½-inch wire netting bottom on your pit to keep the moles from ravaging it. Planking, shiplap, or a thin layer (one inch) of concrete will do. The sides can be similar wood, four-inch concrete walls, or concrete blocks. An overall height of two feet provides room for 10 to 12 inches of compost on the bottom and protective layers of dry leaves, wilted grass, or hay, to shield the worms from the elements.

We stock our own commercial-size concrete pit with 100,000 earthworms. It has produced millions more and hundreds of dollars' worth of "the good earth."

In your outdoor pit, of course, you will not be restricted to soil, peat moss, and manure for your compost. In fact, we avoid peat moss altogether in our outdoor culture. There's so much more other material to use: all the weeds on the place, fallen and waste fruits and leftovers from the vegetable garden, and tablescraps; everything and anything. But always be sure you are putting in your full one-third of screened, clean earth, and one-third of fairly fresh animal manure. Work out your own dividing and cast-harvesting methods, based on what you've learned by working with the worm in the culture box. Don't bother other people about these techniques—learn by trying and doing, and you'll simply love it!

A New Angle on Worms

by Ken Bernsohn

A two-by-two-foot box, sticking up just six inches above ground level, will provide some high nitrogen "supersoil" as well as enough angleworms to make us avid anglers squirm with pleasure. And best of all, total investment is as little as four hours to get the box into production, ten minutes maintenance a week, and no cash at all.

Our two-foot cube was made from scrap shiplap left from reroofing the house, though almost any worm-proofed container will do. Some people use washing machine tubs, bathtubs, or old TV cabinets. Just make sure that whatever you scrounge will keep the worms in, but let excess water seep out the bottom. Our box has cracks between boards, but if the openings are large—like where the picture tube went in that old TV set—you can cover them with window screening. Or drill some small holes in solid bottomed boxes.

Once you've wormproofed and taken care of drainage, put the box where temperatures will be moderate enough to

Ken Bernsohn's handy and effective breeding box was sited where it would get partial shade. The board covers, removed here, also protect the worms from heat and birds. Ken reports that the worms, which came from his garden, thrive on their diet of garbage.

avoid baking the worms in summer or freezing them in winter. We buried ours in the backyard, though just putting the box in the basement is said to work well. If you do bury yours in the ground, leave a six-inch collar sticking up. Boards loosely laid over the top let worms survive despite days over 100°F since they shade the inside, regulate the amount of rain that gets into the box, and stop the early birds from getting the worms. But good results have been reported by people using window screening, a burlap bag tossed over the bedding, or even a shingled roof that disguises the worm box as a wishing well.

Recommended worm beddings include sphagnum moss at $1.50 per pound. But we started with equal four-inch layers; soil, a mix of grass clippings, carrot tops, coffee grounds and leaves, more soil, more nonwoody vegetable matter, and a final four inches of earth. Our care wasn't really necessary. A mixture of half earth, one-quarter clippings and one-quarter kitchen wastes should work fine as long as you end up with soil on top. Manure, which usually arrives with worms in it, can be added as long as you don't go overboard. Too much manure and/or decaying vegetable matter can raise the temperature above the moist coolness that makes worms thrive.

Now you're ready for worms. We found ours in the garden, under bricks and flagstones, and laid a few pieces of plywood down on weeds so worms would come to the surface since the wood shaded the ground and trapped moisture. By checking the plywood and bottoms of bricks edging our garden every few days, we collected literally thousands of worms in the spring.

However you get your worms, don't harvest from your worm box for a month or two after you start it. The amount of kitchen wastes you can recycle depends directly on the size of your worm population. At first you'll probably only be able to dump a half-gallon of coffee grounds, tea leaves, potato parings, and apple skins a week into the box. But, as the worms multiply, so will the amount you can recycle.

Scraping some of the worm bedding over the trash you dump in, and an occasional sprinkling to keep the ground moist, are the only maintenance needed in spring and summer. When you use a trowel or shovel to turn the bedding so you can harvest fishing worms, you'll be halting buildup of a hardpan layer, and can't fail to notice soil conditions throughout the box.

In the fall, after harvest, I usually dump the bedding on a sheet of plywood, remove the worms big enough to be noticeable, then put new bedding in the box, plus the large worms, and a few scoops of old bedding with tiny worms. Then it's time to fill the box to the top with grass clippings, cornstalks, leaves, and if necessary, shredded newspaper. This 18-inch layer of insulation will help your worms survive the winter, though they will, of course, become torpid.

Which means you won't have to disturb the insulation to feed them until the spring thaw.

The fall emptying of the worm bedding, a spring emptying just before planting the garden, and another emptying about two months later when vegetables are just beginning to ripen, provides enough supersoil to enrich a six-by-twelve foot plot in our garden. And since the box takes so little attention, I have more time in the summer to let the surplus worms provide trout to go with the vegetables they've enriched.

Our Worm Projects

by Gladys S. Geddes

A couple of years ago I bought 2,500 red wiggler worms from an ad in *Organic Gardening and Farming*, thinking to go into the business. However, we've been doing so many things with these marvelous little creatures that there haven't been any left over to sell.

My husband is a pipe organ designer and builder, and since we have big wooden crates for shipping the delicate metal pipes, we use every board of these for some project or other.

I commandeered two crates about two feet deep, two wide and eight long. The outside bottoms were covered with metal screening to keep snakes and moles out, while the inside bottoms were lined with tongue-and-groove boards to keep the worms in. (I now question the necessity of these boards.) Then, about four inches of sand were added, and the rest of the boxes were filled with a mixture of ground leaves, aged horse manure (itself full of worms), and sawdust. This was watered thoroughly two weeks before adding the worms, and lightly each week thereafter.

The worm shipment was divided into the two large boxes. Every two weeks I added about one pound of dolomite lime, sprinkling it atop the beds. I made a small ditch

As this picture shows, you don't need an elaborate setup to grow a crop of worms. The pipe organ crates are two feet wide, two feet deep, and eight feet long.

lengthwise down the middle of each bed and sprinkled about a pound of ground cornmeal on each box.

Every three or four weeks, I added aged horse manure and ground leaves or sawdust. It was surprising how quickly the supply needed replenishing.

257

The beds were kept covered with burlap bags, and these were covered with old plastic shower curtains or used plastic leaf bags. Garbage was put in only one end of each box, but garden refuse like pods, cabbage leaves, and weeds were spread anywhere in the beds. There was never the slightest odor from the boxes.

During the summer months we took a small can of worms out of the beds almost every day for fishing bait. The refuse from cleaning the fish was put into the worm beds, and this was their favorite food.

In the fall, after the garden was cleaned and covered with a blanket of mulch, but before real cold weather, I waited for a warm, sunny day and emptied the entire contents of one worm box onto the vegetable garden. These worm castings sell for about a dollar a quart, so you can guess the price of the material I put on the garden—about six big wheelbarrows full, plus millions of worms, which quickly disappeared into the mulch.

The second box was emptied on another bright, warm day.

This past spring I planned to buy more red wigglers to start the worm boxes again. However, I discovered a surprise in the garden. I'd laid corrugated cardboard to kill the maze of roots in a new part, and upon turning a piece of this cardboard over, I found thousands of red wigglers gathered in the shallow trenches of the cardboard. All I had to do to replace the worm population in the boxes was pick up the big worms from the cardboard, put them into a can, and deposit them in the boxes.

There were many more worms under various plastic bags of leaves I'd used to keep the cold frame from freezing and to protect various delicate shrubs. There was no need to buy more worms to replenish the boxes.

Using the same procedures of feeding and adding the horse manure and leaves as the year before, I found the worms thrived and multiplied again this past season. We fed our wide-mouth bass several big helpings of worms in late summer and fall. Before putting the boxes of castings on the garden, some was used for houseplants and around new azaleas, rhododendrons, roses, and a new peony bed. I find it necessary not to overfertilize some things, the castings are so rich.

We're going to have a new chicken coop and baby chicks this spring. I'll try feeding some worms to the chickens. I've not read material for such a procedure but we'll try it, going slowly at first. Since worms represent a good source of protein, we should be able to cut down on some of the expensive high-protein commercial chicken feed.

Maybe some year we'll have enough worms to be able to advertise them for sale in *Organic Gardening and Farming*. Until then, they certainly are adding a wealth of good things to our organic homesteading.

His Earthworms
Work for Him

by Paula Delfeld

Huge earthworms in two compost boxes do most of the gardenwork around the Austin homestead near Madison, Wisconsin.

Bob Austin runs two boxes alternately so he never runs out of compost for his ornamentals. They are made of redwood, which weathers well, and have air spaces at the sides to help the worms along with the chore of converting the organic materials inside into ripe, rich growing soil.

"I put in about a foot of leaves, and then some topsoil," he explains, "plus some chicken droppings mixed with crushed corncobs. Continue with a layer of droppings, then leaves, topsoil and more droppings until the box is full."

Bob Austin usually has a surplus of leaves and uses all he possibly can. "The secret of the thing is to keep turning it. I leave it until spring, and then get in there and turn it and aerate it, and shake it up so the air gets to it, and then the bac-

Bob Austin with one of his two compost boxes. He uses them alternately, using the older one first, and holding the fresher in reserve for late top and side booster feedings.

teria go to work and break down the leaves, and then that's how you get your compost.

"There are a lot of earthworms in there," he continues. "Just huge ones. They like those leaves of course. When I use the compost, I take the earthworms out and put them back in the compost, and make them work some more, see?"

Bob also goes to the local sewage disposal plant. "They have these beds, you know. After the sludge tanks are filled, they run it out on these beds and it dries. And then every so often they empty these beds. If you get it in the spring, that's the best time. In the fall, it's dried out, and it's real hard. But in the spring, it has had some snow on it and it has been kept real moist. It works out real well and breaks up nicely. I just put in a layer of that and go through the same process until the box is full."

Bob puts an inch or two of finished compost in each hole when he plants his bulbs—tulips, narcissus, and daffodils—in the fall. "It's a good idea," he says, "to mix it in with a little soil, and then add some bone meal. In the spring, when they're finished blossoming, I feed them again. Then they make their new growth for next year's blooms."

When he plants perennials, he also puts several handfuls in the bottom of each hole, and then in the spring he "feeds everything. Give all the perennials as much as you want to, or have time to give them—several handfuls each. Organic matter won't burn the plants, so use as much as you can."

Bob also has a large bed of ferns on the north side of the house. In the fall he puts the fronds down and lets the leaves that have accumulated lie on top of the ferns for winter protection. Then in spring he adds several inches of compost. He says, "This holds the fronds down and helps keep the moisture in as well as feeding the plants. This more or less simulates the forest condition where they grow naturally."

His wife, Juanita, adds: "Don't forget the tea leaves and coffee grounds. We don't use much coffee except when we have a party or something, but tea is our long suit. I'm from the South, and we have to have iced tea in the summertime, starting in the early spring. And in winter we have it hot." Both husband and wife agree that the brewed tea and the leaves are good for the soil.

All the time he is talking and explaining his composting operations and what they do for the garden, Bob keeps sifting handfuls of soil through his fingers. Juanita says he spends "half his working time here running compost through his fingers."

Bob smiles in agreement. "People who come fishing here," he says, "want to know if they can have some earthworms. I'd be glad to give them some, but I need them here working for me. I figure they're more valuable this way, and also if folks want to go fishing—they can also find the time to dig themselves a few worms."

They Wormed
Their Way
into a Business

by George "Doc" and Katy Abraham

Our acquaintance with the three wild worm women of Webster (that's how they were jokingly introduced to us) began four years ago when we had ecology-minded organic gardener Fran Ferguson of Rochester, New York, on our TV program to demonstrate how to make fertile compost in a garbage can just by tossing in all your after-meal scraps. Fran has two garbage cans in her cellar all winter long to take care of the table scraps produced by her family of four. She doesn't empty them until spring and they don't smell! That's a guarantee. We were converted and ours don't smell either. She keeps them outdoors during summer, performing the same recycling process.

Fran emptied beautiful dark fertile soil onto our table in the studio and casually poked around to expose some of the red worms, a species of earthworm also called red wigglers. They quickly scooted back into the soil to escape the bright lights. Fran pointed out that this aversion to light makes it easy for home gardeners to scoop out the humus without scooping out the worms. Just remove the cover of the garbage can and they burrow deeper, remove a layer, then wait a few minutes until they have gone further toward the bottom.

These worms are the same kind fishermen find so valuable when trout season opens. They're also in the same family as "manure worms," which are found in barnyards or wherever manure is broken down into soil.

The TV show with Fran created such a stir that we received over one thousand requests for the recycling bulletin put out by the Environmental Education Committee of Rochester on how to make garbage can compost. Almost every letter contained a "P.S." asking: "Where do we get the red worms to add to our garbage can?"

The trail led straight to Webster, New York, a suburb of

Rochester, and on to the door of LPF Enterprises, where three "girls" in the worm business had been endorsed by the Environmental Committee. Shirley (Chic) Leschorn, her sister Betty Peachy, and a friend, Carol Fogg, started LPF Enterprises on a dare with each other after seeing an ad in one of mother Pauline Leschorn's crocheting magazines.

"Mother wasn't too impressed," according to Chic. "She kept saying: 'What in heaven's name are we going to do with a thousand hybrid worms?' " As fate would have it, the question took on more import when the worms were delivered on April 20, 1973, just as 35 guests were arriving to help celebrate Mother Leschorn's 76th birthday.

L., P., and F. had already situated an ordinary washtub full of moist peat moss in the basement, with a box of corn-meal nearby for food. Although they watered and fed faithfully, their dreams of the worm population doubling in six months were shattered about a week or so later when they noted a peculiar smell coming from the tub. Investigation showed their investment had expired in soggy peat.

Chic emphasizes: "We learned that worms need to be kept moist but not soggy. Good drainage in the container is important." After a conference, the corporate owners decided they should not be easily discouraged and with a unanimous vote they decided to order another thousand worms. The spring fishing season was in full swing and word got around that Leschorn, Peachy, and Fogg had some fine worms for bait. Making a quick calculation of their sales rate, they decided to order another fifteen thousand worms. This time they built two bins four feet by four feet by two feet high, out of plywood. As their worm population grew they began transferring larger worms to Styrofoam picnic baskets which made it easier for them to count out orders for their growing list of customers. The worms can still breed in these but are handier to get at.

It was one of those Styrofoam picnic baskets that Chic, Betty, and Carol brought to show on our "Green Thumb" TV show. We showed how they could be used to make garbage can compost, and also showed the worms in all stages of growth. The results were impressive. When the cameras moved up and magnified those little fellows, with their tiny white young ones and even some of the eggs, viewers got a people's eye view of what it's like to be a red worm.

One enthusiastic viewer wrote: "We always watch your program at lunchtime. Even though we were eating spaghetti for lunch, I became so fascinated with those worms and what they could do to eliminate our garbage problems that I went right out and took off for Webster to get a batch. Before the afternoon was out I had two garbage cans setting on cement blocks, with drainage holes in the bottoms, a little soil and a few scraps, and my little humus factory was already working."

Mother Pauline L. no longer doubted the possibilities of the worm business but began assisting the trio by taking orders and coordinating schedules. LPF gave good measure, hand counting orders of big fat worms, and business increased. They still count out smaller orders but they also sell by the pound, always making sure that folks get the quality they expect and good measure to boot.

From the washtub in the corner of their basement, Leschorn, Peachy, and Fogg have expanded to a 10-foot by 20-foot garage, insulated against freezing. They no longer feed cornmeal, but use chicken mash in 100-pound lots, augmented by manure. Feed is put into the pit in a center trench, and ½ pound of mash will feed about 2,000 worms for three or four days. They tell us that under ideal conditions the adult worm population will double in about six months. Thus they have worms in all stages of development at all times. They keep two pits undisturbed. About one to three inches of manure and sludge are put on top of the pits and worms are able to feed from underneath.

We asked L., P., and F. how many worms they have at present. "That would be hard to say," they responded, "because our little friends are reproducing continually. Earthworms are bisexual and each can produce eggs after copulation. It takes from 21 to 30 days for worms to hatch, depending upon the conditions in the pit. The cooler the temperature, the slower the worms reproduce. In fact, the bedding must be kept above freezing or the worms will not survive. This applies to the garbage can compost also. Cans must be kept in an area that does not go below freezing or sunk into the ground up to the rim, with an extra covering in very cold climates. We find a cool garage or basement that is kept above freezing is ideal."

Another important precaution: do not add vinegar-soaked food or too many citrus skins to the garbage cans. Acids in excess amounts could kill the worms. Hold off altogether on onions unless you want your worms climbing the walls. L., P., and F. found this out to their dismay when they temporarily moved a bushel of onions into the basement. Very shortly they found red worms all over the floor crawling in the opposite direction. They soon found out that garbage can composters had had the same experience when they added onion scraps to the can.

Chic, Betty, and Carol are shipping worms to customers who live too far away to come and get them, but Chic reminds us that shipping costs are expensive even though containers cost only a few pennies.

We asked the girls if they would recommend worm raising as a profitable home business. "That all depends upon location and ambition." Bait customers are repeat customers. Garbage can composters make up a good portion of the business but don't repeat too often since they have to replenish only when too many are scooped out with the compost or when something happens to the worms, such as poor drainage or freezing. However, composters have been quick to recommend LPF to their friends and converts to garbage composting. In an area as large as Rochester and its environs this can go on for a long time.

They suggest that novices start with between 1,000 and 5,000 breeder worms. If the business pans out like theirs has, then they can easily build more breeder bins and increase their stock. Chic, Betty, and Carol started it as a part-time venture, since they were all working, but when the recession hit, Chic and Carol were furloughed. This was the push they needed to go into the business full time. Their customers are satisfied because they know they will get their full count and a few besides. Even on large orders the girls have gauged it so that customers get full weight and a little extra for their money. As one customer put it: "I know I'm going to get good fresh, lively worms and if I order 500 I know I will get 500 plus."

As to our query: "Do you have any advice for beginners?" they were quick to say: "You can't always go by the book. Many things are trial and error. What may work in one part of the country might not in another location, but persistence pays off." Incidentally, you can't be squeamish about handling worms, either.

For those who want to try garbage can composting here is a list of the most often asked questions:

Can a plastic container be used or must it be metal?
Either heavy plastic or galvanized cans can be used as long as you have a tight-fitting cover and make sure several holes the diameter of a large-sized nail are punched in the bottom.

How much soil do I add in the bottom of the can?
About three inches.

How many red worms should I use per can?
About 500 to 1,000 for each large can.

Will liquid seep out of the holes?
Yes, you should put something underneath to catch it. You can use it to water your plants.

Suppose I have added several days' garbage and there is some odor. Is there anything I can use to offset it?

Yes. It is better to add a light sprinkling of soil or shredded leaves or shredded newspapers every couple of days after garbage has been put in the can. Coffee grounds are good also to neutralize odor.

Can grease and meat scraps be added?

In moderate amounts these items do no harm, and will break down along with other materials. A family of four with a normal diet would probably not have more than can be integrated satisfactorily.

How about bones such as steak bones or chicken bones?

These can be included but probably will not break down very much. They will add some calcium and can be turned under in the garden in small quantities.

How many cans does a family need to go through the winter?

A family of four, with two school-age children, would need two cans. They can be started simultaneously or one can be added later in the season as the other becomes nearly full.

Once you start garbage can composting you'll wonder why the whole world isn't turning their garbage into rich earth for plants to grow in.

Getting Started
in the Worm Business

by Steve Dubie

We started our worm business four years ago, on the advice of an old gentleman who kept telling us to get out there, pick those night crawlers, and sell them.

Worms had been planted on our two acres in southern Oregon 20 years ago, and at one time had been sold from this

property. So it wasn't too hard to go into business, in an ig-
norant sort of a way. What we knew about worms didn't quite
fill a thimble. We would pick a few at night, put them in a box
filled with dirt, and sell them to fishermen who came to the
house. Our first worms were sold in tin cans and cottage
cheese containers. The dirt proved to be messy—always too
wet or too dry. We didn't know how to store worms, package
them, or feed them.

As business began to pick up, we had to find a better way
to handle worms. For the first couple of years, our customers
were fishermen and bait outlets interested only in night
crawlers. But this changed. Now our customers include
farmers, organic gardeners, orchardists, and fishermen who
want red wigglers as well. Raising night crawlers is nothing
like raising reds, so I'll describe the procedures separately.

Although red wigglers are usually raised in beds, the
only way to raise night crawlers is in a couple of fertile acres.
While we were fortunate to have them growing at our place
when we bought it, here's how you would start from scratch:

First, cultivate the soil, and seed it with grass and clover.
Night crawlers like clover particularly. Then plant the area
with worms. If you want a fast start, you might plant 100,000.
Even then you wouldn't want to pick any for a full year. After
a year, you could harvest that initial 100,000 and, by the next
year, maybe five times that. In bulk shipments, crawlers sell
for $20 per thousand.

One nice thing about night crawlers is that you don't
have to feed them. All you have to do is cut the grass periodically (not letting it get more than three inches high), water
it, and pick the worms. When the nights are warm enough
(40°F or more) and the ground is moist, the worms will
emerge to breed and eat dead grass. That's when you catch
them.

Our method for harvesting worms is still the same:
creeping around on our hands and knees with flashlights, trying to keep quiet so we don't frighten them back into their
holes. A night crawler will always keep its tail in the hole so

he can escape if anything approaches. When you grab him, you have to be careful not to pull too hard. He might break in two, or be stretched far enough to cause internal injury. If injured, he will likely die in a day or two, and cause other worms to die, too. When you're pulling on a crawler who refuses to let go of his hole, loosen your grip and place your hand on the ground next to the hole. When he contracts, he will loosen up, and can then be pulled out with ease.

On a warm night (50° to 70°F) an experienced person can pick 800 or more worms in an hour. One of our daughters is a champion worm picker in these parts, catching more than 1,000 worms per hour. In general, our girls seem to do a better job of picking than the boys. They pick more and break fewer worms; it could be that their smaller hands are not as clumsy as the boys'.

We catch night crawlers on our two acres and on the nearby high school football field. After harvesting, we sort the worms. Dumping them on a table, my family and I go through them, packing only the big ones, and putting the smaller ones in a large concrete fattening bed outside. Night crawlers need to be kept cool, and they like a bedding of shredded, moistened newspaper. After a lot of experimentation, I found that I could get perfect bedding by running soaking-wet newspaper through a W-W Shredder-Grinder fitted with a ¼-inch screen. We pack the crawlers in 500-worm wax-lined cartons and in regular fish-bait containers, a dozen worms in the 10-ounce size, and two dozen in the 16-ounce size.

We used to keep the cartons and containers in secondhand refrigerators, but now we mostly use an insulated eight-foot by eight-foot storage room built off of the garage. It is cooled to about 45° with a used, one-room air-conditioning unit. The worms can be kept refrigerated this way for months, but they will eat the newspaper, which has to be checked and replaced every week or so.

As far as selling worms is concerned, we began by running ads in some local newspapers, and by going around and talking with store owners. Now I have a couple of routes, and people come by or call me up. The best advertising you can get is word-of-mouth. If I find a carton of our worms in a store, and the newspaper bedding is about gone, I'll exchange cartons. We'll bring the worms home, sort through them, and repack in fresh bedding if they look good. If they don't look so good, we'll put them in the concrete fattening bed outside for a while.

Compared to night crawlers, red wigglers are very hardy. They can easily be raised in beds. Their eggs don't mind being exposed to air. In fact, their eggs are often frozen, shipped halfway around the world, and when returned to the right growing environment and watered, they will revive and hatch.

If you want to raise red wigglers, you don't even need a piece of land or a lot of money. You can raise them in your garage or basement. Build small beds, maybe about the size of an apple box—15 by 20 by 5 inches. Fill these beds with bedding mix (which I'll describe later), seed with a couple hundred worms each, and stack them. They will need to be watered every few days and fed kitchen wastes or cornmeal. This way of raising reds is fine for someone who doesn't have any land, but it's more work than raising them outside in large beds. Outside, you don't have to worry about the stack of boxes falling over, or the compost getting too wet, or the floor going muddy.

Worm beds come in all different sizes. If you don't have a lot of space, you can make small 3 by 6 by 2-foot-deep beds. I've had them in all shapes and sizes, but now my preference is for beds that are 3½ feet wide, 8 feet long, and 3 feet deep. Some people like to use raised, wooden beds for red wigglers, but I prefer a sunken bed. It stays cool and moist in the summer, warm in the winter, and is easier to fork over when you're digging for worms or cleaning it out. I start by digging a trench that is a little larger than the finished bed, build a four-sided wooden box (without top or bottom) and place it in the trench. Then I add an inch of gravel for drainage, and place a loose-fitting floor of planks on top of the gravel. If your soil doesn't drain well, dig a deeper trench and put more gravel in the bottom.

Next, fill the frame with a bedding mixture and water it well. I use roughly equal parts manure and soil. Rabbit manure is the best because it doesn't heat up too much, but it isn't always easy to find. I have a source of steer manure, free for the hauling. And because it's often green when I get it, I have to let the bed compost itself for at least 10 days, until the temperature drops below 90°. At that time, you can seed the bed with worms.

Seeding consists of putting anywhere from 2,500 to 10,000 worms in each bed, depending on how fast you want salable results. You can seed with breeders—mature worms with distinct bands—that sell for $12 per thousand; or, if you're not in a hurry, you can start with a bed-run assortment of breeders, young worms and eggs—for about $7 per thousand. With a capital outlay of $150 in the late summer (10,000 breeders for $120 and $30 for lumber), you can divide each bed into two new beds every three months, and by the next summer, you would have 16 beds worth at least $5,000—a good sum.

It takes about three months for a bed to regenerate itself—from eggs to a new generation of full-grown breeders. After three months, you can either start selling worms or start new beds with them. Maintenance of a bed consists of adding fresh or composted manure periodically and keeping it well watered. (If you add composted manure, dig it directly into the beds; but if you add green manure, pile it in a row down the center, or all on one end, so that the worms can work towards it without getting burned.) Every couple of weeks, we turn all of our kitchen wastes into the beds as well.

During the summer, we keep the beds covered with tar paper, cardboard, or plywood, which we remove when watering and then replace. If the beds get too dry or too warm, the worms will burrow deeper and deeper—and this can mean an awful lot of digging when you want to catch them.

When cold weather approaches, I pile about six inches of

fresh steer manure on top of the beds, and don't have to worry about their freezing. As long as you don't break that "hot cap" open, the worms will continue to thrive and multiply underneath, even if the outside temperature drops down to zero.

In the early spring, we clean out all of the beds. This consists of removing everything, clear down to the board floor. Each forkful of compost is screened, and all the worms removed. The largest worms can be packaged for sale, or put into special fattening beds of moistened peat moss and cornmeal, then kept in the refrigerator. Smaller worms and egg capsules should be returned to the beds after filling them with fresh bedding mix. Once the worms have been returned, you are left with 24 to 30 cubic yards of worm compost from each bed. It isn't pure castings, because we are always adding more food to the bed, turning it over, and so on. But it's a fine compost, one that you can sell or use in your own vegetable garden.

We harvest worms from our beds nine months of the year, from March through November. We remove only the number of worms that we think we're going to sell in the next week or so, leaving the rest to grow and to reproduce. The worms we remove are placed in fattening beds (small trays or produce bins) and kept refrigerated until ready for boxing. Fresh cornmeal is sprinkled over these fattening beds every few days.

Red wigglers are packed and sold in the same kind of containers as night crawlers, only instead of being bedded in ground-up newspaper, the reds are packed in moistened peat moss. I buy Canadian peat moss, mix it with water in a five-gallon bucket, and let the mixture soak overnight. Before being used, it should be squeezed out well.

As we do with night crawlers, we exchange cartons of red wigglers that have been sitting around in a store for a couple of weeks. This way you don't lose any worms, and the customer is always satisfied.

The worm business isn't my only source of income—I'm

disabled. But without it, we'd starve . . . or else go on welfare . . . and raising worms sure beats welfare! It's our own business. The whole family participates—working the beds, catching the worms, sorting and selling them.

It's hard work, but we enjoy it. During the last four years, we've met people from all over the United States . . . right here on our doorstep in Rogue River, Oregon. If anyone needs help or advice in starting their own worm business, feel free to write us (Steve's Worm Farm, 819 Pine Street, Rogue River, Oregon 97537). The worm business won't make anyone rich, but it's a good, honest way to make some money.

Making Money
with Earthworms

by Maurice Franz

"There is constant demand for domesticated earthworms. We have enjoyed a successful shipping business, sending orders to New York, Honolulu, Canada, and Australia. We have developed a simple and successful shipping technique, and many others have set themselves up in business to enjoy the same privileges as we."

That's what Mary R. Roethl reported in the April 1954 issue of *Organic Gardening and Farming* when she wrote "How to Run a Successful Worm Business." Today we feel there is plenty of room and opportunity to make extra money—side-income money—out of your homestead by putting its assets to work. Here are some of the things Mary Roethl told us back in 1954.

"Measuring the success of this business by the trend of events," she begins, "we find many large farm projects in it. An excellent opportunity was offered to us to expand in this field on one of California's largest projects, a 900-acre ranch which grew from a homestead to a gigantic operation . . . . This farm raises, processes, and markets thousands of rainbow trout, 400 steers, as well as many acres of alfalfa. To this farm we transplanted 1,000 cultures of earthworms and supervised the project until it has now resulted in 21 earthworm ground pits—all of which are 12 feet wide and 225 feet long—covering a space of five acres. All contain active, squirming earthworms."

Mary Roethl is not the only woman to go into the earthworm-breeding business. Gladys Pederson and Minerva Cutler did it up in Maine as we shall subsequently see. But earthworm-raising is not exclusively a woman's occupation. Roy L. Donahue, Chairman of the Department of Agronomy of the University of New Hampshire, reported "roping in 50,000 earthworms from a 20-by-40-foot plot makes for good business with fishermen—and wonderfully fertile, productive soil in the garden."

Professor Donahue's interest in marketing earthworms began when he found that his garden soil was teeming with so many worms that he put up a sign "Worms" and sold 100 worms in his first day. Later, he reports, the children took over the business and "operated it with success for three seasons."

But not without organic effort, he stresses. Each year his family added 50 bales of hay to a 20-by-40 plot, and on occasion "bought and added poultry manure, dried molasses, and cornmeal.

"Always we kept the surface of the soil covered with hay or manure," he adds, "since drying kills earthworm egg capsules. In dry weather, we watered the earthworm bed, but it never got too wet, even in rainy weather. With plenty of hay as a cover, the worms lived in the hay when the soil became too wet."

The "harvest" from the well-tended 20-by-40 bed was about 50,000 worms with "as many worms there now as when we started four years ago." Worms always get scarce in the driest part of the summer, he notes, so he would obtain several loads of chicken manure and dump it nearby. When the soil became too dry, he would find his worms in the manure.

274

The repeating fish bait business is said to be particularly good, other breeders report. A. L. Dunn reported selling worms full-time, and has produced more than ten million worms in a year in glass houses and outdoor beds on his one-acre plot in San Leandro, California.

But you don't have to live in California to raise worms successfully or operate an organic farmstead. Captain C. E. Misener was raising earthworms back in 1952 in Wellfleet, Canada, and using their castings to step up soil fertility and boost crop yield and quality.

"The demand for my organic pure foods is forcing me to grow 25 acres of vegetables," he reported. "I have increased my raspberries to 32 acres, and my strawberries to 7 acres. But now I have to put in 20 more acres of raspberries, 10 more of strawberries, 5 acres of black currants, and 5 acres of black raspberries. The Grand Valley Canners have asked me to boost my acreage ten times."

In order to keep pace with the increased acreage burden and maintain or improve soil fertility, Capt. Misener made use of the indefatigable earthworm.

"My original worm population of 1,200 red wigglers imported from Hughes Worm Ranch in Savannah, Tennessee, has increased to 100,000,000," he reported. Capt. Misener provided food for his numerous brood by running two digesters filled with fresh manure which he allowed to age for a month, and then mixed with such farm wastes as sawdust, grain dust and corncobs. He "spiked" this with rock phosphate and used all his wood ashes for potash, added a little lime rock and then "put the mass in big beds about 3 by 3 by 75 feet.

"The red wigglers take over from here," he added, "and really do a job. The labor cost is negligible when one considers the great benefits. My yields have been tripling, and the products are of such high grade, they command as much as double the market prices. And the demand is growing."

Such is Capt. Misener's report, made over 20 years ago.

We believe it has a real message for today's organic homesteader. What he did 25 years ago in Canada can be done now because the organic movement enjoys a prestige it never had before.

In addition to their castings, worms are in great demand among fishermen and bird breeders. And you don't need a lot of money to get started. You can begin part-time, with a small cash investment just as Gladys Pederson and Minerva Cutler did in West Brooksville, Maine.

Their business reportedly grew so rapidly in one year that one of the partners gave up her teaching job, so they could devote full time to the project. The investment will vary; you can buy 1,200 red worms for $5.25, or 5,000 for $20. You can also get 10,000 bedrun of pit-run worms for $27.50. Pit-run is favored by many breeders, particularly when it contains a good proportion of large worms plus egg capsules. Pit-run may take 30 to 60 days longer to attain production but it's worth the extra time. Worms in all stages of growth are recommended because the young ones adapt themselves quickly to change.

Cost of culture boxes and even the rather king-sized outdoor pits should not be prohibitive. But the boxes—you most probably can obtain what you need free from your local shopping center stores and work them into shape—should be kept indoors, which means you'll have to keep them in a fairly warm place, such as the cellar or garage. Be sure to take this factor into consideration when making your plans. Also, the outdoor pit should be shaded and have covers or overhead shelter during the winter.

Additional costs include shipping boxes or cartons, and peat moss in which the worms are shipped. Holes should be punched in the cartons, and the peat moss soaked in water for 12 hours and squeezed dry. The Misses Pederson and Cutler reported using ice-cream cartons—a quart handles 250 to 300 worms, and a gallon holds 1,500 to 2,000 worms.

While most professional earthworm growers prefer outdoor pits with some sort of overhead shelter, it might be a good idea to start with boxes which can be placed in the cellar, the shed, or even the garage. This will give you a chance to find out what you have to do, and what the market potential is before investing in a fairly expensive permanent installation.

Noted earthworm breeder Thomas J. Barrett favored vegetable lug boxes stacked in twelve-box (three stacks, each four boxes high) setups on a wooden base. He used two-by-twos to separate the boxes for aeration and ventilation, and drilled quarter-inch holes in the box bottoms for drainage. When necessary, he reinforced the boxes to prevent sagging from the weight of the contents, and attached a simple lath handle to the sides for easy, safe handling. Finally, he labeled or numbered his boxes to keep track of production and tabulate results.

Getting the boxes ready for the worms is a simple, commonsense operation. After making sure the bottom of each box allows drainage and can take the weight of the contents, it is lined with either burlap or newspaper. Then, the box is filled with the compost/bedding mixture.

Worms need moisture because they can only get oxygen by its dissolving directly on their skins. On the other hand, they can drown in too much, so it's a good idea to fluff up your compost mixture until it can be compressed in the fist into a ball, "wet but not dripping." Then layer the bottom of the box with grass clippings or dried leaves and fill in with compost to within three inches of the top.

Next, dump 500 breeders into each box or one-half pound of pit-run worms, turning on a strong light immediately over them to make them go down into the compost quickly. (If you're working outdoors, sunlight will do.) Next the box should be filled with compost to within one inch of the top and cornmeal and coffee grounds added to it. Finally the box should be filled with grass clippings or dried leaves, and a wet cloth or burlap tucked in over them *with all the ends tucked inside the box to keep the worms inside*.

If you're confident enough to work with an outdoor pit

(preferably after you've been able to raise worms successfully in boxes), the experience of Hans D. Birk should be of real value because he's been raising worms outdoors in Canada where the winters are really severe.

"I have built pits," he reported, "four feet square and four feet deep using cement block for overwintering the worms." The pit has a cement floor with drain although a good layer of gravel will also work well. When filling a new pit, he piles a "good amount" of old straw or rough material on the bottom, and adds the contents of an old pit or compost pile with lots of worms in it.

Into this he empties every day the contents of the family garbage pail which consists of table scraps and vegetable peelings. He spreads the refuse carefully over the entire surface with a rake, and is careful not to let any piles accumulate that hinder good aeration and cause bad odors. He stresses that "decaying material needs lots of air the first few days and, if it is provided, there will be no flies." He keeps his pit covered with both a fly screen and slanted roof to keep out pests, rain, and snow. Once a week he gives the pit a good soaking and, "once in a while," adds a sprinkling of manure, leaf mold, coffee grounds "and even old flour from local mills."

In this continuously growing heap, Birk's worms thrive, "multiplying and working much harder than they possibly could outside in the garden. The pit is always slightly warm," he notes.

When winter comes, Birk tops the pit with a bale of straw spread over the entire surface. He makes sure "there is no hole that would let warmth escape," and then closes the roof, which he doesn't open until the following April. "The worms thrive all through the winter," he reported, "and multiply 200-fold by next spring."

When the weather warms up in the spring he removes the finished compost, usually "adding some sugar water or molasses to bring the worms to the surface." Then the upper layers are taken out carefully and emptied in cone-shaped piles onto plastic sheets and exposed to the sun. The worms retreat to the mossy centers of the piles, allowing him to remove the outside portions of finished compost, which he applies to the garden.

Birk's description of this rich compost—for which a market exists—is worth repeating here in full. Greenhouse operators and nurserymen can be made into "repeating" customers, once you demonstrate the excellence of your worms' output. Here is what Hans Birk has to say:

"Actually this pit-compost is so rich that I only fertilize the planting holes of vegetables and a circle around the trunks of trees. I also use it as an activator in starting new compost heaps above ground, so they break down faster. Remember, the pit method is used mainly for composting garbage and other wastes that might be a nuisance.

"My worm compost never seems too rich or too sour. It shows a steady pH 7, and the phosphate and potash content is always quite high."

Getting Started. Mary Roethl set up a successful earthworm business and has based it on a very simple and inexpensive operation—unlined "ground earthworm pits." First, dig a trench six inches deep, two feet wide, and three feet long which will give you enough room for 1,000 breeders. Fill it with manure and soil mixed equally, using the soil from the pit. Mound up well and dampen until there is a "thorough penetration of water."

Next, empty the 1,000 worms on top and immediately cover with a light top dressing of straw or leaves to conserve moisture and also to avoid "hot" materials. The worms will promptly descend and occupy the entire pit. It will take them about three weeks to become established after which they should receive a top dressing of food such as cottonseed meal, cornmeal, coffee grounds, and manure.

A cold climate is no problem as far as the ground pit method is concerned, although the Roethl experience seems to have been mostly in California. Sash frames such as storm doors or windows can be applied when more housing or protection is needed, and extra application of top dressing will encourage the worms to feed constantly and multiply satisfactorily.

Of all the countless varieties of earthworms, you most likely will work with the red wigglers or *Eisenia foetida*, raising them and then selling them or their castings. Red wigglers are active, most prolific and reproduce throughout the year and, judging from the orders coming through the mail, are preferred as bait by the majority of fishermen.

According to the wildlife researchers at Texas A.&M. University, 50 to 100 worms are enough to start a small bed. They recommend feeding the worms leaves of celery, cabbage, lettuce, and turnips, chopped up and worked into the bed. They also prefer one part of cottonseed meal mixed into two parts of alfalfa meal.

Many breeders count out their worms into "fattening boxes" because they feel that they do not attain the full size in the pits. Since the worms are already counted—500 to the box—the grower is able to quickly fill wholesale orders.

Can Money Be Made by Breeding Earthworms?   Based on the experiences of readers of *Organic Gardening and Farming* quoted here, we believe extra income can be made from earthworms. We also believe that there is a place for one or more earthworm pits in the organically functional homestead—it is probably the best way to safely and effectively recycle the family garbage. So you're urged to study the area in which you live and also the resources of your home grounds. We have seen that Professor Donahue had a veritable "mine" of fishing worms growing naturally in his soil that only had to be dug up. If you live in or near a fishing resort, the answer is obvious—concentrate on the red wigglers and put up a sign.

If there are greenhouses or houseplant growers within a reasonable hailing and hauling distance, contact the proprietors. It's hard to believe they won't have use for your earthworm castings. One quart of castings in the past sold for 26 cents (which seems low today) and it must be assumed that wholesale bulk orders will be somewhat lower. But the castings should be reckoned with as a source of income, and also a sure way to improve the soil fertility of your home grounds. Just remember what Captain Misener has done in Canada.

And finally, there is the mail-order earthworm business, which will take some organizing and study. You'll have to advertise and find ways to reach a steady, repeating market; only experience plus trial and error will show you the best way to do it.

But it's been done and it's being done. Like Earl Shields who many years ago wrote *Raising Earthworms for Profit*, we believe that "The earthworm-growing industry has zoomed to multi-million-dollar proportions and is still growing. It is providing comfortable living incomes or supplementary earnings for thousands of families."

In addition, it's a good, clean, organic business that really "belongs" in the national ecology. Good luck to you.

Earthworm Gardening in the Desert

by Lynn Fuller

We are organic gardeners who live in the "not-so-dust-free" area just south of Tucson. Surrounding our humus-laden growing beds the sun-baked, hard-packed gravel sits atop a layer of cementlike hardpan—"caliche" we call it.

Nevertheless, thanks to organic practices, including the liberal use of earthworms, we have transformed our "scrabble-patch" into growing beds of fertile, humus-rich soil. Starting with our own seeds, we have even raised date palms as well as our own orange and lemon trees.

In addition we grow enough salad greens to keep our table continuously supplied with fresh, green vitamins. We also have a more-than-adequate stock of radishes, onions, chives, garlic, scallions, and leeks plus beets, chard, squash, and to-matoes.

It wasn't always like this. The Arizona desert isn't so easily tamed. Progress has by no means been continuous and there have been setbacks, times when our faith in organic gardening was severely tested.

For instance there was the time when the chard and beets were six inches high—and swarming with clouds of little green leafhoppers. We were still neophytes and frankly skeptical of the "No-Poison" idea. However, although we were new to true organic gardening, we decided to follow the law to the letter and let Nature find its own balance.

We were happy we did because within a couple of days we noticed zebra-tailed lizards darting in and out of the greens. Then our friendly horned toads started making their visits to the growing beds—regularly. Within a week we had trouble finding even a dozen hoppers.

This not only amazed but thrilled us as well. We felt we could depend on Nature to protect our garden.

Then, about three or four weeks later, we had a large influx of grasshoppers. Again, for about two weeks, our faith in Nature was pretty badly strained. But one day we noticed the cardinals and wrens making their morning visits through the beds as the grasshoppers steadily diminished in number and then vanished. Our faith in organics was vindicated.

But we were lucky because, at the very beginning, we stumbled onto the earthworm as an assistant in building fertility into our most unlikely soil.

I had been looking for an easy way to retire and had decided to raise earthworms. But that plan was almost completely changed when we looked into the raising and cultivation of the domesticated earthworm.

After a protracted session of study and reading on earthworm culture, we suddenly realized we had stumbled upon the one sure way of building a year-round garden—we would mellow and cure our starved, sick land with earthworms!

"We needed fill in front of the house, so we filled one side to the necessary height and placed four-inch cement blocks to make planting beds, each measuring three by ten feet."

283

It took some time to get started because our limited budget held us down to an initial order of 500 breeders from a Georgia supplier. They weren't babied or pampered. From the very beginning they received only one bedding. But they did get plenty of food: dried horse manure, well trampled and with the dirt mixed right in, plus a daily supply of garbage or kitchen refuse. The worms throve on it.

We took the well-trampled manure—it is well aged and doesn't heat up—and soaked it thoroughly. Then we dumped the worms on top of it and forgot about them except once each week when we soaked the bed and added more manure—about an inch at a time.

Our first colony was started in a washtub. Before long it had spread out to two tubs, then into a packing box measuring four by six by four feet. This we buried in the ground about two feet deep to reduce evaporation. Here the worms stayed in the ground all summer. By August they had to spread out quick.

The need for a new and larger home was so urgent that we were literally forced to develop a simple pit which could be made quickly and cheaply. An open pit evolved, about 18 inches deep and as wide and long as the terrain permitted. This we edged with four-inch blocks to reduce side leaching. Since we were in need of considerable fill in the front of the house, we decided to build our first pits there in the form of large planter beds at ground level.

We loosened the gravel with a pick and put scrap board down for a bottom base for two good reasons. First, it gives the worms a place in which to hide if it gets too hot and dry, and, second, it makes it a lot easier to clean out the beds when it is time to harvest the worms.

On top of the boards we placed about two inches of straw and filled the bed with the dried horse manure mixed with dirt and sand, four to one.

We finished three beds in this way, each three by ten feet, and spread the castings and egg capsules from the old bed on top of these pits. This was finished by the end of

August and has since provided us with the highest-quality topsoil we could wish for.

For our first garden we decided on quick-growing vegetables. In 20 days we were eating tender radishes and lettuce and even had a tasty meal of Swiss chard. We planted beets, but they never reached maturity because we prefer the young beet tops as greens mixed with the Swiss chard.

We've had fresh salads every day for months and we plant every month to insure a continuous supply. One full bed consists of multiplying onions, the chives, garlic, scallions, and leeks. This, combined with the above plantings of leaf and Bibb lettuce, provides us with a constant source of salad material. These were the things we missed and wanted most— and now have in full abundance.

As arid-region gardeners we are forced to keep a close watch on the weather. In the hot days, the beds have to be watched to prevent drying. So we mulch heavily with straw to conserve soil moisture and use the runoff from our cooler during the hot part of the day.

But, by using the straw mulch, we have eliminated the need for constant watering which plagues so many desert gardeners.

What impresses my wife most is the fact that we never lack for special potting mixtures now. All we do is scoop some of the soil from the worm bed right into the pot. This is the only secret you have to know in order to become a never-failing, green thumb gardener.

This mellow, rich, fertile, humus-laden soil has allowed us to take cuttings from the most expensive roses—which we could never afford. We place them in the shaded worm bed, cover them with fruit jars and water once a week. They have never lost a leaf nor withered, and are now prospering and growing rapidly.

Summing it up, we can only pay tribute here to earthworms whose ceaseless activity has helped us turn this arid, sun-stricken soil into fertile growing beds packed with loamy humus. We know now that we can depend on Nature to build the land, protect our garden, and maintain a soundly organic balance.

Are we happy with our hobby?

You bet we are.

Domestic Rabbits, Earthworms, and the Organic Homestead

by Avery R. Jenkins

The domestic rabbit came into its own on the West Coast during World War II, during meat rationing, and proved to thousands that it was more than an animal just to be admired or kept as a pet. In the past 30 years, rabbit raising has become an increasingly popular homestead venture—and for good reasons. Rabbits are cheaper to raise, take less time and work than chickens; a 50- by 100-foot area will hold 200 rabbits and their litters; rabbit meat is more widely appreciated, and their skins and furs bring a good price.

When we began raising rabbits, sanitation was a minor problem, as the droppings from only three rabbits were not enough to worry about. Then the young ones came along and made their daily contributions to make it quite an arduous task at times to keep this space underneath the hutches clean and odorless.

To conquer this problem, we decided to be lazy about it and to attempt something we had heard of, a way to sneak up on nature—or rather to let nature assist us. We first nailed some boards around the bottom of the hutch legs to catch the droppings, and as they continued to accumulate, we spread some agricultural lime and peat moss on top of them to help control any disagreeable odor. This proved very effective.

More droppings continued to fall, and when there were enough of them, we used lime and peat moss to cover them until this reached a depth of about six inches. When we removed the nestbox materials, we added them to the bedding under the hutches, and occasionally a few leaves were added. This mixture could have been taken from under the hutches and put into our vegetable garden with excellent results, but we had other plans for it before it finally reached our garden.

We purchased enough pit-run brandling earthworms to average about 100 per square foot of space, and put them under the hutches. They were not scattered over the bedding, but a small trench was opened up down the middle and the earthworms were placed in this trench. I covered the trench lightly with bedding, thoroughly sprinkled with a garden hose, and allowed the worms to go their own way for a few more weeks before checking. To our surprise, in some places of the bedding, the earthworms were very numerous, and in others not a worm could be found. However, after a number of years of breeding brandling earthworms, we still find this to be true, no matter how many there may be in the beds.

These worms multiplied at an astonishingly fast rate, making the proverbial breeding of the rabbits seem slow by comparison, and soon we could tell a big difference in the bedding in which the worms were living and breeding. It had assumed a very different form, and when visitors came into our rabbitry, which by now numbered around 100 animals, they would ask "Where is the odor?"

Numbers of visitors stated that they had been skeptical about visiting a domestic rabbitry, or rabbit ranch, and also of eating domestic rabbit meat because of the imagined uncleanness about them and their habitat. Everyone is greatly surprised to learn that with just a little effort on the part of the owner, and with the help of the earthworms, it is a pleasure to visit and learn just how easily the rabbits and earthworms may be raised.

The earthworms do an amazing job of converting the rabbit droppings into a rich, black, humus, with an actually pleasing aroma. This compost-humus can now be mixed with garden soil and you can expect (and get) excellent growth from all your plants. To prove its mildness, we have sown seeds directly into it. They were not burned as they would have been in almost any other kind of rich manure of equal age.

Domestic rabbits offer an enjoyable and profitable hobby for many; they have even developed into a full-time business for some. I believe you will agree with me that raising rabbits and earthworms together make a perfect combination for the organic grower. I've found we all work fine together.

New California Retirement Business— Angleworms Combined with Rabbits

by Robert J. Wyndham

Raising rabbits and angleworms together has everything to recommend it. Not only is sanitation around the rabbit cages and hutches improved, but real money is to be made.

Angleworms often sell at two-thirds of a cent each, and one California breeder—Leslie Zadany of Fontana—sold over two million worms in 1967 for an estimated gross take of over $13,000. Although rabbit-meat prices are up, many homesteaders are saying that "the worm has turned" in rabbit raising and that "the worm's tail is now wagging the rabbit."

As a result, rabbit raisers are now expanding production of angleworms. Worm-raising beds are no longer under the rabbit cages but have been moved up on tables where they are more easily reached. Here's how the method works.

Zadany and Gretchen Swarthwood, another Fontana rabbit breeder, prepare their wormbeds with peat moss that is water soaked for 72 hours and then covered with rabbit manure. After two weeks, the bed is watered again and seeded with angleworms. The average wormbed, 2½ feet wide by 4 feet long and 10 inches deep, takes 10 to 12 pounds of worms. The eggs hatch out in two to three weeks, and under ideal conditions, the original 10 to 12 pounds will produce a ton of angleworms. Theoretically—space permitting—1,000 worms could multiply themselves into one billion offspring in two years.

But, as the California dealers say, that's strictly up to the rabbits—they've got to keep producing too.

Worms—A Safe, Effective Garbage Disposal

by Mary Appelhof

Using worms for garbage disposal is good, commonsense gardening.

Here's how it's done: Set up a container large enough to hold several thousand worms where they will not freeze in the winter. You fill the container to about two-thirds capacity with loose, organic bedding—leaves, peat moss, manure, shredded newspaper. Then add a couple of thousand worms, and put a burlap bag, hunk of old carpet, or straw on top to retain moisture. Every week or so you bury your household garbage in the bedding, stir it up a bit, and water it. This rids you of your garbage and feeds the worms. The worms do the rest, namely, reduce the garbage and ingredients of the bedding to produce a potting soil which will, in turn, help to produce healthier plants.

The advantages, important to both the household and the garden, are worth citing. Here they are:

1. Odorless reduction of kitchen wastes;

2. Creation of nutrient-rich worm castings both for the garden row and potting soil;

3. A surplus of worms which can be added to the compost pile, the planting row and your houseplant containers, where they may be of help but will not necessarily flourish;

Bedding for worms should be moist, not soaked. Turn it occasionally to keep it from massing or packing.

4. You'll have worms for fishing all year-round;

5. You'll be helping the environment—not running it down.

In comparison, the disadvantages are minor:

1. You spend a few dollars for worms to get started;

2. You use up some household space for worm bins;

3. You expend some time and energy on the project.

What we are trying to accomplish is to get rid of our garbage and enrich the soil. We're asking earthworms to do it. Feed them just about anything organic which is already dead. They will do the rest—turn the soil, aerate it, make nutrients available to plants, reproduce, and expand the army of workers.

A farm-size operation describing the extent to which this materials handling can develop is given by the late Dr. George Sheffield Oliver in T. J. Barrett's book, *Harnessing the Earthworm*, a book highly recommended for homesteaders. Dr. Oliver describes a barnyard pit of the 1800s, 50 by 100 feet, two feet deep, especially designed to provide for the breeding of earthworms. Daily droppings from about 50 horses, plus cattle, sheep and hogs, were transported from the barn to the pit by means of an overhead trolley. A flock of ducks and about 500 chickens continuously scratched in the barnyard, adding their droppings to the pit. Bedding and straw were added to the pits, the barnyard was scraped and raked, and the entire material distributed in an even layer on the compost. Clay, rich in mineral elements, was added, and the entire area was occasionally flooded with water from the nearby creek to add moisture.

Millions of earthworms were continually feeding upon and breeding in this compost, transforming a mixture of manure, urine, litter, and clay into a dark, fertile, crumbly soil. In the spring, tons of the earthworm- and capsule-laden compost were spread on the soil and rapidly plowed under, placing worms and nutrients where they would be available for the crops to be planted. Dr. Oliver thus described a technique permitting the continual addition of millions of worms to the soil on a 160-acre self-sustaining farm which never knew a crop failure. A method follows which will enable you, on a smaller homestead, to start with a few thousand worms, eventually enabling you to produce millions.

A satisfactory worm for this purpose is the red worm, sometimes referred to as the red wiggler, brandling, or hybrid red worm. A mature worm will range from 1½ to 3 inches long, and is ³/₁₆ inch in diameter. Its reproductive capacity is phenomenal! Under ideal conditions, one thousand can procreate one million in one year.

Here's a good way to get your earthworm "ranch" started: For indoor propagation of a sufficient quantity of worms to reduce your household garbage to fine potting soil, find or build a container big enough for about 1,000 to 2,000 breeders. Following the guideline of four square feet of surface area, 8 to 18 inches deep, for 1,000 breeders, this container accommodates about 1,500 or 1½ pounds of breeders and offspring for the winter months.

By spring, all worms can then be transferred to larger outside pits. An old discarded trough with holes is fine—saves you the work of drilling a hole or two for drainage. Worms require moisture, but they won't fare well in a soaking-wet bedding. A properly constructed pit will let water percolate through and the excess drain off. Buckets underneath the holes can catch the drips.

Limestone gravel as a bottom layer in the bin helps to facilitate drainage. It may also help to offset the acidity generated by rapid decomposition of garbage. Worms can be injured or killed by an environment which is too acid. Limestone gravel, and the use of powdered lime in the pits helps to counteract this acidity.

Planks placed over the limestone make it easier to work the bin using either a pitchfork or your hands. Turning the compost isn't as discouraging as it sounds, and the feel and smell of the rich, moist, dark humus is really quite satisfying. Don't worry, the worms don't bite.

Bedding mixtures vary, and experimentation is encouraged. A satisfactory one is a mixture of about one-half ground peat moss and one-half rotted manure. After the bin is set up and wet down, it is advisable to wait a couple of days before the worms are placed on top and allowed to work down into the bedding. You don't want to run the risk of getting them cooked if the freshly moistened manure heats up!

Worms can be purchased from a number of suppliers who advertise in gardening and sportsman's magazines. They are shipped at all times of the year, and indoor pits can be started at any time, even in the northern states. It will probably be easier to buy worms from a southern supplier if you set up in the middle of the winter. The supplier should provide some recommendations about how to set up bins, what to do with the worms when they arrive. After you are set up, you can bury your kitchen garbage in your bins and let the worms eat it up!

Once you have made the plunge, and have worms propagating in your bins, start thinking about how you'll use your ever-increasing quantities of worms. Use worms in your compost pile. After it has gone through its initial heating (hot enough to kill worms), add worms. Let them work up and down through your pile, digesting the decaying, decomposing organic material, making tunnels to help get air to lower layers. They save you turning the pile, and do a better job, anyhow.

Use worms and worm castings in your houseplants. The worms help to keep the soil tilled, let water seep down more readily, permit air to circulate around the roots, put nutrients into more soluble form for the plants. Feed your worms in your flower pots, too! Coffee grounds, apple cores, vegetable scrapings. Watch your plants thrive with such industrious tillers of the soil.

For continued rapid propagation during spring and summer, you probably will want to set up a more extensive pit system outside. Dig a trench, line it with cement blocks, or wood planks held in by stakes, or pour some concrete over wire mesh and make yourself a concrete-lined trench. Three feet wide by 15 long is a common size, and can produce about 50,000 worms in a season. Techniques vary, and lots of things work.

Haul in some manure (or get it from the barn), mix it with some peat moss if you want, wet it down, and let it pass through the heating period. Divide your household bin contents between this pit and your compost pile. Add the worms, capsules, young worms, the castings, and bedding. Keep the bedding moist, not soaked. Keep rodents out if they are a problem, turn bedding with a pitchfork occasionally, and add more garbage and more manure as the worms seem to be working the rest into a packed mass of castings. Worms move with difficulty in packed soil or bedding.

When the worms seem to be too crowded, you can construct new pits and divide the contents of the old ones. Or you can spread castings—worms, capsules, and all—out under your heavily mulched orchard trees or in your gardens. Or give Dr. Oliver's homestead farm technique a try, and use worms and composted animal manures by the ton to apply to the fields in the spring. Or develop a market and begin selling worms. Be sure to keep enough to set up your inside bins in winter. And bed down the outside pits with lots of manure, and vegetation. An 18-inch layer of straw or hay will help to insulate the pits from zero temperatures. In northern states, it is best not to crack the frozen layer of hay or straw until all danger of severe cold is past.

So, worms can help you to simplify your life, or to make it more complicated. With the money you save on fertilizers and pesticides, you can buy yourself some excellent reading material on how to go at this homesteading more sensibly using worms to help you out. Highly recommended is Barrett's book, *Harnessing the Earthworm*, previously mentioned. One of these days I'll even get into Darwin's classic on worms, *The Formation of Vegetable Mould through the Action of Worms with Observations on their Habits*. At the moment, I'm still looking for those long winter evenings when there's time to work through my ever-increasing list of "Books to Read." But I'm getting there, and worms are going to help me do it!

Build Your Own Earthworm-Casting "Factory"

by R. N. Coffman

Earthworm castings make the finest compost available, and you can get the worms to produce them for you in abundance by building this simple six-box kit which costs less than $5. Here's how we've been doing it down in Texas for years.

Starting with minimum production of earthworm castings, you will need: 1,000 ordinary, red worms (red wigglers, available by mail from many suppliers) all of bait size; three compost boxes in which the end product is produced; one screen box; one ⅛-inch mesh shaker screen; one ¼-inch mesh shaker screen; one sack black Michigan peat moss; and one small sack of dried commercial cattle manure. (Be certain this manure has not been chemically treated.)

A complete earthworm-casting kit consists of six boxes, with the same size inside dimensions—15-by-11-by-3⅞ inches. Use galvanized ring-type nails, tacks and hardware cloth to lap the corners, nailing both ways to make a strong, durable frame.

We work with ½-by-8-inch redwood which is reasonably priced, does not warp, is easily handled, and moisture resistant. We rip the ½-by-8 in half, which gives us two boards, each 3⅝ inches wide. Working with #6 galvanized nails, we predrill with a ³/₃₂-inch bit to avoid splitting, setting three nails to the corner.

Check the frame for squareness before nailing on the bottom—two 1-by-8-inch pieces, 12 inches long, plus another piece the same length, ripped to the needed width. Use the drill bit for nail holes for a better job, and tack a small cleat on each end for easier handling. (See fig. 19.)

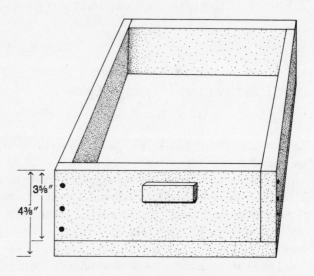

Figure 19 Earthworm Box Dimensions

The screen box is made just the same with 3⅝-inch boards but with a ⅛-inch hardware cloth bottom tacked into place with galvanized carpet tacks.

The shaker screen boxes also have the same inside dimensions. One nail to a corner is enough. Square the frame and tack on a piece of ⅛-inch mesh hardware cloth, cinching it into place with ½-by-½-inch wood stripping. Follow the same procedure for the #2 screen box, using ¼-inch mesh.

Shake enough Michigan peat through the ¼-inch screen to fill a compost box to within a half-inch of the top. Pieces that do not fall through freely should be discarded. Place 500 worms on top of the peat, and when they have gone down into it—takes just a few minutes—cover the peat with ⅜ inch of dried cattle manure.

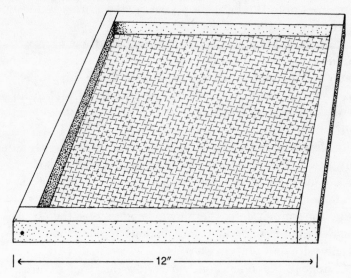

Figure 20 Shaker Screen for Earthworm Box

Use an ordinary garden sprinkling can to sprinkle this filled box evenly with four pints—no more and no less—of clean tap water. Then prepare the second compost box exactly the same, including the 500 worms.

Stack the two boxes, one above the other, and place the third—empty—compost box on top, bottom down, to serve as a cover. Set the stack where it will not be in contact with the ground, sheltered from direct sunlight and weather, and where it will not become too hot or too cold. Any temperature between 50° and 90°F will be suitable for good production.

Do not disturb the boxes for 10 days; leave them strictly alone.

On the tenth day, fill the empty compost box up to within a half inch of the top with Michigan peat shaken through the ¼-inch screen. Set the screen on top of the filled

297

compost box and put them to one side. Then transfer by hand a quantity of castings and worms from one of the two processed compost boxes into the ⅛-inch shaker screen, placed flat on the bench. Shake the castings through the finer screening onto the bench top, leaving the worms and roughage on the screen.

Then, working as quickly as possible—the worms will go through the ⅛-inch mesh and are hard to dislodge—dump them and the leftovers into the ¼-inch screen box, which has been placed on the newly filled compost box. Don't be afraid to shake hard—the worms are tough. Repeat the operation until all the castings and worms are out of the first box.

As the worms go down into the peat in the newly filled box, use the fingers every 5 minutes to rake off the top layer of rough material in the screen box, placing it in a separate container. In about 30 minutes all the worms will have passed from the screen into the newly loaded box below. Then remove the screen, add ⅜-inch manure topping, and sprinkle evenly with four pints of water.

Repeat the operation, emptying the second boxful of worms into the first box. Again, you will have two boxes full of worms with the empty one serving as a cover—and nothing more to do for 10 days.

However you will have 12 to 14 quarts of pure earthworm castings—the finest compost ever produced—and can count on having that much more rich fertilizer within another 10 days. This compost is practically odorless.

You will have no problem in finding uses for this soil enricher, and it is certain that these earthworm castings supply everything a plant needs just as nature intended.

Once you start applying earthworm castings to your soil, I doubt you will ever be satisfied with other fertilizers. But, if your present soil does not have plenty of organic food for earthworms, they will go elsewhere in search of it—no matter how many boxcar-loads of them are dumped on your land. So, keep on using their castings as they are produced, and add all the other organic material you can find.

Appendix

The Earthworm Grower's Library: Suggested Readings

Technical materials

Biology of Earthworms, by C. A. Edwards and J. R. Lofty. 299 pp., illus. London: Chapman and Hall, Ltd., 1972. Without doubt, the best recent book on the subject, presented with a minimum of technical jargon. A massive amount of scientific research is condensed and presented here in a terse and clear fashion.

The Challenge of Earthworm Research, edited by Robert Rodale. 102 pp., illus. Emmaus, Pa.: Soil and Health Foundation, 1961. Twelve classic articles reprinted in a single volume.

The Physiology of Earthworms, by M. S. Laverack. 216 pp., illus. New York: Pergamon Press, 1963. An excellent treatise, covering biochemical architecture, metabolism, calciferous glands, the axial field, nitrogenous excretion, water relations, respiration, regeneration, neurosecretion, the nervous system, and behavior. Not for the layman.

What Every Gardener Should Know about Earthworms, by Henry Hopp. 40 pp., illus. Charlotte, Vt.: Garden Way Publishing Co., 1973. Many of Hopp's findings are presented in this small book, a valuable one for the farmer and gardener.

The classics

Earthworms: Their Intensive Propagation and Use in Biological Soil-Building, by Thomas J. Barrett. 9th ed., 1948. 64 pp., illus. Barrett's "Earthmaster System" of organic homesteading is explained here, including his plan for a two-acre self-contained plot ("Security Acres"), generous helpings of sound philosophy, and a 14-page earthworm production manual. (Published privately by Thomas J. Barrett; now out of print.)

The Formation of Vegetable Mould through the Action of Worms with Observations on their Habits, by Charles Darwin. 1881; London: Faber & Faber, Ltd., 1949. 153 pp., illus. The earthworm book of all earthworm books.

Harnessing the Earthworm, by Thomas J. Barrett. Boston: Wedgwood Press, 1947; 1959. Described by the author as "a practical inquiry into soil-building, soil conditioning, and plant nutrition through the action of earthworms, with instructions for intensive propagation and use of Domesticated Earthworms in biological soil-building."

Our Friend, the Earthworm, by George Sheffield Oliver. 103 pp., illus. Emmaus, Pa.: Rodale Press, 1937; 1954. Oliver ties in the raising of earthworms with a strong philosophy for man's happiness.

Help for growers

The ABCs of the Earthworm Business, by Ruth Myers. The author draws on 10 years of experience in building one of California's biggest worm farms to give information the newcomer wants to know. (Shields Publications, Box 472, Elgin, IL 60120.)

The Complete Book of Composting, by J. I. Rodale and the staff of *Organic Gardening and Farming*. 1,008 pp., illus. Emmaus, Pa.: Rodale Press, 1960. Plenty of information about using earthworms in composting, in this all-encompassing volume.

Earthworm Feeds and Feeding, by Charlie Morgan. 84 pp. 1961. A work manual of feed preparation and use. (Shields Publications.)

Earthworm Harvester Plans and Instructions. The developers say, "The harvester can pick and pack up to 200,000 worms in one day and one man operating it. No hard work either." (Eco-Enterprises, Rt. 6, Box 755, Sequim, WA 95382.)

Earthworm Selling and Shipping Guide, by Charlie Morgan. 82 pp. Essential reference volume for all commercial raisers; explains licenses and postal regulations, packages and packaging materials and where to get them. (Shields Publications.)

Earthworms for Ecology & Profit, by Ronald E. Gaddie Sr., and Donald E. Douglas. Vol. 1, *Scientific Earthworm Farming*; 192 pp., illus. 1975. Vol. 2, *Earthworms & the Ecology*; 190 pp., illus. 1977. A good two-volume set, containing a wealth of data not only on commercial raising but on a whole range of topics, including farming and gardening. (Bookworm Publishing, Box 3037, Ontario, CA 91761.)

Facts about Night Crawlers, by George Sroda. 112 pp., illus. An all-around manual written by "The Worm Czar." Chapters on harvesting, holding, and managing night crawlers, transporting worms for fishing, the red worm, soil building, and merchandising worms. (George Sroda, Amherst Jct., WI 54407.)

How to Sell Fishworms by Mail, by Robert Williams. 24 pp. A complete working manual on the advertising and marketing of fishworms by mail. (Shields Publications.)

Larger Red Worms, by George H. Holwager. 36 pp., illus. 1952. (Shields Publications.)

Let an Earthworm Be Your Garbage Man. This report by Home, Farm & Garden Research Associates, Inc., includes complete directions for building a northern worm pit to handle a family's kitchen refuse all winter long. Also contains material by Henry Hopp which appears in *What Every Gardener Should Know about Earthworms*. (Available from Shields Publications.)

Over 300 Questions and Answers on Raising Worms, by Hugh Carter. Practical advice from the owner of one of America's biggest worm operations. (Carter Worm Farm, Plains, GA 31780.)

Profit from Earthworms, by Herb and Les Lanser. 159 pp., illus. A complete guide to raising earthworms for market. (Clear Creek Farms, Inc., 5300 Clark Rd., Paradise, CA 95969.)

Profitable Earthworm Farming, by Charlie Morgan. Much information on earthworm biology, history, types, classifications, and reproductive processes, plus practical suggestions for raising. (Shields Publications.)

Raising the African Night Crawler, by Charlie Morgan. 54 pp., illus. 2d ed. 1970. All you need to know to grow the finicky African. (Shields Publications.)

Raising Earthworms for Profit, by Earl B. Shields. 128 pp., illus. A good, basic book for the beginning grower, offering a wide range of advice on nearly every practical topic. This book has gone through 15 editions and is still the most popular guide to raising commercial species. (Shields Publications.)

Personal experiences

A-Worming We Did Go!, by Ruth Myers. 72 pp., illus. 1968; 1975. Essential reading for anyone who contemplates entering the earthworm-raising business. A light book with loads of practical knowledge learned through experience. (Shields Publications.)

With Tails We Win!, by Mary B. Crowe and Gladys S. Bowen. 32 pp., illus. 1954. A composting adventure with earthworms. (Shields Publications.)

The Worm Farm, by Charlie Morgan. 76 pp., illus. 1962. A diary, described by the author as the "complete story of building and operating a $20,000 worm business." (Shields Publications.)

Bibliography

Adey, W. R. 1951. The nervous system of the earthworm *Megascolex. J. Comp. Neurol.* 45:57–103.

Adolph, E. F. 1927. The regulation of volume and concentration in the body fluids of earthworms. *J. Exp. Zool.* 47:31–62.

————. 1943. *Physiological Regulations*. Lancaster, Pa.: Jaques Cattell Press, 502.

Agarwal, G. W.; Rao, K. S. K.; and Negi, L. S. 1958. Influence of certain species of earthworms on the structure of some hill soils. *Curr. Sci.* 27:213.

Allee, W. C.; Torvik, M. M.; Lahr, J. P.; and Hollister, P. L. 1930. Influence of soil reaction on earthworms. *Physiol. Zool.* 3,2:164–200.

Allen, R. W. 1960. Relative susceptibility of various species of earthworms to the larvae of *Capillaria annulata. Proc. Helminthol. Soc. Wash.* 17,2:58–64.

Amassian, V. E., and Floyd, W. F. 1946. Repetitive discharge of giant nerve fibres of the earthworm. *Nature, Lond.* 157:412–13.

Ambache, N.; Dixon, A. St. J.; and Wright, E. A. 1945. Some observations on the physiology and pharmacology of the nerve endings in the crop and gizzard of the earthworm with special reference to the effects of cooling. *J. Exp. Biol.* 21:46–57.

Anderson, J. C. 1956. Relations between metabolism and morphogenesis during regeneration in *Tubifex tubifex* II. *Biol. Bull. Wood's Hole* 110:179–89.

Appelhof, Mary. Worms—a safe, effective garbage disposal. *Organic Gardening and Farming*, Aug. 1974, 65–69.

Arbit, J. 1957. Diurnal cycles and learning in earthworms. *Am. Assoc. Adv. Sci.* 126:654–55.

Arrhenius, O. 1921. Influence of soil reaction on earthworms. *Ecology* 2:255–57.

Arthur, D. R. 1965. Form and function in the interpretation of feeding in Lumbricid worms. *Viewpoints in Biology* 4:204–51.

Atlavinyte, O., and Vanagas, J. 1973. Mobility of nutritive substances in relation to earthworm numbers in the soil. *Pedobiologia* 13:5.

Bahl, K. N. 1919. On a new type of nephridia found in Indian earthworms of the genus *Pheretima*. *Quart. J. Micr. Sci.* 64.

———. 1922. On the development of the 'enteronephric' type of nephridial system found in Indian earthworms of the genus *Pheretima*. *Quart. J. Micr. Sci.* 66:49–103.

———. 1927. On the reproductive processes of earthworms. Part 1. The process of copulation and exchange of sperms in *Eutyphoeus waltoni mich*. *Quart. J. Microscopy* 71:479.

———. 1945. Studies on the structure, development and physiology of the nephridia of Oligochaeta. VI. The physiology of excretion and the significance of the enteronephric type of nephridial system in Indian earthworms. *Quart. J. Micr. Sci.* 85:343–89.

———. 1947. Studies on the structure, development and physiology of the nephridia of Oligochaeta. VIII. Biochemical estimations of nutritive and excretory substances in the blood and coelomic fluid of the earthworm, and their bearing on the role of the two fluids in metabolism. *Quart. J. Micr. Sci.* 87:357–71.

———. 1947. Excretion in the Oligochaeta. *Biol. Rev.* 22:109–47.

———. 1950. *The Indian Zoological Memoirs. I. Pheretima.* 4th ed. Lucknow, India: Lucknow Pub. House.

Bailey, P. L. 1930. The influence of the nervous system in the regeneration of *Eisenia foetida* Savigny. *J. Exp. Zool.* 57:473–509.

Baker, W. L. 1946. DDT and earthworm populations. *J. Econ. Ent.* 39:404–5.

Baldwin, F. M. 1917. Diurnal activity of the earthworm. *J. Anim. Behav.* 7:187–90.

Ball, R. C., and Curry, L. L. 1973. *Culture and Agricultural Importance of Earthworms.* Mich. St. Univ. Ext. Bul. E766.

Barker, R. J. 1958. Notes on some ecological effects of DDT sprayed on elms. *J. Wildl. Manage.* 22:269–74.

Barley, K. P. 1959. The influence of earthworms on soil fertility. II. Consumption of soil and organic matter by the earthworm *Allolobophora caliginosa*. *Aust. J. Agr. Res.* 10,2:179–158.

———. 1959. Earthworms and soil fertility. IV. The influence of earthworms on the physical properties of a red-brown earth. *Aust. J. Agr. Res.* 10,3:371–76.

———. 1961. The abundance of earthworms in agricultural land and their possible significance in agriculture. *Adv. Agron.* 13:249–68.

Barley, K. P., and Jennings, A. C. 1959. Earthworms and soil fertility. III. The influence of earthworms on the availability of nitrogen. *Aust. J. Agr. Res.* 10,3:364–70.

Barley, K. P., and Kleinig, C. R. 1964. The occupation of newly irrigated lands by earthworms. *Aust. J. Sci.* 26, 9:290.

Barnes, Frank. Millions of worms raised commercially at Jones Worm Farm. *Oklahoma County News*, 15 April 1976, 11.

Barrett, T. J. 1959. *Harnessing the Earthworm*. Boston: Wedgwood Press.

Bates, G. H. 1933. The distribution of wild white clover (*Trifolium repens*) in relation to the activity of earthworms (*Lumbricidae*). *Welsh F. of Agriculture* 9:195–208.

Bather, E. A. 1920. *Pontoscolex latus*, a new worm from Lower Ludlow, Beds. *Ann. Mag. Nat. Hist.* 9:5.

Baweja, K. D. 1939. Studies of the soil fauna with special reference to the recolonisation of sterilised soil. *J. Anim. Ecol.* 8,1:120–61.

Baylis, H. A. 1914. Preliminary account of *Aspidodrilus*, a remarkable epizoic Oligochaete. *Ann. Mag. Nat. Hist.* 8:16.

————. 1915. A new African earthworm collected by Dr. C. Christy. *Ann. Mag. Nat. Hist.* 8:16.

Beadle, L. C. 1957. Respiration of the African swampworm *Alma emini* Mich. *J. Exp. Biol.* 34:1–10.

Bean, C. 1972. We need these soil tillers. *Ecologist* 2:2.

Beddard, F. E. 1912. *Earthworms and Their Allies*. Cambridge: Cambridge Univ. Press.

Benham, W. B. 1896. On *Kynotus cingulatus*, a new species of earthworm from Imerina in Madagascar. *Quart. J. Micr. Sci.*, 38.

————. 1898. A re-examination of Hutton's types of New Zealand earthworms. *Transactions of the New Zealand Institute* 21:156–63.

————. 1922. Oligochaeta of Macquarie Island. *Australian Antarctic Expedition. Sci. Reports, Zool. and Bot.* 6.

Bergmann, W. 1949. Comparative biochemical studies on the lipids of marine invertebrates, with special reference to the sterols. *J. Mar. Res.* 8:137–76.

Bernsohn, Ken. A new angle on worms. *Organic Gardening and Farming*, May 1975, 138–40.

Bharucha-Reid, R. P. 1956. Latent learning in earthworms. *Science* 123:222.

Bhat, J. V. 1974. Suitability of experimental diets for earthworm culture. *Current Sci.* 43:9.

Bigger, J. H., and Decker, G. C. 1966. Controlling root-feeding insects on corn. *Ill. Univ. Agr. Exp. Stn. Bull.* 716.

Birk, Hans D. I use earthworms for fast composting. *Organic Gardening and Farming*, Dec. 1964, 39–41.

Black, C. A. 1965. Methods of soil analysis, part 2. Chemical and microbiological properties. Amer. Soc. of Agron., Madison, Wis.

Blaisdell, Harold F. 1977. *The Art of Worm Fishing*. New York: Alfred A. Knopf.

Blaschko, H., and Himms, J. M. 1953. Amine oxidase in the earthworm. *J. Physiol.* 120:445–48.

Block, W., and Banage, W. B. 1968. Population density and biomass of earthworms in some Uganda soils. *Rev. Ecol. Biol. Sol.* 5,3:515–21.

Bocock, K. L.; Gilbert, O.; Capstick, C. K.; Twinn, D. C.; Waid, J. S.; and Woodman, M. G. 1960. Changes in leaf litter when placed on the surface of soils with contrasting humus types. I. Losses in dry weight of oak and ash leaf litter. *Soil Sci.* 11:1–9.

Boyd, J. M. 1957. The ecological distribution of the Lumbricidae in the Hebrides. *Proc. R. Soc. Edinb.* 66:311–38.

———. 1958. The ecology of earthworms in cattle-grazed machair in Tiree Argyll. *J. Anim. Ecol.* 27:147–57.

Bradway, W. E., and Moore, A. R. 1940. The locus of the action of the galvanic current in the earthworm, *Lumbricus terrestris*. *J. Cell. Comp. Physiol.* 15:47–54.

Bray, J. R., and Gorham, E. 1964. Litter production in forests of the world. *Adv. Ecol. Res.* 2:101–57.

Bretnall, G. H. 1927. Earthworms and spectral colours. *Science* 66:427.

Brown, B. R.; Love, C. W.; and Handley, W. R. C. 1963. Protein-fixing constituents of plants. *Rep. For. Res. London, Part III*, 90–93.

Brown, D. M. 1944. The cause of death in submerged worms. *J. Tenn. Acad. Sci.* 19,2:147–49.

Buahin, G. K. A., and Edwards, C. A. 1964. The recolonisation of sterilised soil by invertebrates. *Rep. Rothamsted Exp. Stn. for 1963*, 149–50.

Bullock, T. H. 1945. Functional organization of the giant fibre system of *Lumbricus*. *J. Neurophysiol.* 8:55–71.

———. 1947. Problems in invertebrate electrophysiology. *Physiol. Revs.* 27:643–64.

———. 1951. Facilitation of conduction rate in nerve fibres. *J. Physiol.* 114:89–97.

Bullock, T. H.; Cohen, M. J.; and Faulstick, D. 1950. Effect of stretch on conduction in single nerve fibres. *Biol. Bull. Wood's Hole* 99:320.

Bullock, T. H., and Turner, R. S. 1950. Events associated with conduction failure in nerve fibres. *J. Cell. Comp. Physiol.* 36:59–81.

Buntley, C. J., and Papedick, R. I. 1960. Worm-worked soils of eastern South Dakota, their morphology and classification. *Soil Sci. Soc. Amer. Proc.* 24:128–32.

Bunyea, Hubert. 1931. Diseases and parasites of poultry. USDA Farmers' Bulletin 1652:63.

Bureau of Sport Fisheries and Wildlife. 1970. *Earthworms for Bait.* U.S. Fish and Wildl. Ser., Div. of Fish Hatcheries Leaflet FL-23.

Byzova, Yu B. 1965. Comparative rate of respiration in some earthworms. *Rev. Ecol. Biol. Sol.* 2:207-16.

Carson, Rachel. 1962. *Silent Spring.* Boston: Houghton Mifflin Co.

Carter, G. S. 1940. *A General Zoology of the Invertebrates.* 4th ed.

Causey, D. 1961. The earthworms of Arkansas, in *The Challenge of Earthworm Research*, ed. R. Rodale. Emmaus, Pa.: Soil and Health Foundation, 43-56.

Cernosvitov, L., and Evans, A. C. 1947. *Synopses of the British Fauna (6) Lumbricidae.* London: Linn. Soc.

Chadwick, L. C., and Bradley, J. 1948. An experimental study of the effects of earthworms on crop production. *Proc. Amer. Soc. Hort. Sci.* 51:552-62.

Chapman, G. 1950. On movement of worms. *J. Exp. Biol. Cambridge* 27:29-39.

———. 1958. The hydrostatic skeleton in the invertebrates. *Biol. Revs.* 33:338-71.

Chawla, O. P., and Nijhawan, S. D. 1972. Effect of aggregates and burrows made by earthworms in the yield of wheat. *Agric. Agro-Ind. J.* 5:12.

Clark, A. M. 1957. The distribution of carbonic anhydrase in the earthworm and snail. *Aust. J. Sci.* 19:205-7.

311

Cline, Martin G. 1955. *Soils and Soil Associations of New York*. Cornell Ext. Bull. 930:1–72.

Cockerell, T. D. A. 1924. Earthworms and the cluster fly. *Nature, Lond.* 113,2832:193–94.

Coffman, R. N. Build your own earthworm-casting "factory." *Organic Gardening and Farming*, May 1969, 58–61.

Cohen, S., and Lewis, H. B. 1949. Nitrogenous metabolism of the earthworm *(L. terrestris)*. *Fedn. Proc. Fedn. Am. Soc. Exp. Biol.* 8:191.

———. 1950. The nitrogenous metabolism of the earthworm *(Lumbricus terrestris)*. *J. Biol. Chem.* 184:479–84.

Collier, H. O. J. 1938. The immobilization of locomotory movements in earthworm, *Lumbricus terrestris. J. Exp. Biol.* 15:339–57.

———. 1939. Central nervous activity in the earthworm. 1. Responses to tension and to tactile stimulation. *J. Exp. Biol.* 16:286–99.

———. 1939. Central nervous activity in the earthworm. 2. Properties of the tension reflex. *J. Exp. Biol.* 16:300–312.

Collier, J. C. 1947. Relations between metabolism and morphogenesis during regeneration in *Tubifex tubifex. Biol. Bull. Wood's Hole* 92:167–77.

Comfort, A. 1956. *The Biology of Senescence*. New York: Rhinehart.

Cooper, E. L. 1968. Transplantation immunity in annelids. I. Rejection of xenografts exchanged between *Lumbricus terrestris* and *Eisenia foetida. Transplantation* 6:322.

———. 1968. Multinucleate giant cells, granulomata and "myoblastomas" in annelid worms. *Journal of Invertebrate Pathology* 11:123.

———. 1969. Chronic allograft rejection in *Lumbricus terrestris. Journal of Experimental Zoology* 171:69.

———. 1969. Neoplasia and transplantation immunity in annelids. *National Cancer Institute Monographs* 31:655.

Cooper, E. L.; Acton, R. T.; Weinheimer, P.; and Evans, E. E. 1969. Lack of a bactericidal response in the earthworm *Lumbricus terrestris* after immunization with bacterial antigens. *Journal of Invertebrate Pathology* 14:402.

Cooper, E. L., and Baculi, B. S. 1968. Degenerative changes in the annelid, *Lumbricus terrestris. Journal of Gerontology* 23:375.

Cooper, E. L.; Beller, J.; and Hayes, S. 1970. A successful medium for maintaining earthworms. *Laboratory Animals* 4,1:25–28.

Cooper, E. L., and Rubilotta, L. M. 1969. Allograft rejection in *Eisenia foetida. Transplantation* 8:220.

Cragg, J. B. 1961. Some aspects of the ecology of moorland animals. *J. Anim. Ecol.* 30:205–54.

Crompton, E. 1953. Grow the soil to grow the grass. Some pedological aspects of marginal land improvement. *J. Minist. Agric. Fish.* 50,7:301–8.

Crossley, D. A.; Reichle, D. E.; and Edwards, C. A. 1971. Intake and turnover of radioactive cesium by earthworms (Lumbricidae). *Pedobiologia* 11:71–76.

Crowe, Mary B., and Bowen, Gladys S. 1970. *With Tails We Win!* 6th ed. Waverly, Ohio: Wonder Worm Farms, dist. Shields Publications.

Danielli, J. F., and Pantin, C. F. A. 1950. Alkaline phosphatase in protonephridia of terrestrial nemertines and planarians. *Quart. J. Mic. Sci.* 91:209–14.

Danielson, R. N. 1937. In *Culture Methods for Invertebrate Animals*, ed. J. Needham. New York: Dover Publications.

Darwin, C. R. 1881. *The Formation of Vegetable Mould through the Action of Worms with Observations on their Habits*. London: John Murray and Co.

Davey, S. P. 1963. *Effects of chemicals on earthworms: a review of the literature*. Special Scientific Report. Wildlife 74. U.S.D.I. Fish and Wildlife Service.

Davis, A. G., and Cooper, M. M. 1953. White clover trail. V. Earthworm population. *J. Br. Grassld. Soc.* 8:125–27.

Davis, B. N. K. 1968. The soil macrofauna and organochlorine residues at twelve agricultural sites near Huntingdon. *Ann. Appl. Biol.* 61:29–45.

Davis, B. N. K., and French, M. C. 1969. The accumulation and loss of organochlorine insecticide residues by beetles, worms, and slugs in sprayed fields. *Soil Biol. Biochem.* 1:45–55.

Davis, B. N. K., and Harrison, R. B. 1966. Organochlorine insecticide residues in soil invertebrates. *Nature, Lond.* 211:1424–25.

Davis, J. G., and Slater, W. K. 1928. The anaerobic metabolism of the earthworm *(Lumbricus terrestris).* *Biochem. J.* 22:338–45.

Dawson, A. B. 1920. The intermuscular nerve cells of the earthworm. *J. Comp. Neurol.* 32:155–71.

Dawson, R. C. 1947. Earthworm microbiology and the formation of water-stable aggregates. *Soil Sci.* 69:175–84.

Day, G. M. 1950. The influence of earthworms on soil microorganisms. *Soil Sci.* 69:175–84.

Delfeld, Paula. His earthworms work for him. *Organic Gardening and Farming*, Aug. 1970, 71–74.

Dennell, R. 1949. Earthworm chaetae. *Nature, Lond.* 164:370.

de Robertis, E. D. P., and Bennett, H. S. 1955. Some features of fine structure of cytoplasm of cells in the earthworm nerve cord. *Union Int. Sci. Biol. B.* 21:261–73.

————. 1955. Some features of the sub-microscopic morphology of synapses in frog and earthworm. *J. Biophys. Biochem. Cytol.* 1:47–58.

Dhawan, C. L.; Sharma, R. L.; Singh, A.; and Handa, B. K. 1955. Preliminary investigations on the reclamation of saline soils by earthworms. *Proc. Natn. Inst. Sci. India* 24:631–36.

Dhennin, L. et al. 1963. Investigations on the role of *Lumbricus terrestris* in the experimental transmission of foot and mouth disease virus. *Bull. Acad. Vet. France* 36:153–55.

Doane, C. C. 1962. Effects of certain insecticides on earthworms. *J. Econ. Ent.* 55:416–18.

Dobson, R. M. 1956. *Eophila oculata* at Verulamium: a Roman earthworm population. *Nature, Lond.* 177:796–97.

Dobson, R. M., and Lofty, J. R. 1956. Rehabilitation of marginal grassland. *Rep. Rothamsted Exp. Stn. for 1955.*

————. 1965. Observations of the effect of BHC on the soil fauna of arable land. *Congr. Int. Sci. Sol. Paris* 3:203–5.

Doeksen, J. 1950. An electrical method of sampling soil for earthworms. *Trans. 4th Int. Congr. Soil Sci.*, 129–31.

————. 1964. Notes on the activity of earthworms. 1. The influence of *Rhododendron* and *Pinus* on earthworms. *Jaarb. I.B.S.*, 177–80.

————. 1964. Notes on the activity of earthworms. 3. The conditioning effect of earthworms on the surrounding soil. *Jaarb. I.B.S.*, 187–91.

————. 1967. Notes on the activity of earthworms. V. Some causes of mass migration. *Meded. Inst. Biol. Scheik. Ouderz LandbGewass* 353:199–221.

————. 1968. Notes on the activity of earthworms. VI. Periodicity in the oxygen consumption and the uptake of feed. *Meded. Inst. Biol. Scheik. Ouderz LandbGewass* 354:123–28.

Doeksen, J., and van Wingerden, C. G. 1964. Notes on the activity of earthworms. 2. Observations on diapause in the earthworm *A. caliginosa. Jaarb. I.B.S.*, 181–86.

Donahue, R. L. 1961. *Our Soils and Their Management*. Interstate Printers and Publishers.

Downs, James S. The right to wiggle—provides us with compost. *Organic Gardening and Farming*, July 1968, 77.

Dubie, Steve. Getting started in the worm business. *Organic Gardening and Farming*, Sept. 1973, 78–82.

Dustman, E. H., and Stickel, L. F. 1966. Pesticide residues in the eco-system. 'Pesticides and their effects on soils and water.' *Am. Soc. of Agronomy Spec. Publ.* 8:109–21.

Dutt, A. K. 1948. Earthworms and soil aggregation. *Amer. Soc. Agron. Jour.* 40:407–10.

Duweini, A. K., and Ghabbour, S. I. 1965. Population density and biomass of earthworms in different types of Egyptian soils. *J. Appl. Ecol.* 2:271–87.

Dzangaliev, A. D., and Belousova, N. K. 1969. Earthworm populations in irrigated orchards under various soil treatments. *Pedobiologia* 9:103–5.

Eaton, T. H., Jr. 1942. Earthworms of the Northeastern United States. *J. Wash. Acad. Sci.* 32, 8:242–49.

Eaton, T. H., and Chandler, R. F. 1942. The fauna of forest-humus layers in New York. *Mem. 247. Cornell Agr. Exp. Stn.*

Eccles, J. C.; Granit, R.; and Young, J. Z. 1933. Impulses in the giant fibres of earthworms. *J. Physiol.* 77:23–25.

Edwards, C. A. 1965. Effects of pesticide residues on soil in-vertebrates and plants. *5th Symp. Brit. Ecol. Soc.* Blackwell, Oxford, 239–61.

———. 1970. Persistent pesticides in the environment. *Critical Reviews in Environmental Control.* Chem. Rubber Co., 6–68.

———. 1970. Effects of herbicides on the soil fauna. *Proc. 10th Weed Control Conf. 1970* 3:1052–62.

Edwards, C. A., and Arnold, M. 1966. Effects of insecticides on soil fauna. *Rep. Rothamsted Exp. Stn. for 1965*, 195–96.

Edwards, C. A., and Dennis, E. B. 1960. Some effects of Al-drin and DDT on the soil fauna of arable land. *Nature, Lond.* 188,4572:767.

Edwards, C. A.; Dennis, E. B.; and Empson, D. W. 1967. Pesticides and the soil fauna. 1. Effects of Aldrin and DDT in an arable field. *Ann. Appl. Biol.* 59,3:11–22.

Edwards, C. A., and Heath, G. W. 1963. The role of soil ani-mals in breakdown of leaf material. In *Soil Organisms*, eds. J. Doeksen and J. van der Drift. Amsterdam: North Holland Publishing Co., 76–80.

Edwards, C. A., and Lofty, J. R. 1969. Effects of cultivation on earthworm populations. *Rep. Rothamsted Exp. Stn. for 1968*, 247–48.

———. 1969. The influence of agricultural practice on soil micro-arthropod populations. In *The Soil Ecosystem*. Systematics Association publication No. 8, ed. J. G. Sheals, 237–47.

———. 1972. *Biology of Earthworms*. London: Chapman and Hall, Ltd., dist. Harper and Row.

Edwards, C. A.; Thompson, A. R.; and Benyon, K. 1967. Some effects of chlorfenvinphos, an organophosphorus insecticide, on populations of soil animals. *Rev. Ecol. Biol. Sol.* 5,2:199–214.

Edwards, C. A.; Whiting, A. E.; and Heath, G. W. 1970. A mechanized washing method for separation of invertebrates from soil. *Pedobiologia* 10,5:141–48.

Ehlers, W. 1975. Observations on earthworm channels and infiltration on tilled and untilled loess soil. *Soil Sci.* 119:3.

El-Duweini, A. K., and Ghabbour, S. I. 1965. Population density and biomass of earthworms in different types of Egyptian soils. *J. Appl. Ecol.* 2:271–87.

Ellenby, C. 1945. Influence of earthworms on larval emergence in the potato root eelworm, *Heterodera rostochrensis* Wollenweber. *Ann. Appl. Biol.* 31,4:332–39.

Ennor, A. H., and Morrison, J. F. 1958. Biochemistry of the phosphagens and related guanidines. *Physiol. Rev.* 38:631–74.

Ennor, A. H.; Rosenberg, H.; Rossiter, R. J.; Beatty, I. M.; and Gaffney, T. 1960. The isolation and characterization of D-serine ethanolamine phosphodiester from earthworms. *Biochem J.* 75:179–82.

Escritt, J. R. 1955. Calcium arsenate for earthworm control. *J. Sports Turf Res. Inst.* 9,31:28–34.

Escritt, J. R., and Arthur, J. H. 1948. Earthworm control—a resumé of methods available. *J. Bd. Greenkeep. Res.* 7, 23:49.

Euler, U. S. von. 1948. Preparation, purification and evaluation of nonadrenaline, and adrenaline in organ extracts. *Arch. Int. Pharmacodyn Ther.* 77:477–85.

———. 1961. Occurrence of catecholamines in acrania and invertebrates. *Nature, Lond.* 190:170–71.

Evans, A. C. 1946. Distribution of numbers of segments in earthworms and its significance. *Nature, Lond.* 158:98.

———. 1947. Some earthworms from Iowa, including a description of a new species. *Ann. Mag. Nat. Hist.* 14, 11:514.

———. 1947. Method of studying the burrowing activity of earthworms. *Ann. Mag. Nat. Hist.* 11,14:643–50.

———. 1948. Studies on the relationships between earthworms and soil fertility. II. Some effects of earthworms on soil structure. *Ann. Appl. Biol.* 35:1–13.

———. 1948. Relation of worms to soil fertility. *Discovery,* Norwich 9,3:83–86.

———. 1948. Identity of earthworms stored by moles. *Proc. Zool. Soc. Lond.* 118:1356–59.

Evans, A. C., and Guild, W. J. Mc. L. 1947. Some notes on reproduction in British earthworms. *Ann. Mag. Nat. Hist.* 654.

———. 1947. Cocoons of some British Lumbricidae. *Ann. Mag. Nat. Hist.* 714–19.

———. 1947. Studies on the relationships between earthworms and soil fertility. I. Biological studies in the field. *Ann. Appl. Biol.* 34:307–30.

————. 1948. Studies on the relationships between earthworms and soil fertility. IV. On the life cycles of some British Lumbricidae. *Ann. Appl. Biol.* 35,4:471–84.

————. 1948. Studies on the relationships between earthworms and soil fertility. V. Field populations. *Ann. Appl. Biol.* 35,4:485–93.

Ewer, D. W., and Hanson, J. 1945. Some staining reactions of invertebrate mucoproteins. *J. R. Micr. Soc.* 65:40–43.

Feigel, Edith Elizabeth. Angleworms as pepper-uppers. *Organic Farming and Gardening*, Aug. 1942.

Fenton, G. R. 1947. Ecological note on worms in forest soil. *J. Anim. Ecol.* 16:76–93.

Finlayson, D. G.; Campbell, C. J.; and Roberts, H. A. 1975. Herbicides and insecticides: their compatibility and effects on weeds, insects, and earthworms in the minicauliflower crop. *Ann. Appl. Biol.* 79,1:95–108.

Fleming, W. E., and Hadley, C. H. 1945. DDT ineffective for control of an exotic earthworm. *J. Econ. Ent.* 38:411.

Fleming, W. E., and Hanley, I. M. 1950. A large-scale test with DDT to control the Japanese beetle. *J. Econ. Ent.* 43:586–90.

Ford, J. 1935. Soil communities in Central Europe. *J. Anim. Ecol.* 6:197–98.

Fox, C. J. S. 1964. The effects of five herbicides on the numbers of certain invertebrate animals in grassland soils. *Can. J. Pl. Sci.* 44:405–9.

Fox, H. M. 1940. Function of chlorocruorin in *Sabella* and of haemoglobin in *Lumbricus*. *Nature, Lond.* 145:781–82.

———. 1945. The oxygen affinities of certain invertebrate haemoglobins. *J. Exp. Biol.* 21:161–65.

Fox, H. M., and Taylor, A. E. R. 1955. The tolerance of oxygen by aquatic invertebrates. *Proc. Roy. Soc.* B. 143:214–25.

Franz, H., and Leitenberger, L. 1948. Biological-chemical investigations into the formation of humus through soil animals. *Ost. Zool. Z.* 1,5:498–518.

Franz, Maurice. Making money with earthworms. *Organic Gardening and Farming*, Mar. 1972, 68–74; Apr. 1972, 104–8.

French, C. E.; Liscinsky, S. A.; and Miller, D. R. 1957. Nutrient composition of earthworms. *J. Wildlife Mgmt.* 21:348.

Fuller, Lynn. Earthworm gardening in the desert. *Organic Gardening and Farming*, Mar. 1960, 53–55.

Gabbay, K. H. 1958. An investigation of the calciferous glands in *Lumbricus terrestris*. *Biol. Rev. City Coll. N. Y.* 21:16–19.

Garner, M. R. 1953. The preparation of latex casts of soil cavities for the study of the tunneling habits of animals. *Science* 118:380–81.

Garrey, W. L., and Moore, A. R. 1915. Peristalsis and co-ordination in the earthworm. *Amer. J. Physiol.* 39:139–48.

Gaskell, J. F. 1920. Adrenalin in annelids. *J. Gen. Physiol.* 2:13–85.

Gast, J. 1937. Contrast between the soil profiles developed under pines and hardwood. *J. For.* 35:11–16.

Gates, G. E. 1929. The earthworm fauna of the United States. *Science* 70:266–67.

————. 1937. The genus *Pheretima* in North America. *Bull. Mus. Comp. Zool.* 80,8:339–73.

————. 1954. On regenerative capacity of earthworms of the family Lumbricidae. *Ann. Midl. Nat.* 50, 2:414–19.

————. 1959. On a taxonomic puzzle and the classification of the earthworms. *Bull. Mus. Comp. Zool. Harv.* 121:229–61.

————. 1961. Ecology of some earthworms with special reference to seasonal activity. *Am. Midl. Nat.* 66:61–86.

————. 1962. An exotic earthworm now domiciled in Louisiana. *Proc. Louisiana Acad. Sci.* 25:7–15.

————. 1963. Miscellanea Megadrilogica. VII. Greenhouse earthworms. *Proc. Biol. Soc. Wash.* 76:9–18.

————. 1966. Requiem for Megadrile Utopias. A contribution toward the understanding of the earthworm fauna of North America. *Proc. Biol. Soc. Wash.* 79:239–54.

Geoghegan, M. J., and Brain, R. C. 1948. Aggregate formation in soil. I. Influence of some bacterial polysaccharides on the binding of soil particles. *Biochem. J.* 43:5–13.

Gerard, B. M. 1964. *Synopses of the British Fauna* (6) *Lumbricidae*. London: Linn. Soc.

―――. 1967. Factors affecting earthworms in pastures. *J. Anim. Ecol.* 36:235–52.

Gersch, M. 1954. Effect of carcinogenic hydrocarbons on the skin of earthworms. *Naturwissenschaften* 41:337.

Ghabbour, S. I. 1966. Earthworms in agriculture: a modern evaluation. *Rev. Ecol. Biol. Soc.* 111,2:259–71.

Ghilarov, M. S. 1956. Significance of the soil fauna studies for the soil diagnostics. *6th Congr. Sci. Sol. Paris* 3:130–44.

―――. 1963. On the interrelations between soil dwelling invertebrates and soil microorganisms. In *Soil Organisms*, eds. J. Doeksen and J. van der Drift. Amsterdam: North Holland Publishing Co., 255–59.

―――. 1965. Zoological methods in soil diagnostics. In 'Nauka', Moscow, 278.

Gibbons, Euell. I'm going out in the garden and eat worms! *Organic Gardening and Farming*, Dec. 1966, 62–64.

Gish, C. D. 1970. Organochlorine insecticide residues in soils and soil invertebrates from agricultural land. *Pest. Mon. J.* 3,4:241–52.

Goodrich, E. S. 1945. The study of nephridia and genital ducts since 1895. *Quart. J. Micr. Sci.* 86:113–392.

Graff, O. 1953. Investigations in soil zoology with special reference to the terricole Oligochaeta. *Z. PflErnähr. Düng* 61:72–77.

———. 1967. Translocation of nutrients into the subsoil through earthworm activity. *Landw. Forsch.* 20:117–27.

Graff, O., and Satchell, J. E. 1967. *Progress in Soil Biology Pub*. Amsterdam: North Holland Publishing Co.

Grant, W. C. 1955. Studies on moisture relationships in earthworms. *Ecology* 36,3:400–407.

———. 1955. Temperature relationships in the megascolecid earthworm, *Pheretima hupeiensis*. *Ecology* 36,3:412–17.

———. 1956. An ecological study of the peregrine earthworm, *Pheretima hupeiensis* in the Eastern United States. *Ecology* 37,4:648–58.

Gray, J., and Lissmann, H. W. 1938. Studies in animal locomotion. VII. Locomotory reflexes in the earthworm. *J. Exp. Biol.* 15:506–17.

Griffiths, D. C.; Raw, F.; and Lofty, J. R. 1967. The effects on soil fauna of insecticides tested against wireworms (*Agriotes* spp.) in wheat. *Ann. Appl. Biol.* 60:479–90.

Grove, A. J., and Newell, G. E. 1962. *Animal Biology*. London: University Tutorial Press.

Guild, W. J. Mc. L. 1948. Effect of soil type on populations. *Ann. Appl. Biol.* 35,2:181–92.

———. 1951. Earthworms in agriculture. *Scot. Agric.* 30, 4:220–23.

———. 1951. The distribution and population density of earthworms (Lumbricidae) in Scottish pasture fields. *J. Anim. Ecol.* 20,1:88–97.

———. 1952. Variation in earthworm numbers within field populations. *J. Anim. Ecol.* 21,2:169.

———. 1952. The Lumbricidae in upland areas. 11. Population variation on hill pasture. *Ann. Mag. Nat. Hist.* 12, 5:286–92.

———. 1955. Earthworms and soil structure. In *Soil Zoology*, ed. D. K. Mc. E. Kevan. London: Butterworths, 83–98.

Gunston, David. The worm's good turn. *Organic Gardening and Farming*, Dec. 1955, 42–46.

Gurianova, O. Z. 1940. Effect of earthworms and of organic fertilizers on structure formation in chernozem soils. *Pedology* 4:99–108.

Hama, K. 1959. Some observations on the fine structure of the giant nerve fibres of the earthworm *Eisenia foetida*. *J. Biophys. Biochem. Cytol.* 6:61–66.

Hamblyn, C. J., and Dingwall, A. R. 1945. Earthworms. *N.Z. Jl. Agric.* 71:55–58.

Hanson, J. 1957. The structure of the smooth muscle fibres in the body wall of the earthworm. *J. Biophys. Biochem. Cytol.* 3:111–22.

Hanson, J., and Lowy, J. 1960. Contractile apparatus in invertebrate animals. In *Structure and Function of Muscle*, ed. G. Bourne. New York: Academic Press.

Harker, J. E. 1958. Diurnal rhythms in the animal kingdom. *Biol. Revs.* 33:1–52.

————. 1960. Internal factors controlling the sub-oesophageal ganglion neurosecretory cycle in *Periplaneta americana* L. *J. Exp. Biol.* 37:164–70.

Harmsen, G., and van Schreven, D. 1955. Mineralisation or organic nitrogen in soil. *Adv. Agron.* 7:299–398.

Harrington, N. R. 1899. The calciferous glands of the earthworm, with appendix on the circulation. *J. Morph.* 15, suppl.

Harvey, Sara J. Six boxes of earthworms in the cellar. *Organic Gardening and Farming*, Oct. 1973, 65.

Hasenbein, G. 1951. A pregnancy test on earthworms. *Arch. Gynakol.* 181:5–28.

Haswell, W. A., and Hill, J. P. 1894. A proliferating cystic parasite of the earthworms. *Proc. Linn. Soc. N. S. Wales* 8,2:365–76.

Haughton, T. M.; Kerkut, G. A.; and Munday, K. A. 1958. The oxygen dissociation and alkaline denaturation of haemoglobins from two species of earthworm. *J. Exp. Biol.* 35:360–68.

Hawke, P. B.; Oser, B. L.; and Summerson, W. H. 1954. *Practical Physiological Chemistry*. London: Churchill, 1439.

Headstrom, Richard. Earthworms in winter quarters. *Organic Gardening*, Mar. 1945, 21–23. Reprinted from *Horticulture Magazine*.

Heath, G. W. 1962. The influence of ley management on earthworm populations. *J. Br. Grassld. Soc.* 17,4:237–44.

————. 1965. The part played by animals in soil formation. In *Experimental Pedology*, eds. E. G. Hallsworth and D. V. Crawford. London: Butterworths, 236–43.

Heath, G. W.; Arnold, M. K.; and Edwards, C. A. 1966. Studies in leaf litter breakdown. 1. Breakdown rates among leaves of different species. *Pedobiologia* 6:1–12.

Heath, G. W., and King, H. G. C. 1964. The palatability of litter to soil fauna. *Proc. VIII Int. Congr. Soil Sci. Bucharest*, 979–86.

Heimburger, H. V. 1924. Reactions of earthworms to temperature and atmospheric humidity. *Ecology* 5:276–83.

Hertzberg, Will. Gold in the ground: how to make a fortune raising worms. *Sports Afield*, Mar. 1975.

Hess, W. N. 1924. Reactions to light in the earthworm, *Lumbricus terrestris. J. Morph.* 39:515–42.

————. 1925. Nervous system of the earthworm, *Lumbricus terrestris. J. Morph.* 40:235–60.

————. 1925. Photoreceptors of *Lumbricus terrestris*, with special reference to their distribution, structure and function. *J. Morph.* 41:63–93.

————. 1937. In *Culture Methods for Invertebrate Animals*, ed. J. Needham. New York: Dover Publications.

Heungens, A. 1969. The physical decomposition of pine litter by earthworms. *Pl. Soil* 31,1:22–30.

Hewett, Dorothy. The story of the earthworm. *Organic Gardening and Farming*, Dec. 1957, 36–38; Jan. 1958, 48–53; Feb. 1958, 60–68.

Hirst, J. M.; Storey, Ward, W. C.; and Wilcox, H. G. 1955. The origin of apple scab epidemics in the Wisbech area in 1953 and 1954. *Pl. Path.* 4:91.

Hodgson, E. S. 1955. Problems in invertebrate chemoreception. *Quart. Rev. Biol.* 30:331–47.

Hoeksema, K. J.; Jongerious, A.; and K. van der Meer. 1956. On the influence of earthworms on the soil structure in mulched orchards. *Boor en Spade* 8:183–201.

Hogg, John Edwin. Harnessing earthworms. *Organic Farming and Gardening*. Oct. 1942.

Holwager, George H. 1952. *The Production and Sale of Earthworms*. Elgin, Ill.: Shields Publications.

Home, Farm, and Garden Research Associates. *Let An Earthworm Be Your Garbage Man*. Elgin, Ill.: Shields Publications.

Hopkins, A. R., and Kirk, V. M. 1957. Effects of several insecticides on the English red worm. *J. Econ. Ent.* 50, 5:699–700.

Hopp, Henry. 1946. Earthworms fight erosion too. *Soil Conserv.* 11:252–54.

———. 1947. The ecology of earthworms in cropland. *Soil. Sci. Soc. Amer. Proc.* 12:503–7.

———. 1973. *What Every Gardener Should Know about Earthworms*. Charlotte, Vt.: Garden Way Publishing Co.

Hopp, H., and Hopkins, H. T. 1946. Earthworms as a factor in the formation of water-stable aggregates. *J. Soil Water Conserv.* 1:11–13.

———. 1946. The effect of cropping systems on the winter populations of earthworms. *J. Soil Water Conserv.* 1, 1:85–88,98.

Hopp, H., and Slater, C. S. 1948. Influence of earthworms on soil productivity. *Soil. Sci.* 66:421–28.

———. 1949. The effect of earthworms on the productivity of agricultural soil. *J. Agric. Res.* 78:325–39.

Horridge, G. A., and Roberts, M. B. V. 1960. Neuro-muscular transmission in the earthworm. *Nature, Lond.* 186:650.

Howard, Sir Albert. The earthworm. *Organic Gardening*, May 1944, 5–6.

———. Pasture improvement by earthworms. *Organic Gardening*, Apr. 1946, 5–6.

Howell, C. D. 1939. The responses to light in the earthworm, *Pheretima agrestis* Goto and Hatai, with special reference to the function of the nervous system. *J. Exp. Zool.* 81:231–59.

Hoy, H. M. 1955. Toxicity of some hydrocarbon insecticides to earthworms. *N.Z. Jl. Sci. Technol.* (A) 37,4:367–72.

Hunt, L. Barrie. 1965. Kinetics of pesticide poisoning in Dutch Elm Disease control. *U.S. Fish Wildl. Serv. Circ.* 226:12–13.

———. 1969. Physiological susceptibility of robins to DDT poisoning. *Wilson Bulletin* 81,4:407–18.

Hunt, L. B., and Sacho, R. J. 1969. Response of robins to DDT and methoxychlor. *J. Wildlife Manage.* 33:267–72.

Hurwitz, S. N. 1910. The reactions of earthworms to acids. *Proc. Amer. Acad.* 46:67–81.

Hutchinson, S. A., and Kamel, M. 1956. The effect of earthworms on the dispersal of soil fungi. *J. Soil Sci.* 7, 2:213–18.

Hyche, L. L. 1956. Control of mites infesting earthworm beds. *J. Econ. Ent.* 49:409–10.

Hyman, L. H. 1916. An analysis of the process of regeneration in certain microdrilous Oligochaetes. *J. Exp. Zool.* 20:99–163.

———. 1940. Aspects of regeneration in Annelids. *Am. Nat.* 74:513–27.

Ibbotson, H. Compost from earthworms. *Organic Gardening and Farming*, Feb. 1968, 40–42.

Ireland, M. P. 1975. The effect of the earthworm *Dendrobaena rubida* on the solubility of lead, zinc, and calcium in heavy metal contaminated soils in Wales. *J. Soil Sci.* 26:3.

Issidorides, M. 1956. Ultrastructure of the synapse in the giant axons of the earthworm. *Exp. Cell Res.* 11:423–36.

Jacks, G. V. 1963. The biological nature of soil productivity. *Soils & Fert.* 26,3:147–50.

Jackson, C. M. 1926. Storage of water in various parts of the earthworm at different stages of exsiccation. *Proc. Soc. Exp. Biol., N.Y.* 23:500–504.

Jefferson, P. 1956. Studies on the earthworms of turf. *J. Sports Turf Res. Inst.* 9:166–79.

———. 1956. Studies on the earthworms of turf. B. Earthworms and soil. *J. Sports Turf Res. Inst.* 9,31:6–27.

Jewell, M. E., and Lewis, H. B. 1918. The occurrence of lichenase in the digestive tract of invertebrates. *J. Biol. Chem.* 33:161–67.

Joachim, A. W. R., and Panditesekera, D. G. 1948. Soil fertility studies. IV. Investigations on crumb structure on stability of local soils. *Trop. Agric.* 104:119–39.

Johnson, M. L. 1942. The respiratory function of the haemoglobin of the earthworm. *J. Exp. Biol.* 18:266–77.

Johnstone-Wallace, D. B. 1937. The influence of wild white clover on the seasonal production and chemical composition of pasture herbage and upon soil temperatures. Soil moistures and erosion control. *4th Int. Grassl. Congr. Rep.*, 188–96.

Joshi, N. V., and Kelkar, B. V. 1952. The role of earthworms in soil fertility. *Indian J. Agric. Sci.* 22:189–96.

Kahsnitz, H. G. 1922. Investigations on the influence of earthworms on soil and plant. *Bot. Arch.* 1:315–51.

Kalmus, H. 1955. On the colour forms of *Allolobophora chlorotica* Sav. *Ann. Mag. Nat. Hist. Ser.* 12,8:795.

Kalmus, H.; Satchell, J. E.; and Bowen, J. C. 1955. On the colour forms of *Allolobophora chlorotica* Sav.(Lumbricidae). *Ann. Mag. Nat. Hist. Ser.* 12,8:795–800.

Kamat, D. N. 1955. The nature of the intestinal proteinase of the earthworm, *Pheretima elongata* (Steph). *J. An. Morph. Physiol.* 2:79–86.

Kao, C. Y. 1956. Basis for after-discharge in the median giant axon of the earthworm. *Science* 123:803.

Kao, C. Y., and Grundfest, H. 1957. Postsynaptic electrogenesis in septate giant axons. 1. Earthworm median giant axon. *J. Neurophysiol.* 20:553–73.

Keilin, D. 1920. On the pharyngeal or salivary gland of the earthworm. *Quart. J. Micr. Sci.* 65:33–61.

————. 1925. Parasitic autotomy of the host as a mode of liberation of coelomic parasites from the body of the earthworm. *Parasitology* 17:70–72.

Kelsey, J. M., and Arlidge, G. Z. 1968. Effects of Isobenzan on soil fauna and soil structure. *N.Z. Jl. Agric. Res.* 11:245–60.

Kennedy, G. Y. 1959. A porphyrin pigment in the integument of *Arion ater* (L). *J. Mar. Biol. Ass..U.K.* 38:27–32.

Kennedy, G. Y., and Vevers, H. G. 1953. The biology of *Asterias rubens*. V. A porphyrin pigment in the integument. *J. Mar. Biol. Ass. U.K.* 32:235–47.

Kennerly, A. B. He makes earthworm fertilizer. *Organic Gardening and Farming*, Mar. 1965, 64–66.

Kerkut, G. A. 1960. *Implications of Evolution*. Oxford and London: Pergamon Press, 174.

Kerr, Dallas P. Grow your own! Do-it-yourself worm bed. *Pennsylvania Angler*, Mar. 1969.

Kevan, D. K. Mc. E., ed. 1955. *Soil Zoology*. London: Butterworths, 23–28, 452–88.

Khambata, S. R., and Bhatt, J. V. 1957. A contribution to the
study of the intestinal microflora of Indian earthworms.
Arch. Mikrobiol. 28:69–80.

King, H. G. C., and Heath, G. W. 1967. The chemical
analysis of small samples of leaf material and the relationship between the disappearance and composition of
leaves. *Pedobiologia* 7:192–97.

Kobatake, M. 1954. The antibacterial substance extracted
from lower animals. 1. The earthworm. *Kekkabu (Tu-
berculosis)* 29:60–63.

Kollmannsperger, F. 1956. Lumbricidae of humid and arid
regions and their effect on soil fertility. *VI Congr. Int.
Sci. Sol. Rapp*. C., 293–97.

Kollmannsperger, G. 1934. The Oligochaeta of the Bellinchen
Region. Inaugural dissertation. Dillingen (Saargebiet).

Kominz, D. R.; Saad, F.; and Laki, K. 1957. Vertebrate and
invertebrate tropomyosins. *Nature, Lond*. 179:206.

Kring, J. B. 1969. Mortality of the earthworm *Lumbricus terrestris* L. following soil applications of insecticides to a
tobacco field. *J. Econ. Ent*. 62,4:963.

Krivanek, J. O. 1956. Habit formation in the earthworm,
Lumbricus terrestris. Physiol. Zool. 29:241–50.

Kubiena, W. L. 1955. Animal activity in soils as a decisive factor in establishment of humus forms. In *Soil Zoology*,
ed. Kevan. London: Butterworths, 73–82.

Kühnelt, Wilhelm. 1961. *Soil Biology: With Special Reference to the Animal Kingdom*. Emmaus, Pa.: Rodale Books, Inc., 95–107.

Kurcheva, G. F. 1960. The role of invertebrates in the decomposition of the oak leaf litter. *Pocvovedenie* 4:16–23.

Kurtz, I., and Schrank, A. R. 1955. Bioelectrical properties of intact and regenerating earthworms, *Eisenia foetida*. *Physiol Zool*. 28:322–30.

Ladell, W. R. S. 1936. A new apparatus for separating insects and other arthropods from the soil. *Ann. Appl. Biol*. 23:862–79.

Lakhani, K. H., and Satchell, J. E. Production by *Lumbricus terrestris* (L.). *J. Anim. Ecol*. 39:473–92.

Lal, L.; Mukherji, S. P.; and Katiyar, O. P. 1971. The role of earthworms on soil fertility and yield of crops. *Farm Journal* (Calcutta) 13:2.

Langdon, F. E. 1895. The sense organs of *Lumbricus agricola* Hoffm. *J. Morph*. 11:193–234.

Langway, Lynn, and Sciolino, Elaine. Worming away. *Newsweek*, 21 June 1976, 67–68.

Lauer, A. R. 1929. Orientation in the earthworm. *Ohio. J. Sci*. 29:179.

Laverack, M. S. 1960. Tactile and chemical perception in earthworms. I. Responses to touch, sodium chloride, quinine and sugars. *Comp. Biochem. Physiol*. 1:155–63.

———. 1960. The identity of the porphyrin pigments of the integument of earthworms. *Comp. Biochem. Physiol.* 1, 4:259–66.

———. 1961. II. Response to acid pH solutions. *Comp. Biochem. Physiol.* 2:22–34.

———. 1961. Effect of temperature changes on the spontaneous nervous activity of the isolated nerve cord of *Lumbricus terrestris*. *Comp. Biochem. Physiol.* 3:136–40.

———. 1963. *The Physiology of Earthworms*. Vol. 15 in the Zoology Div., Series on Pure and Applied Biology. New York: Pergamon Press.

Lawrence, R. D., and Millar, H. R. 1945. Protein content of earthworms. *Nature, Lond.* 155:517.

Lee, K. E. 1951. Role of earthworms in New Zealand soil. *Tuatara* 4,1:22–27.

———. 1959. A key for the identification of New Zealand earthworms. *Tuatara* 8,1:13–60.

Legg, D. C. 1968. Comparison of various worm-killing chemicals. *J. Sports Turf Res. Inst.* 44:47–48.

LeRay, W., and Ford, N. 1937. In *Culture Methods for Invertebrate Animals*, ed. J. Needham. New York: Dover Publications.

Lidgate, H. J. 1966. Earthworm control with chlordane. *J. Sports Turf Res. Inst.* 42:5–8.

Liebmann, E. 1942. The role of the chloragogue in regeneration of *Eisenia foetida* (Sav.). *J. Morph.* 70:151–87.

———. 1942. The coelomocytes of lumbricidae. *J. Morph.* 71:221–49.

———. 1946. On trephocytes and trephocytosis: a study on the role of leucocytes in nutrition and growth. *Growth* 10:291–330.

Lipa, J. J. 1958. Effect on earthworm and Diptera populations of BHC dust applied to soil. *Nature, Lond.* 181:863.

Logsdon, Gene. 1975. *The Gardener's Guide to Better Soil*. Emmaus, Pa.: Rodale Press, Inc., 144–45.

Long, W. H.; Anderson, H. L.; and Isa, A. L. 1967. Sugarcane growth responses to chlordane and microarthropods, and effects of chlordane on soil fauna. *J. Econ. Ent.* 60:623–29.

Low, A. J. 1955. Improvements in the structural state of soils under leys. *J. Soil Sci.* 6:179–99.

Lukose, J. 1960. A note on an association between two adult earthworms. *Curr. Sci.* 29:106–7.

Lund, E. E.; Wehr, E. E.; and Ellis, D. J. 1963. Role of earthworms in transmission of *Heterakis* and *Histomonas* to turkeys and chickens. *J. Parasit.* 49,5:50.

Lunt, H. A., and Jacobson, G. M. 1944. The chemical composition of earthworm casts. *Soil Sci.* 58:367.

M'Dowall, J. 1926. Preliminary work towards a morphological and physiological study of the calciferous glands of the earthworm. *Proc. Phys. Soc. Edinb.* 21:65–72.

MacKay, Alastair I. 1950. *Farming and Gardening in the Bible*. Emmaus, Pa.: Rodale Press.

McKey-Fender, Dorothy. 1970. Concerning native earthworms from southwestern Washington and northwestern Oregon. *Northwest Science* 44,4:225–34.

McLeod, J. H. 1954. Note on a staphylinid (Coleoptera) predator of earthworms. *Canad. Ent.* 86:236.

MacMunn, C. A. 1886. On the presence of haematoporphyrin in the integument of certain invertebrates. *J. Physiol.* 7:240–52.

McRill, M. 1974. The ingestion of weed seed by earthworms. *Proc. Br. Weed Control Conf.* 12,2.

Madge, D. S. 1966. How leaf litter disappears. *New Scientist* 32:113–15.

———. 1969. Field and laboratory studies on the activities of two species of tropical earthworms. *Pedobiologia* 9:188–214.

Maloeuf, N. S. R. 1940. Osmo- and volume regulation in the earthworm with special reference to the alimentary tract. *J. Cell. Comp. Physiol.* 16:175–87.

Mamytov, A. 1953. The effect of earthworms on the water stability of mountain-valley serozem soils. *Pochvovederie* 8:58–60.

Mangold, O. 1951. Experiments in analysis of the chemical senses of earthworms. 1. Methods and procedure for leaves of plants. *Zool. Jb. (Physiol.)* 62:441–512.

Manwell, C. 1959. Alkaline denaturation and oxygen equilibrium of annelid haemoglobins. *J. Cell. Comp. Physiol.* 53:61–74.

Marapao, B. P. 1959. The effect of nervous tissue extracts on neurosecretion in the earthworm *Lumbricus terrestris*. *Catholic U. Amer. Biol. Stud.* 55:1–34.

Marbut, C. F. 1935. Soils of the United States. In *Atlas of American Agriculture*, Part 3. Washington, D.C.: USDA Bureau of Chem. and Soils.

Marshall, V. G. 1972. Effects of soil arthropods and earthworms on the growth of Black Spruce. *Proc. 4th Int. Congr. Soil Zool.*

Martin, A. W. 1957. Recent advances in knowledge of invertebrate renal function. *Invertebrate Physiol*, ed. B. T. Scheer. Univ. of Oregon Pub., 247–76.

Mast, S. O. 1917. The relation between spectral colours and stimulation in the lower organisms. *J. Exp. Zool.* 22:471–528.

Meldrum, N. U., and Roughton, F. J. W. 1934. Carbonic anhydrase, its preparation and properties. *J. Physiol.* 80:113–70.

Mellanby, K. 1961. Earthworms and the soil. *Countryside* 14, 4:1.

Michon, J. 1949. Influence of desiccation on diapause in Lumbricids. *C.r. hebd. Séanc. Acad. Sci., Paris* 228, 18:1455–56.

————. 1951. Supernumerary regeneration in *A. terrestris* f. *typica. C.r. hebd. Séanc. Acad. Sci., Paris* 232:1449–51.

Miles, H. B. 1963. Soil protozoa and earthworm nutrition. *Soil Sci.* 95:407–9.

————. 1963. Heat-death temperature in *Allolobophora terrestris* f. *longa* and *Eisenia foetida*. *Nature, Lond.* 199:826.

Millard, A., and Rudall, K. M. 1960. Light and electron microscope studies of fibres. *J. Roy. Mic. Soc.* 79:227–31.

Miller, Jim. The warbling worm. *Organic Gardening and Farming*, Jan. 1964, 82–84.

Miller, J. A., and Ting, H. P. 1949. The role of the subepidermal nervous system in the locomotion of the earthworm. *Ohio J. Sci.* 49:109–14.

Millott, N. 1943. The visceral nervous system of the earthworm. II. Evidence of chemical transmission and the action of sympathomimetic and parasympathomimetic drugs on the tone of the alimentary canal. *Proc. Roy. Soc.* B. 131:362–73.

————. 1944. The visceral nerves of the earthworm. III. Nerves controlling secretion of protease in the anterior intestine. *Proc. Roy. Soc.* B. 132:200–212.

Minnich, Jerry. The earthworm—man's best friend. *Organic Gardening and Farming*, Sept. 1976, 127–29.

————. Have you thanked an earthworm today? *Countryside*, Apr. 1977, 32–34.

Moment, G. B. 1949. On the relation between growth in length, the formation of new segments, and electric potential in an earthworm. *J. Exp. Zool.* 112:1–12.

————. 1953. On the way a common earthworm, *Eisenia foetida*, grows in length. *J. Morph.* 93:489–507.

————. 1953. The relation of body level, temperature and nutrition to regenerative growth. *Physiol. Zool.* 26:108–17.

Moore, A. R. 1921. Chemical stimulation of the nerve cord of *Lumbricus terrestris. J. Gen. Physiol.* 4:29–31.

————. 1923. Galvanotropism in the earthworm. *J. Gen. Physiol.* 5:453–59.

————. 1923. Muscle tension and reflexes in the earthworm. *J. Gen. Physiol.* 5:327–33.

Moore, B. 1922. Earthworms and soil reaction. *Ecology* 3:347–48.

Morgan, Charlie. 1962. *The Worm Farm: A Diary*. Charlie Morgan, dist. by Shields Publications.

————. 1970. *Raising the African Night Crawler or Tropical Giant Worm*, revised ed. Charlie Morgan, dist. by Shields Publications.

————. 1972. *Earthworm Feeds and Feeding*, 6th ed. Charlie Morgan, dist. by Shields Publications.

————. 1972. *Earthworm Selling and Shipping Guide*, 3rd ed. Charlie Morgan, dist. by Shields Publications.

————. 1975. *Profitable Earthworm Farming*, revised ed. Charlie Morgan, dist. by Shields Publications.

Morgan, T. H., and Dimon, A. C. 1904. An examination of the problems of physiological polarity and electrical polarity in the earthworm. *J. Exp. Zool.* 1:331–47.

Morris, H. M. 1922. Insect and other invertebrate fauna of arable land at Rothamsted. *Ann. Appl. Biol.* 9,3–4:282–305.

Morrison, F. O. 1950. The toxicity of BHC to certain microorganisms. Earthworms and arthropods. *Ontario Ent. Soc. Ann. Rep.* 80:50–57.

Muldal, S. 1949. Cytotaxonomy of British earthworms. *Proc. Linn. Soc. Lond.* 161:116–18.

Murchie, W. R. 1955. A contribution on the natural history of *Allolobophora minima*, Muldal. *Ohio J. Sci.* 55,4:241–44.

––––––. 1956. Survey of the Michigan earthworm fauna. *Mich. Acad. Sci. Arts. Let.* 151:53–72.

––––––. 1958. Biology of the Oligochaete *Eisenia rosea* (Savigny) in an upland forest soil of southern Michigan. *Am. Midl. Nat.* 66,1:113–31.

––––––. 1958. A new megascolecid earthworm from Michigan with notes on its biology. *Ohio J. Sci.* 58, 5:270–72.

––––––. 1959. Redescription of *Allolobophora muldali* Omodeo. *Ohio J. Sci.* 59,6:229–32.

––––––. 1960. Biology of the Oligochaete *Bimastos zeteki* Smith and Gittins (Lumbricidae) in northern Michigan. *Am. Midl. Nat.* 64,1:194–215.

––––––. 1961. A new diplocardian earthworm from Illinois. *Ohio J. Sci.* 61,6:367–71.

––––––. 1961. A new species of Diplocardia from Florida. *Ohio J. Sci.* 61,3:175–77.

––––––. 1963. Description of a new diplocardian earthworm, *Diplocardia longiseta*. *Ohio J. Sci.* 63,1:15–18.

————. 1965. *Diplocardia gatesi*, a new earthworm from North Carolina. *Ohio J. Sci.* 65,4:208–11.

Myers, Ruth. 1969. *The ABC's of the Earthworm Business.* Elgin, Ill.: Shields Publications.

————. 1975. *A-Worming We Did Go*, revised. Elgin, Ill.: Shields Publications.

Needham, A. E. 1957. Components of nitrogenous excreta in the earthworms *Lumbricus terrestris* L. and *Eisenia foetida* (Savigny). *J. Exp. Biol.* 34:425–46.

————. 1958. The pattern of nitrogen-excretion during regeneration in Oligochaetes. *J. Exp. Zool.* 138:369–430.

————. 1960. The arginase activity of the tissues of the earthworms *Lumbricus terrestris* L., and *Eisenia foetida* (Savigny). *J. Exp. Biol.* 37:775–82.

————. 1962. Distribution of arginase activity along the body of earthworms. *Comp. Biochem. Physiol.* 5:69–82.

————. 1962. Arginase activity in earthworms. *Comp. Biochem. Physiol.* 5:96–103.

Nelson, J. M., and Satchell, J. E. 1962. The extraction of Lumbricidae from soil with special reference to the hand-sorting method. *Progress in Soil Zoology*, ed. P. Murphy. London: Butterworths, 294–99.

Nelson, Lewis, Jr., et al. 1974. *Earthworm Biology and Production.* Univ. of Calif. Coop. Ext.

Newell, G. E. 1950. The role of the coelomic fluid in the movements of earthworms. *J. Exp. Biol.* 27:110–21.

Nicol, J. A. C. 1948. The giant axons of annelids. *Quart. Rev. Biol.* 23:291–323.

Nielsen, G. A., and Hole, F. D. 1964. Earthworms and the development of coprogenous Al horizons in forest soils of Wisconsin. *Soil Sci. Soc. Amer. Proc.* 28:426–30.

Nielson, R. L. 1952. Earthworms and soil fertility. *N.Z. Grassl. Assoc. Proc.* 158–67.

————. Effect of soil minerals on earthworms. *Organic Gardening*, June 1953, 30–33, 46. Reprinted from *Compost Magazine* (New Zealand).

————. 1953. Recent research work. Earthworms. *N.Z. Jl. Agric.* 86:374.

Nijhawan, S. D., and Kanwar, J. S. 1952. Physiochemical properties of earthworm castings and their effect on the productivity of soil. *Indian J. Agric. Sci.* 22:357–73.

Nye, P. H. 1955. Some soil-forming processes in the humid tropics. IV. The action of soil fauna. *J. Soil Sci.* 6:78.

O'Brien, B. R. A. 1947. Studies in the metabolism of normal and regenerating tissue of the earthworm. Part 1. Factors affecting the endogenous oxygen consumption of normal and regenerating muscle tissue. *Proc. Linn. Soc. N.S.W.* 72:367–78.

————. 1957. Evidence in support of an axial metabolic gradient in the earthworm. *Aust. J. Exp. Biol. Med. Sci.* 35:83–92.

————. 1957. Tissue metabolism during posterior regeneration in the earthworm. *Aust. J. Exp. Biol. Med. Sci.* 35:373–80.

Ogg, W. G., and Nicol, H. 1945. Balanced manuring. *Scot. J. Agric.* 25,2:76–83.

Oldham, C. 1915. *Testacella scutulum* in Hertfordshire. *Trans. Herts Nat. Hist. Soc.* 15:193–94.

Olds, Jerome. Earthworm farming for extra income. *Organic Gardening and Farming*, Aug. 1959, 82–87.

———. Winterize your earthworms and microbes. *Organic Gardening and Farming*, Dec. 1967, 80–81.

Oliver, George Sheffield. More about earthworms. *Organic Farming and Gardening*, Dec. 1942.

———. 1954. *Our Friend, the Earthworm. Organic Gardening and Farming* Library no. 26. Emmaus, Pa.: Rodale Press.

Olson, H. W. 1928. The earthworms of Ohio. *Ohio Biol. Survey Bull. 17. The Ohio State Univ. Bull.* 33:47–90.

Pant, R. 1959. Isolation of lombricine and its enzymic phosphorylation. *Biochem. J.* 73:30–33.

Parker, G. H., and Parshley, H. M. 1911. The reactions of earthworms to dry and to moist surfaces. *J. Exp. Zool.* 11:361–63.

Parle, J. N. 1963. Micro-organisms in the intestines of earthworms. *J. Gen. Microbiol.* 31:1–13.

———. 1963. A microbiological study of earthworm casts. *J. Gen. Microbiol.* 13:13–23.

Peachey, J. E. 1963. Studies on the Enchytraeidae (Oligochaeta) of moorland soil. *Pedobiologia* 2:81–95.

Perkins, M. 1929. Growth gradients and the axial relations of the animal body. *Nature, Lond.* 124:299–300.

Peterson, A. E., and Dixon, R. M. 1971. Water movement in large soil pores: validity and utility of the channel system concept. *College of Agr. and Life Sci., Univ. of Wis. Res. Rep.* 75.

Petrov, B. C. 1946. The active reaction of soil (pH) as a factor in the distribution of earthworms. *Zool. Jour.* 25,1:107–10.

Phillips, E. F. 1923. Earthworms, plants and soil reactions. *Ecology* 4:89.

Picken, L. E. R.; Pryor, M. G. M.; and Swann, M. M. 1947. Orientation of fibrils in natural membranes. *Nature, Lond.* 159:434.

Polivka, J. B. 1951. Effect of insecticides upon earthworm populations. *Ohio J. Sci.* 51:195–96.

Pomerat, C. M., and Zarrow, M. X. 1936. The effect of temperature on the respiration of the earthworm. *Proc. Nat. Acad. Sci., Wash.* 22:270–73.

Powell, V. E. 1951. Alkaline phosphatase in the regenerating annelid. *Anat. Rec.* 111:101–7.

Powers, W. L., and Bollen, W. B. 1935. The chemical and biological nature of certain forest soils. *Soil Sci.* 40:321–29.

Prabhoo, N. R. 1960. Studies on Indian Enchytraeidae (Oligochaeta: Annelida). Description of three new species. *J. Zool. Soc. India* 12,2:125–32.

Prosser, C. F. 1933. Correlation between development of behaviour and neuromuscular differentiation in embryos of *Eisenia foetida* Sav. *J. Comp. Neurol.* 58:603–41.

Prosser, C. L. 1934. The nervous system of the earthworm. *Quart. Rev. Biol.* 9:181–200.

———. 1934. Effect of the central nervous system on responses to light in *Eisenia foetida* Sav. *J. Comp. Neurol.* 59:61–92.

———. 1935. Impulses in the segmental nerves of the earthworm. *J. Exp. Biol.* 12:95–104.

Prosser, C. L.; Brown, F. A.; Bishop, D. W.; Jahn, T. L.; and Wulff, V. J. 1950. *Comparative Animal Physiology.* New York: Saunders.

Puh, P. C. 1941. Beneficial influence of earthworms on some chemical properties of the soil. *Contr. Biol. Lab. Sci. Soc. China* 15:147–55.

Puttarudriah, M., and Sastry, K. S. S. 1961. A preliminary study of earthworm damage to crop growth. *Mysore Agric. J.* 36:2–11.

Ragg, J. M., and Ball, D. F. 1964. Soils of the ultra-basic rocks of the Island of Rhum. *J. Soil Sci.* 15,1:124–34.

Ralph, C. L. 1957. Persistent rhythms of activity and O_2 consumption in the earthworm. *Physiol. Zoöl.* 30:41–55.

Ramsay, J. A. 1949. The osmotic relations of the earthworm. *J. Exp. Biol.* 26:46–56.

————. 1949. The site of formation of hypotonic urine in the nephridium of *Lumbricus. J. Exp. Biol.* 26:65–75.

Ratner, S. C., and Miller, K. R. 1959. Classical conditioning in earthworms, *Lumbricus terrestris. J. Comp. Physiol. Psychol.* 52:102–5.

Raw, F. 1959. Estimating earthworm populations by using formalin. *Nature, Lond.* 184:1661.

————. 1960. Observations on the effect of hexoestrol on earthworms and other soil invertebrates. *J. Agric. Sci.* 55,1:189–90.

————. 1960. Earthworm population studies: a comparison of sampling methods. *Nature, Lond.* 187,4733:257.

————. 1961. The agricultural importance of the soil meso-fauna. *Soils & Fert.* 14:1–2.

————. 1962. Studies of earthworm populations in orchards. I. Leaf burial in apple orchards. *Ann. Appl. Biol.* 50:389–404.

————. 1965. Current work on side effects of soil applied organophosphorus insecticides. *Ann. Appl. Biol.* 55:342–43.

————. 1966. The soil fauna as a food source for moles. *J. Zool., Lond.* 149:50–54.

Raw, F., and Lofty, J. R. 1959. Earthworm populations in orchards. *Rep. Rothamsted Exp. Stn. for 1958*, 134–35.

Reed, R., and Rudall, K. M. 1948. Electron microscope studies on the structure of earthworm cuticles. *Biochim. Biophys. Acta.* 2:7–18.

Reynoldson, T. B. 1955. Observations on the earthworms of North Wales. *North Wales Nat.* 3:291–304.

————. 1966. The ecology of earthworms with special reference to North Wales habitats. *Rep. Welsh Soils Discuss. Grp.*, 25–32.

Reynoldson, T. B.; O'Connor, F. B.; and Kelly, W. A. 1955. Observations on the earthworms of Bardsey. *Bardsey Obs. Rep.*, 9.

Rhee, J. A. van. 1963. Earthworm activities and the breakdown of organic matter in agricultural soils. In *Soil Organisms*, eds. J. Doeksen and J. van der Drift. Amsterdam: North Holland Publishing Co., 55–59.

————. 1965. Earthworm activity and plant growth in artificial cultures. *Pl. and Soil* 22:45–48.

————. 1967. Development of earthworm populations in orchard soils. In *Progress in Soil Biology*, eds. O. Graff and J. Satchell. Amsterdam: North Holland Publishing Co., 360–71.

————. 1969. Inoculation of earthworms in a newly drained polder. *Pedobiologia* 9:128–32.

————. 1969. Development of earthworm populations in polder soils. *Pedobiologia* 9:133–40.

————. 1972. Some aspects of the productivity of orchards in relation to earthworm activities. *Proc. 4th Int. Congr. Soil Zool.*

Rhee, J. A. van, and Nathans, S. 1961. Observations on earthworm populations in orchard soils. *Neth. J. Agric. Sci.* 9,2:94–100.

Ribaudcourt, E., and Combault, A. 1907. The role of earthworms in agriculture. *Bull. Soc. for. Belg.*, 212–23.

Richards, J. G. 1955. Earthworms (recent research work). *N.Z. Jl. Agric.* 91:559.

Richardson, H. C. 1938. The nitrogen cycle in grassland soils: with special reference to the Rothamsted Park grass experiment. *J. Agric. Sci., Camb.* 28:73–121.

Richter, G. 1953. The action of insecticides on soil macrofauna. *NachrBl. dt. PflSchutzdienst, Berl.* 7:61–72.

Riegel, Barbara. Earthworms: the composting factories chemicals close down. *Maine Times*, 7 May 1976.

Roberts, M. B. V. 1960. Giant fibre reflex of the earthworm. *Nature, Lond.* 186:167.

Robertson, J. D. 1936. The function of the calciferous glands of earthworms. *J. Exp. Biol.* 13:279–97.

Robinson, J. S. 1953. Stimulus substitution and response learning in the earthworm. *J. Comp. Physiol. Psychol.* 46:262–66.

Robinson, R. R. *Earthworms in Relation to Soil Productivity.* USDA report, Feb. 1964.

Rodale, J. I. Raising chickens by feeding earthworms. *Organic Gardening*, Mar. 1943, 6–8.

———. Earthworms and evolution. *Organic Gardening and Farming*, Aug. 1963.

———. What's an earthworm worth? *Organic Gardening and Farming*, Oct. 1968.

Rodale, Robert. 1948. Do chemical fertilizers kill earthworms? *Organic Gardening* 12,2:12–17.

————. All earthworms are not alike. *Organic Gardening and Farming*, Jan. 1961.

————. Exploring the unknown earthworm. *Organic Gardening and Farming*, Dec. 1962.

Rogers, C. G., and Lewis, E. M. 1914. The relation of the body temperature of the earthworm to that of its environment. *Biol. Bull. Wood's Hole* 27:262–68.

Roots, B. I. 1955. The water relations of earthworms. 1. The activity of the nephridiostome cilia of *Lumbricus terrestris* L. and *Allolobophora chlorotica* Savigny, in relation to the concentration of the bathing medium. *J. Exp. Biol.* 32:765–74.

————. 1956. The water relations of earthworms. 2. Resistance to desiccation, immersion and behaviour when submerged and when allowed a choice of environment. *J. Exp. Biol.* 33:29–44.

————. 1957. Nature of chloragogen granules. *Nature, Lond.* 179:679–80.

————. 1960. Some observations on the chloragogenous tissue of earthworms. *Comp. Biochem. Physiol.* 1:218–26.

Roots, B. I., and Phillips, R. R. 1960. Burrowing and the action of the pharynx of earthworms. *Med. Biol. Illus.* 10:28–31.

Rosenberg, H., and Ennor, A. H. 1959. The isolation of lombricine and its possible biological precursor. *Biochem. J.* 73:521–26.

————. 1960. Occurrence of free D-serine in the earthworm. *Nature, Lond.* 187:617–18.

Rossiter, R. J.; Gaffney, T. J.; Rosenberg, H.; and Ennor, A. H. 1960. Biosynthesis of lombricine. *Nature, Lond.* 185:383–84.

————. 1960. The formation in *vivo* of lombricine in the earthworm *Magascolides cameroni*. *Biochem. J.* 76:603–10.

Rushton, W. A. H. 1945. Action potentials from the isolated nerve cord of the earthworm. *Proc. Roy. Soc.* B. 132:423–37.

————. 1946. Reflex conduction in the giant fibres of the earthworm. *Proc. Roy. Soc.* B. 133:109–20.

Rushton, W. A. H., and Barlow, H. B. 1943. Single fibre response from an intact animal. *Nature, Lond.* 152:597–98.

Russell, E. J. 1909. The effect of earthworms on soil productiveness. *Jour. Agr. Sci.* (England) 3(II):246–57.

————. 1950. *Soil Conditions and Plant Growth*. 8th ed. Revised by E. W. Russell. London: Longmans.

Salomon, K. 1941. Studies on invertebrate haemoglobins (Erythrocruorins). *J. Gen. Physiol.* 24:367–75.

Sanders, Eric E. (undated) *The Worm and I*.

Saroja, K. 1959. ●Studies on the oxygen consumption in tropical Poikilotherms. 2. Oxygen consumption in relation to body size and temperature in the earthworm *Megascolex mauritii* when kept submerged in water. *Proc. Ind. Acad. Sci.* B. 49:183–93.

Satchell, J. E. 1955. *Allolobophora limicola*. An earthworm new to Britain. *Ann. Mag. Nat. Hist.* 8,12:224.

————. 1955. The effects of BHC, DDT and parathion on the soil fauna. *Soils & Fert.* 18,4:279–85.

————. 1955. An electrical method of sampling earthworm populations. In *Soil Zoology*, ed. D. K. Mc. E. Kevan. London: Butterworths, 356–64.

————. 1956. Some aspects of earthworm ecology. *Soil Zoology*, 180–201.

————. 1958. Earthworm biology and soil fertility. *Soils & Fert.* 21,4:209–39.

————. 1960. Earthworms and soil fertility. *New Scientist* 7:79–81.

————. 1963. Nitrogen turnover by a woodland population of *Lumbricus terrestris*. In *Soil Organisms*, eds. J. Doeksen and J. van der Drift. Amsterdam: North Holland Publishing Co., 60–66.

————. 1967. Lumbricidae. In *Soil Biology*, eds. A. Burgess and F. Raw. London and New York: Academic Press, 259–322.

————. 1969. Studies on methodical and taxonomical questions. *Pedobiologia* 9:20–25.

Satchell, J. E., and Lowe, D. G. 1967. Selection of leaf litter by *Lumbricus terrestris*. In *Progress in Soil Biology*, eds. O. Graff and J. E. Satchell. Amsterdam: North Holland Publishing Co., 102–19.

Saussey, M. 1957. A case of commensalism in the lumbricids. *Bull. Soc. Ent. Fr.* 62,1–2:15–19.

Schaller, F. 1958. *Soil Animals*. Ann Arbor: Univ. of Mich. Press.

Scheer, B. T. 1948. *Comparative Physiology*. New York: Wiley.

Schmid, L. A. 1947. Induced neurosecretion in *Lumbricus terrestris. J. Exp. Zool.* 104:365–77.

Schmidt, H. 1955. Behaviour of two species of earthworm in the same maze. *Science* 121:341–42.

Schmidt, P. 1927. Anabiosis of the earthworm. *J. Exp. Zool.* 27:57–72.

Schneiderman, H. A., and Gilbert, L. I. 1958. Substances with juvenile hormone activity in crustacea and other invertebrates. *Biol. Bull. Wood's Hole* 115:530–35.

Schread, J. C. 1952. Habits and control of the oriental earthworm. *Bull. Connect. Agric. Exp. Stn.* 556:5–15.

Scott, H. E. 1960. Control of mites in earthworm beds. *North Carolina State Agr. Ext. Serv. Ext. Folder* 181.

Scrickhande, J. C., and Pathak, A. N. 1951. A comparative study of the physico-chemical characters of the castings of different insects. *Indian J. Agric. Sci.* 21:401–7.

Shaver, E. C. Rabbits and compost—combined! *Organic Gardening and Farming*, June 1964, 39–40.

Shearer, C. 1924. On the oxygen consumption rate of parts of the chick embryo and fragments of the earthworm. *Proc. Roy. Soc. B.* 96:146–56.

———. 1930. A re-investigation of metabolic gradients. *J. Exp. Biol.* 7:260–68.

Shields, Earl B. 1976. *Raising Earthworms for Profit*, 15th ed. Elgin, Ill.: Shields Publications.

Shields, Robert F. 1976. *Earthworm Buyer's Guide, 1976–77.* Elgin, Ill.: Shields Publications.

Shindo, B. 1929. On the seasonal and depth distribution of some worms in soil. *J. Coll. Agric., Tokyo* 10:159–71.

Shiraishi, K. 1954. On the chemotaxis of the earthworm to carbon dioxide. *Sci. Rep. Tôhoku Univ.* 20,4:356–61.

Sims, R. W. 1963. Oligochaeta (earthworms) *Proc. S. Lond. Ent. Nat. Hist. Soc.* 2:53.

————. 1963. A small collection of earthworms from Nepal. *J. Bombay Nat. Hist. Soc.* 60,1:84–91.

————. 1964. Oligochaeta from Ascension Island and Sierra Leone including records of *Pheretima* and a new species of *Ichogaster. Ann. Mag. Nat. Hist.* 7,13:107–13.

————. 1964. Internal fertilization and the functional relationship of the female and the spermathecal systems in new earthworms from Ghana (Eudrilidae: Oligochaeta). *Proc. Zool. Soc. Lond.* 143,4:587–608.

————. 1966. The classification of the megascolecoid earthworms: an investigation of Oligochaete systematics by computer techniques. *Proc. Linn. Soc. Lond.* 177:125–41.

————. 1969. Outline of an application of computer techniques to the problem of the classification of the megascolecoid earthworms. *Pedobiologia* 9,5:35–41.

Sjöstrand, F. S., and Rhodin, J. 1953. The ultrastructure of the proximal convoluted tubules of the mouse kidney as revealed by high resolution electron microscopy. *Exp. Cell. Res.* 5:426–56.

Slater, C. S. 1954. Earthworms in relation to agriculture. *USDA A.R.C. Circ.*

Slater, C. S., and Hopp, H. 1948. Relation of fall protection to earthworm populations and soil physical conditions. *Soil Sci. Soc. Amer. Proc.* (1947) 12:508–11.

———. 1949. The action of frost on the water-stability of soils. *J. Agr. Res.* 78.

Smallwood, W. M. 1923. The nerve net in the earthworm: preliminary report. *Proc. Nat. Acad. Sci. Washington* 9.

———. 1926. The peripheral nervous system of the common earthworm, *Lumbricus terrestris. J. Comp. Neurol.* 42:35–55.

———. 1930. The nervous structure of the annelid ganglion. *J. Comp. Neurol.* 51:377–92.

Smallwood, W. M., and Holmes, M. T. 1927. The neurofibrillar structure of the giant fibres in *Lumbricus terrestris* and *Eisenia foetida. J. Comp. Neurol.* 43:327–45.

Smith, A. C. 1902. The influence of temperature, odors, light and contact on the movements of the earthworm. *Amer. J. Physiol.* 6:459–86.

Smith, F. 1915. Two new varieties of earthworms with a key to described species in Illinois. *Bull. Ill. State Lab. Nat. Hist.* 10,8:551–59.

———. 1928. An account of changes in the earthworm fauna of Illinois. *Bull. Ill. State Nat. Hist. Survey* 17,10:347–62.

Smith, R. D., and Glasgow, L. L. 1965. Effects of heptachlor on wildlife in Louisiana. *Proc. 17th Ann. Conf. S/E Ass. Game and Fish Comm.* 17:140–54.

Smith, R. M., and Thompson, D. O. *Crops and Soils*, Apr.–May 1954.

Soans, A. B., and Soans, J. S. 1969. Earthworm casts as a source of mud for the construction of nest by sphecid wasp. *J. Bombay Nat. Hist. Soc.* 66,1:221–22.

Sroda, George, 1975. *No Angle Left Unturned: Facts about Night Crawlers.* Amherst Junction, Wis.: George Sroda.

Stephenson, J. 1929. Oligochaeta: in reports of an expedition to Brazil and Paraguay, 1926–27. *J. Linn. Soc. (Zool)* 37:291–325.

———. 1930. *The Oligochaeta.* London: Oxford Univ. Press, 978.

Stephenson, W. 1945. Concentration regulation and volume control in *Lumbricus terrestris* L. *Nature, Lond.* 155:635.

Sterba, James P. Worms turn into an expanding, profitable business. *New York Times*, 30 July 1976.

Sternberg, Irma O. Earthworm pits for ailing elms. *Organic Gardening and Farming*, Dec. 1969, 90–92.

Stickel, W. H.; Mayne, D. W.; and Stickel, L. F. 1965. Effects of heptachlor-contaminated earthworms on woodcocks. *J. Wildl. Manage.* 29:132–46.

Stockdill, S. M. J. 1959. Earthworms improve pasture growth. *N.Z. J. Agric.* 98:227–33.

———. 1966. The effect of earthworms on pastures. *Proc. N.Z. Ecol. Soc.* 13:68–74.

Stockdill, S. M. J., and Cossens, G. G. 1966. The role of earthworms in pasture production and moisture conservation. *Proc. N.Z. Grassl. Ass.*, 168–83.

Stokes, B. M. 1958. The worm-eating slugs *Testacella scutulum* Sowerby and *T. haliotidea* Drapernaud in captivity. *Proc. Malac. Soc. Lond.* 33,1:11–20.

Stough, H. B. 1926. Giant nerve fibres of the earthworm. *J. Comp. Neurol.* 40:409–63.

———. 1930. Polarization of the giant nerve fibres of the earthworm. *J. Comp. Neurol.* 50:217–29.

Strehler, B. L. 1962. *Time, Cells, and Ageing.* New York: Academic Press.

Stringer, Austin, and Lyons, Clive H. 1974. The effect of benomyl and thiophanate-methyl on earthworm populations in apple orchards. *Pesticide Science* 5,2:189–96.

Stringer, A., and Pickard, J. A. 1963. The DDT content of soil and earthworms in an apple orchard at Long Ashton. *Long Ashton Res. Sta. Rep.*, 127–31.

Sun, K. H., and Pratt, K. C. 1931. Do earthworms grow by adding segments? *Am. Nat.* 65: 31–48.

Svedberg, T. 1933. Sedimentation constants, molecular weights, and isoelectric points of the respiratory proteins. *J. Biol. Chem.* 103:311–25.

Svendsen, J. A. 1955. Earthworm population studies: a comparison of sampling methods. *Nature, Lond.* 175:864.

———. 1957. The behaviour of lumbricids under moorland conditions. *J. Anim. Ecol.* 26,2:423–39.

Swaby, R. J. 1949. The influence of earthworms on soil aggregation. *J. Soil Sci.* 1,2:195–97.

Swartz, R. D. 1929. Modification of the behaviour of earthworms. *J. Comp. Psychol.* 9:17–33.

Sykes, Friend. 1949. *Humus and the Farmer.* Emmaus, Pa.: Rodale Press.

Takano, S., and Nakamura, Y. 1968. A new host earthworm, *Allolobophora japonica* Michaelsen, (Oligochaeta: Lumbricidae), of the calypterate muscoid fly, *Onesia subalpina* Kurahashi. (Diptera: Calliphoridae.) *Appl. Ent. Zool.* 3,1:51–52.

Tamesis, Pablo T. Earthworms are our friends. *Philippine Farms and Gardens*, Manilla, Dec. 1967.

Tandan, B. K. 1951. Axial gradient in the water content of the body wall of earthworms. *Current Science* 20:214–15.

Taylor, G. W. 1940. The optical properties of the earthworm giant fibre sheath as related to fibre size. *J. Cell Comp. Physiol.* 15:363–71.

Tembe, V. B., and Dubash, P. J. 1961. The earthworms: a review. *J. Bombay Nat. Hist. Soc.* 58,1:171–201.

Tenney, F. G., and Waksman, S. A. 1929. Composition of natural organic materials and their decomposition in the soil. IV. The nature and rapidity of decomposition of the various organic complexes in different plant materials, under aerobic conditions. *Soil Sci.* 28:55–84.

Teotia, S. P.; Duley, F. L.; and McCalla, T. M. 1950. Effect of stubble mulching on number and activity of earthworms. *Neb. Agric. Exp. Sta. Res. Bull.* 165:20.

Thompson, A. R. 1970. Effects of nine insecticides on the numbers and biomass of earthworms in pasture. *Bulletin of Environmental Contamination and Toxicology* 5,6:577–86.

Thorpe, W. H. 1956. *Learning and Instinct in Animals.* London: Methuen, 493.

Tischler, W. 1955. Effect of agricultural practice on the soil fauna. In *Soil Zoology*, ed. D. K. Mc. E. Kevan. London: Butterworths, 125–37.

Tomlin, A. D., and Gore, F. L. 1974. Effects of six insecticides and a fungicide on the numbers and biomass of earthworms in pasture. *Bulletin of Environmental Contamination and Toxicology* 12,4.

Tracey, M. V. 1951. Cellulase and chitinase of earthworms. *Nature, Lond.* 167:776.

Trembley, Dr. F. J. Lowly earthworm an aid to environment. *Sunday Call-Chronicle*, Allentown, Pa., 3 May 1970.

Tromba, F. G. 1955. Role of the earthworm *Eisenia foetida*, in the transmission of *Stephanurus dentatus. J. Parasit.* 41:157–61.

Uhlen, G. 1953. Preliminary experiments with earthworms. *Landbr. Hogsk. Inst. Jordkultur Meld.* 37:161–83.

Urquhart, A. T. 1887. On the work of earthworms in New Zealand. *Trans. N.Z. Inst.* 19:119–23.

Van Brink, J. M., and Rietsema, J. 1949. Some experiments on the active uptake of chlorine ions by the earthworm (*Lumbricus terrestris* L.). *Physiol. Comp. et Oecol.* 1:348–51.

Van Gansen, P. Semal. 1960. Occurrence of a non-fibrillar elastin in the earthworm. *Nature, Lond.* 186:654–55.

Van Hook, R. I. 1974. Cadmium, lead, and zinc distributions between earthworms and soils: potentials for biological accumulation. *Bulletin of Environmental Contamination and Toxicology* 12,4.

Villiard, Paul. 1973. *Raising Small Animals for Fun and Profit*. New York: Winchester Press.

Vimmerstedt, J. P., and Finney, J. R. 1973. Impact of earthworm introduction on litter burial and nutrient distribution in Ohio strip-mine spoil banks. *Proc. Soil Sci. Soc. Am.* 37,3.

Voison, Andre. 1960. *Better Grassland Sward*. London: Crosby Lockwood and Sons, Ltd.

Volz, P. 1962. Contributions to a pedo-zoological study of sites based on observations in the southeastern Palatinate. *Pedobiologia* 1:242–90.

Waite, R. H. 1920. Earthworms. The important factor in the transmission of gapes in chickens. *Maryland Agric. Exp. Bull.* 234:103–18.

Waksman, S. A., and Martin, J. P. 1939. The conservation of the soil. *Science* 90:304–5.

Walker, J. G. 1959. Oxygen poisoning and recovery in the annelid *Tubifex tubifex*. *Dissertation Absts.* 20:719.

Walton, W. R. 1927. Earthworms and light. *Science* 66:132.

———. 1928. Earthworms as pests and otherwise. USDA Farmers' Bulletin 1569, Washington, D.C., 14.

————. 1933. The reaction of earthworms to alternating currents of electricity in the soil. *Proc. Ent. Soc. Wash.* 35:24–27.

Waters, R. A. S. 1952. Earthworms and the fertility of pasture. *Proc. N.Z. Grassl. Ass.*, 168–75.

————. 1955. Numbers and weights of earthworms under a highly productive pasture. *N.Z. J. Sci. Technol.* 36, 5:516–25.

Watkin, B. R. 1954. The animal factor and levels of nitrogen. *J. Br. Grassld. Soc.* 9:35–46.

Watson, M. R. 1958. The chemical composition of earthworm cuticle. *Biochem. J.* 68:416–20.

Watson, M. R., and Silvester, N. R. 1959. Studies of invertebrate collagen preparations. *Biochem. J.* 71:578–84.

Watson, M. R., and Smith, R. H. 1956. The chemical composition of earthworm cuticle. *Biochem. J.* 64:10 P.

Way, M. J., and Scopes, N. E. A. 1968. Studies on the persistence and effects on soil fauna of some soil applied systemic insecticides. *Ann. Appl. Biol.* 62:199–214.

Welsh, J. H., and Moorhead, M. 1960. The quantitative distribution of 5-hydroxytryptamine in the invertebrates, especially in their nervous systems. *J. Neurochem.* 6:146–69.

Went, J. C. 1963. Influence of earthworms on the number of bacteria in the soil. In *Soil Organisms*, eds. J. Doeksen and J. van der Drift. Amsterdam: North Holland Publishing Co., 260–65.

Wheatley, G. A., and Hardman, J. A. 1968. Organochlorine insecticide residues in earthworms from arable soils. *J. Sci. Fd. Agric.* 19:219–25.

Wherry, E. T. 1924. Soil acidity preferences of earthworms. *Ecology* 89–90.

Wherry, R. J., and Sanders, J. M. 1941. Modifications of a tropism in *Lumbricus terrestris. Trans. Illin. Acad. Sci.* 34:237–87.

Whitney, W. K. 1967. Laboratory tests with Dursban and other insecticides in soil. *J. Econ. Ent.* 60:68–74.

Wilcke, D. E. von. 1952. On the domestication of the 'soilution' earthworm. *Anz. Schädlingsk.* 25:107–9.

———. 1955. Critical observations and proposals on the quantative analysis of earthworms populations in soil zoology studies. *Z. PflErnähr. Düng.* 68:44–49.

Wilde, S. A., and Voigt, G. K. 1959. *An Analysis of Soils and Plants for Foresters and Horticulturists.* Ann Arbor, Mich.: J. W. Edwards.

Williams, Robert. 1959. *How to Sell Fishworms by Mail.* dist. Shields Publications.

Wilson, D. M. 1961. The connections between the lateral giant fibres of earthworms. *Comp. Biochem. Physiol.* 4:274–84.

Witkamp, M. 1966. Decomposition of leaf litter in relation to environment, microflora and microbial respiration. *Ecology* 47:194–201.

Wolf, A. V. 1937. Notes on the effect of heat on *L. terrestris. Ecology* 19:346–48.

————. 1938. Studies on the behaviour of *L. terrestris* and evidence for a dehydration tropism. *Ecology* 19:233–42.

————. 1940. Paths of water exchange in the earthworm. *Physiol. Zool.* 13:294–308.

————. 1941. Survival time of the earthworm as affected by raised temperatures. *J. Cell. Comp. Physiol.* 18:275–78.

Woodhead, A. A. 1950. Life history cycle of the giant kidney worm, *Dioctophyma renale* (Nematoda) of man and many other animals. *Trans. Am. Microsc. Soc.* 69:21–46.

Wright, Michael A., and Stringer, Austin. 1973. The toxicity of thiabendazole, benomyl, methyl benzimidazol-2-yl carbamate and thiophanate-methyl to the earthworm, *Lumbricus terrestris. Pesticide Science* 4:431–32.

Wu, K. S. 1939. On the physiology and pharmacology of the earthworm gut. *J. Exp. Biol.* 16:184–97.

————. 1939. The action of drugs, especially acetylcholine, on the annelid body wall (*Lumbricus, Arenicola*). *J. Exp. Biol.* 16:251–57.

Wyndham, Robert J. New California retirement business—angleworms combined with rabbits. *Organic Gardening and Farming*, Mar. 1968, 46.

Yerkes, R. M. 1912. Habit and its relations to the nervous system in the earthworm. *Proc. Soc. Exp. Biol., N.Y.* 10:16–18.

————. 1912. The intelligence of earthworms. *J. Anim. Behav.* 2:332–52.

Zhinkin, L. 1936. The influence of the nervous system on the regeneration of *Rhynchelmis limosella. J. Exp. Zool.* 73:43–65.

Zicsi, A. 1962. Determination of number and size of sampling unit for estimating lumbricid populations of arable soils. In *Progress in Soil Zoology*, ed. P. W. Murphy. London: Butterworths, 68–71.

Index